STRATEGIC INFORMATION TECHNOLOGY

Founded in 1807, John Wiley & Sons is the oldest independent publishing company in the United States. With offices in North America, Europe, Asia, and Australia, Wiley is globally committed to developing and marketing print and electronic products and services for our customers' professional and personal knowledge and understanding.

The Wiley CIO series provides information, tools, and insights to IT executives and managers. The products in this series cover a wide range of topics that supply strategic and implementation guidance on the latest technology trends, leadership, and emerging best practices.

Titles in the Wiley CIO series include:

The Agile Architecture Revolution: How Cloud Computing, REST-Based SOA, and Mobile Computing Are Changing Enterprise IT by Jason Bloomberg

Big Data, Big Analytics: Emerging Business Intelligence and Analytic Trends for Today's Businesses by Michael Minelli, Michele Chambers, and Ambiga Dhiraj

The Chief Information Officer's Body of Knowledge: People, Process, and Technology by Dean Lane

CIO Best Practices: Enabling Strategic Value with Information Technology (Second Edition) by Joe Stenzel, Randy Betancourt, Gary Cokins, Alyssa Farrell, Bill Flemming, Michael H. Hugos, Jonathan Hujsak, and Karl Schubert

The CIO Playbook: Strategies and Best Practices for IT Leaders to Deliver Value by Nicholas R. Colisto

Enterprise Performance Management Done Right: An Operating System for Your Organization by Ron Dimon

Executive's Guide to Virtual Worlds: How Avatars Are Transforming Your Business and Your Brand by Lonnie Benson

IT Leadership Manual: Roadmap to Becoming a Trusted Business Partner by Alan R. Guibord

Managing Electronic Records: Methods, Best Practices, and Technologies by Robert F. Smallwood

On Top of the Cloud: How CIOs Leverage New Technologies to Drive Change and Build Value Across the Enterprise by Hunter Muller

Straight to the Top: CIO Leadership in a Mobile, Social, and Cloud-based World (Second Edition) by Gregory S. Smith

Strategic IT: Best Practices for Managers and Executives by Arthur M. Langer and Lyle Yorks

Transforming IT Culture: How to Use Social Intelligence, Human Factors, and Collaboration to Create an IT Department That Outperforms by Frank Wander

Unleashing the Power of IT: Bringing People, Business, and Technology Together by Dan Roberts

The U.S. Technology Skills Gap: What Every Technology Executive Must Know to Save America's Future by Gary J. Beach

STRATEGIC INFORMATION TECHNOLOGY

BEST PRACTICES TO DRIVE DIGITAL
TRANSFORMATION

SECOND EDITION

Arthur M. Langer

Lyle Yorks

WILEY

For general information on our other products and services or for technical support, please contact our Customer Care Department within the United States at (800) 762–2974, outside the United States at (317) 572–3993, or fax (317) 572–4002.

Wiley publishes in a variety of print and electronic formats and by print-on-demand. Some material included with standard print versions of this book may not be included in e-books or in print-on-demand. If this book refers to media such as a CD or DVD that is not included in the version you purchased, you may download this material at http://booksupport.wiley.com. For more information about Wiley products, visit www.wiley.com.

Library of Congress Cataloging-in-Publication Data is Available:
ISBN 9781119484523 (Hardcover)
ISBN 9781119484554 (ePDF)
ISBN 9781119484547 (ePub)

Cover Design: Wiley
Cover Image: © iSam iSmile/Shutterstock

Printed in the United States of America.

V10002670_073018

I want to thank and acknowledge all of my students at Columbia University for their dedication and inspiration to continue to explore the complexities of the role of the CIO and other technology leaders in a digital-driven world.

— Arthur Langer

To my granddaughters Maya, Zoe, Maisy, Lia, and Ella Josephine, and my grandson Ian. You are all a wonderful part of my life.

— Lyle Yorks

CONTENTS

FOREWORD

After a 44-year career at IBM, as I stated in the first edition, I have experienced many changes in the IT industry and seen how firms struggle to understand the value of IT in general. With over one hundred years of accumulated personal board experience, those controversies are still discussed at board meetings today. The debates over the role of the CIO continue, including issues of where they should report, their specific responsibilities, and whether they can contribute strategically to the business. Most important is the forecast of the CIOs of the future: What will be their titles and responsibilities?

Strategic IT, 2nd Edition, by Drs. Langer and Yorks, deals with the issues that every CIO faces. This second edition addresses three major and critical developments since the first edition, specifically, digital disruption, cyber security, and analytics. Independent of geography, size, business, or purpose, the constant, critical question facing each and every technology leader in the 21st century is: Are you a cost or are you an investment? That is, are you part of the business tactics or part of its strategy? Langer and Yorks have written the complete CIO survival handbook for thriving in the fast-paced and rapidly changing world. Langer and Yorks remind us that *change* is the norm for technology leaders and that time to change is not an ally; rather, speed and demand typically dictate the environment CIOs call home with regard to their scope of responsibilities.

Drs. Langer and Yorks use the rich research and practice they have obtained as faculty at Columbia University where they hold workshops on technology leadership and teach in the Executive Masters of Science program in Technology Management. Therefore, much of their experience with CIOs and other technology leaders and students back up their theories and coursework. Their real-world examples bring life to the A-Z framework of success. Indeed, I have experienced the excitement of participants at their lectures.

Based on my experience, Langer and Yorks touch on the critical issues facing all CIOs today. While CIOs must be experts in technology, have organizational skills, contribute to the bottom line, and have executive presence, the more vital skill today is their need to be enablers of innovation and change agents in their firms. Furthermore, they must keep their organizations safe from cyber threats. Whether we speak about a large or small enterprise, a for-profit or not-for-profit organization, the CIO's success is all about understanding change. The only way to help transform organizations is by having a very agile and focused IT strategy. As a director on a number boards, I understand the complexity of dealing with the multiple perspectives on how to use information technology. I hear all of the different opinions about the value of big data, mobile applications, mobile devices, cyber security, and cloud computing, just to name a few. What is most challenging is that all these new technologies develop and change in the wink of an eye. Yet little if any of these new technologies were discussed, let alone needed, five years ago. And what will be needed five years from now is truly a mystery to most enterprise leaders today.

For all these reasons and many more, the authors' definition of the successful technology leader in *Strategic IT* is "spot on" and a must-read for CIOs that are planning how they will emerge as leaders in a digital-based society. So much of an organization's success depends on whether the CIO and the leadership team work closely together and have a shared vision of the business. *Strategic IT* will give CIOs more than a fighting chance to make a difference in their organizations—a difference that most of them want to accomplish with the tools they need to survive and thrive in today's fast-paced world.

Nicholas Donofrio
IBM Fellow Emeritus & EVP Innovation
and Technology (Ret.)
NMD Consulting, LLC
Executive in Residence, Columbia University
Center for Technology Management

PREFACE

How This Book Is Structured

Four broad themes provide the structure for this book:

1. How is technology organizationally positioned as an effective strategic driver?
2. What challenges are posed by various ways of positioning technology, and what are the implications of how these challenges are resolved?
3. What strategies are used by effective chief information officers (CIOs) in addressing these challenges and strategically positioning technology?
4. How did these CIOs learn these strategies, and what are the implications for developing this capacity in high-potential technology managers?

This book grows out of the work we have done with the CIO Institute conducted at Columbia University and the Executive Master of Science in Technology Management program at Columbia University, along with several projects working with the technology management staff within corporations with the focus of developing their staffs to the strategic realities described earlier. Part of this work has experimented with educational and mentoring strategies with successful CIOs to foster strategic mindsets and the capability of meeting the challenges of navigating into senior executive roles.

Specifically, this book provides a comparative analysis of case studies of organizations with CIOs widely regarded as being at the forefront of addressing the challenge of strategically positioning technology within the business models of their organizations. These CIOs are recognized as having successfully made the transition into the C-suite and having earned their "seat at the table" through integrating technology as a business driver.

Each case study involves interviews with the CIOs, their colleagues in the C-suite, and chief executive officer (CEO), along with archival documents to describe both the personal and organizational transitions that have occurred. The cases involve Procter & Gamble, Covance, Cushman & Wakefield, Merck, and Prudential, among others. Cross-case analysis reveals the essential and unique themes of strategically positioning technology in the organization along with developmental practices for high-potential technology managers.

The remaining chapters of this book develop the remedies as we see them based on best practices from our cases, the integration of theories in the areas of learning and development and how they relate to the successful growth of the CIO position. Here is a brief summary of each chapter.

Chapter 1: The CIO Dilemma

Chapter 1 addresses why CIOs need to make technology an important part of business strategy, and why few of them understand how to accomplish it. In general, we show that most CIOs have a lack of knowledge about how technology and business strategy can and should be linked to form common business objectives. The chapter provides the results of a research study of how chief executives link the role of technology with business strategy. The study captures information relating to how chief executives perceive the role of information technology (IT), how they manage it and use it strategically, and the way they measure IT performance and activities.

Chapter 2: IT Drivers and Supporters

This chapter defines how organizations need to respond to the challenges posed by technology. We present technology as a "dynamic variable" that is capable of affecting organizations in a unique way. We specifically emphasize technology's unpredictability and its capacity to accelerate change—ultimately concluding that technology, as an independent variable, has a dynamic effect on organizational development. This chapter also introduces the theory of driver and supporter and responsive organizational dynamism (ROD), defined as a disposition in organizational behavior that can respond to the demands of technology as a dynamic variable. We establish two core components of ROD: Strategic integration and cultural assimilation. The chapter also provides a perspective of the technology life cycle so that readers can see how ROD is applied on an IT project basis, defining the driver and supporter functions of IT and how it contributes to managing technology life cycles.

Chapter 3: The Strategic Advocacy Mindset

Chapter 3 provides a framework for engaging in strategic advocacy, linking strategic learning practices such as analog reasoning and scenario thinking with political savvy influencing practices in organizations. Distinctions between technological, adaptive, and generative challenges that confront the IT executive are presented along with the implications for effectively building productive relationships with senior executives. Specific practices are provided along with examples from both our research and working with a range of IT executives. How the IT executives' mindset impacts the effectiveness of how they utilize these practices is also developed.

Chapter 4: Real-World Case Studies

In Chapter 4, we provide five case studies of companies that, as a result of the strategically focused business mindset of the CIO, have made the journey transitioning from a service to driver positioning of technology. These cases, among other data sources, have provided the basis for the points made in previous chapters and the more detailed analysis that follows. Emphasis is placed on how the CIO has enabled or is enabling this ongoing transition. Drawn to provide variance in terms of industry and/or markets, the cases are BP, Covance, Cushman & Wakefield, Merck, Procter & Gamble, and Prudential, along with a summary that frames the following chapters.

Chapter 5: Patterns of a Strategically Effective CIO

Chapter 5 provides evidence of why certain CIOs have attained success as strategic drivers of their businesses. This evidence is presented from the case studies and integrates our findings based on our theories of why certain CIOs are more successful than others. These theories have led us to understand the patterns that suggest why these CIOs have been successful in introducing an IT strategy and how they build credibility among C-level peers in their organizations.

Chapter 6: Lessons Learned and Best Practices

This chapter seeks to define best practices to implement and sustain strategic advocacy and success at the CIO level. The chapter sets forth a model that creates separate, yet linked best practices and maturity "arcs" that can be used to assess stages of the learning development of the chief IT executive, the CEO, and the middle management in an organization. We discuss the concept of "common threads," where each best practice arc links through common objectives and outcomes that contribute to overall performance in the CIO suite.

Chapter 7: Implications for Personal Development

In Chapter 7, we provide a framework for the development of high-potential IT talent. The importance of both formal and informal experiential learning of working across a business is emphasized along with development of both strategic learning and influential practices. Specific exercises are provided for fostering these practices. Effective mentoring practices are also presented, again based on experience.

Chapter 8: Digital Transformation and Business Strategy

This chapter explores the effects of the digital global economy on the ways in which organizations need to respond to the consumerization of products and services. From this perspective, digital transformation involves a type of social reengineering that affects the ways in which organizations communicate internally and how they consider restructuring departments. Digital transformation also affects the risks that organizations must take in what has become an accelerated changing consumer market.

Chapter 9: Integrating Gen Y Talent

This chapter focuses on Gen Y employees who are known as "digital natives." Gen Y employees possess the attributes to assist companies to transform their workforce to meet the accelerated change in the competitive landscape. Most executives across industries recognize that digital technologies are the most powerful variable to maintaining and expanding company markets. Gen Y employees provide a natural fit for dealing with emerging digital technologies; however, success with integrating Gen Y employees is contingent upon Baby Boomer and Gen X management to adapt new leadership philosophies and procedures suited to meet the expectations and needs of these new workers. Ignoring the unique needs of Gen Y employees will likely result in an incongruent organization that suffers high turnover of young employees who will ultimately seek a more entrepreneurial environment.

Chapter 10: Creating a Cyber Security Culture

The growing challenges of protecting companies from outside attacks have established the need to create a "cyber security" culture. This chapter addresses the ways in which information technology organizations must further integrate with business operations so that their firms are better equipped to protect against outside threats. Since the general consensus is that no system can be 100% protected and that most system compromises occur as a result of internal exposures, information technology leaders must educate employees on best practices to limit cyber attacks. Furthermore, while prevention is the objective, organizations must be internally prepared to deal with attacks and thus have processes in place should a system be penetrated by a third-party agent.

Chapter 11: The Non-IT CIO of the Future

This chapter explores the future requirements for CIOs, particularly placing an importance on business knowledge and how technology provides competitive advantage and operational efficiencies. We see the role of the CIO becoming more of a chief of operations or chief being functionally responsible for contracts, equipment management, general automation, and outsourcing while having a central role in conversations about strategically leveraging emerging new technologies.

Chapter 12: Conclusion: New Directions for the CIO of the Future

Chapter 12 summarizes the primary implications of the book for the IT field and the implications for other executives in terms of building strategically productive relationship with IT.

ACKNOWLEDGMENTS

There are many colleagues and corporate executives who have provided significant support during the development of this second edition.

We owe much to our colleagues at Columbia University, Teachers College, namely Professor Victoria Marsick and Professor Emeritus Lee Knefelkamp for their ongoing mentorship on adult learning and developmental theories. We appreciate the support of Aarti Subramanian, our graduate assistant, for her participation in the research process, including transcribing interviews, and to Jody Barto, another graduate assistant, who helped with finalizing some of the exhibits. Nicholas Donofrio, emeritus (retired) executive vice president of innovation and technology at IBM, also provided valuable direction on the complex issues surrounding the emerging role of CIOs, especially how they operate with boards of directors.

We appreciate the corporate CIOs who agreed to participate in the studies that allowed us to apply our theories to actual organizational practices (in alphabetical order): Steve Bandrowczak from Xerox; Craig Cuyar from Omnicom; Dana Deasy now CIO of the Department of Defense; Barbara Koster from Prudential Financial; Filippo Passerini, now retired from Procter & Gamble; and Chris Scalet, retired from Merck. All of these executives contributed enormous information on how corporate CIOs can integrate technology into business strategy.

And, of course, we are indebted to our wonderful students at Columbia University. They continue to be at the core of our inspiration and love for writing, teaching, and scholarly research.

CHAPTER 1

The CIO Dilemma

The role of the chief information officer (CIO) continues to be a challenge in many organizations. Unlike the CIO's related "C-suite" colleagues, organizations struggle to understand the need for the role and more importantly how to measure success. We know that most CIOs have short terms, the vast number only lasting about three years. At CIO conferences, many CIOs have coined the CIO acronym as standing for "Career Is Over." Nothing should be further from the truth. We know that technology continues to be the most important factor in strategic advantage among chief executive officers (CEOs). And we also know that there is a population of CIOs that have clearly demonstrated the success of the role by the sheer longevity that they have held their position. We will cover some cases of these individuals later in the book. This chapter focuses on the common dilemmas that face CIOs based on our research and practice.

The isolation of information technology (IT) as a department is nothing new. Technology people have been criticized, and in many cases rightfully so, for their inability to integrate with the rest of the organization.[1] Being stereotyped as "techies" continues to be relevant, and the image seems to have gravitated to the level of the CIO. Even with the widespread importance of IT over the past two decades, CIOs have been challenged to bring strategic value to their companies—and those that have not done so have had short-lived tenures. There is little question about the frustration that exists with CIOs at the CEO level, the reasons for which we will address in this book. Satisfying the CEO is a challenge for most CIOs—it involves the complexity of explaining why IT is so expensive, understanding why projects take so long to complete, and clearly articulating how IT supports the business. Our best evidence of this communication gap between the CEO and CIO was best represented by Carr's 2003 article titled, "IT Doesn't Matter," which was published in the *Harvard Business Review*.[2] The article sharply criticized the IT function and attacked its overall value to organizations. It received instant popularity among chief financial officers (CFOs) and CEOs as many began to review their investments in IT and the role of the CIO in general. The question remains, *why?* Especially since so many CEOs acknowledge that IT is the most important variable of competitive advantage.

Because technology is changing at such a rapid pace, the ability for any CIO to operate in a dynamic business environment is staggering. As we will see in this book, the CIO fights a "two-front war": Keeping technology operational and secure while at the same time attempting to bring strategic advantage for the business. This is certainly not an easy task, as Schein discussed in his 1992 article, "Management and Information Technology: Two Subcultures in Collision." The article disclosed much of the imbalance between the CEO and IT. This "imbalance" has continued to be the key success factor for many CIOs, especially when they attempt to bring strategic value to their organizations.

The results of our research suggest that the CIO's value to the business lies in the following key areas:

- Business integration
- Security
- Data analytics
- Legal exposure
- Cost containment

Business Integration

There is nothing new about the mission for CIOs to figure out how to integrate technology in their respective businesses. The consensus among successful CIOs is that they spend a significant amount of their time meeting and working with key business owners, particularly business heads. However, Langer's research found that line managers were even more important.[3] Line managers are defined as those managers that have ultimate day-to-day responsibility for a business area, so successful CIOs ensure that they are in touch at that level as well. Spending time is one thing; however, accomplishing true integration requires CIOs to commit staff to those line units and even consider permanently moving IT resources to business units. The results of our research show that many CIOs say they are integrated, yet few really are. The key aspect of CIO business integration is relationship building. True relationships mean spending consistent time and becoming part of the challenges of the business unit.

Security

In the past 10 years, security of information has become of top concern for many organizations because of the growth of the Internet, social media, and widespread online accessibility in general. Depending on the industry, protecting data and information are paramount to the lifeblood in such industries as finance, health care, and government. A breach of security can quickly create a loss of client confidence and even result in penalties imposed by various regulatory bodies. So explaining how the CIO and a CISO (Chief Information Security Officer) are protecting the business's information is a very important topic at board meetings.

Data Analytics

"Data analytics," the current term used for understanding the data that the organization owns, has been the most growing area of interest for CIOs because of board-level interests. Knowledge is power, as they say, and being able to aggregate data for competitive advantage is critical for any organization. Data analytics requires CIOs to first be able to figure out the technical challenges of aggregating the data, then being capable enough to learn how best to present what the data mean. The more board members see meaningful data, the more questions they have, which ultimately leads to an ongoing inquiry of questions and responses. The interaction, if done effectively, promotes the importance that the CIO has to the business.

Legal Exposure

IT has many legal exposures; the data they save, the intellectual property they own, and the complexity of contractual relationship they have cause much exposure for any firm. CIOs need to understand how to operate with their organization's corporate counsel and be heavily versed on the international legal terrain. Furthermore, there are growing legal exposures that relate to the information that firms keep, which can be used as part of discovery during legal cases. In addition are the complexities of protecting intellectual property, patents, trademarks, and copyrights, and in many industries such as health care, the overabundance of regulation on protecting and using data. The responsibility for much of all of these issues falls on the CIO.

Cost Containment

Let's not underestimate the value that IT has in reducing certain operational costs. Providing IT shared services is still a significant value proposition to many boards. Squeezing costs to improve shareholder value is another avenue of IT value. Many CIOs can obtain board confidence by showing ways to cut existing costs. There are dangers in trying to do this, particularly with the business units that may be affected, so CIOs need to be very careful how they embark on cost-reduction initiatives. Having a cost-efficient mindset is also impressive to boards, as CIOs historically have been classified as "spenders" and they still represent a very large part of a firm's overall capital expenditures.

When looking at these issues, it seems overwhelming that one individual could ultimately be responsible for all of these functions. Yet while there are other executives involved (e.g., legal counsel), the CIO must be involved in setting the strategy and operational controls that protect the organization and make it competitive at the same time. It seems like the CIO has a two-front war, as we shall discuss in later chapters.

A major IT dilemma is how to design an enterprise IT organization that addresses the factors just discussed. What does this mean? The question really is whether user and consumer expectations toward IT innovations result in significant changes in how technology is delivered and managed within an organization. This question is being raised during a time where there:

- Are disruptions of traditional models being challenged by the market.
- Is greater opportunity for innovation in a global context.
- Is a much more demanding employee base.
- Is a need to accelerate the speed of change.
- Are third-party infrastructures for consideration.

So, the need for IT leadership has never been greater, during a period where there is a shortage of CIO talent!

As Chris Scalet, former CIO of Merck, once stated at Columbia University, "CEO demands from IT are dramatically increasing":

- They want it all—productivity, speed, predictability, cost effectiveness, and innovation.
- Technology as an accelerator and differentiator rather than a speed bump or "gating factor."
- Generation of revenue.
- Market leadership.
- Relevance.
- Tight alignment with the business.

So the CIO now has to rethink IT services to meet these demands. We are at that "fork in the road."

Some History

Much of the CIO leadership, simply by their age, likely began their careers during a different phase of the IT evolution. During the 1970s, the mainframe was king. IT was locked down and was mostly used for accounting and number crunching. By the 1980s, the personal computer (PC) hit the market and for the first time IT could no longer control technology solely inside the walls of the IT department. Unfortunately, IT executives tended to reject the PC as a viable IT solution, coining it more as a toy than a real business solution. However, by the 1990s, distributed computing became a reality, especially with the proliferation of networked PCs—which allowed for the widespread expansion of IT throughout the business. IT could no longer restrict users from working with computers directly. The advent of PC networks also required that IT leaders become enamored with the need to support the end user—those CIOs that provided the best support were the best CIOs. Unfortunately, support in the 1990s meant quick response to user requests within limits that restricted access to certain computers, software, and operating systems. By 2000, the Internet revolution was upon us, the dot-coms had crumbled, but the user also became a consumer, and consumers rule the business. So in the 40-year evolution, IT leaders have needed to make significant shifts in the way they deliver and manage IT services—with an evolution toward "consumerization." Unfortunately, many of those "older" IT executives have found it difficult to adjust and change, which has resulted in a common turnover of CIOs usually in the three-year range. The typical reason is that CIOs formulate a strategy in their first year, implement in their second, and fail to deliver in their third and final year! Not an impressive story, for sure. The dilemma then also relates to past experiences with CIOs that attempt to either ignore or block past IT evolutions.

The consumerization of technology is staggering. Ninety-five percent of employee purchases of technology are used for business. A Unisys study of 2,820 employees reflected that workers are generally dissatisfied with the level of support IT provides for its consumer technologies. While 95% of technologies are self-purchased by employees, 70% of their employers want to standardize technologies for them, thus restricting their abilities to use the technologies they have purchased. Furthermore, 57% of those employers are not interested in providing stipends for employee expenditures.

The Challenge

Today, we see another level of IT evolution that specifically involves cloud computing, mobility, predictive analysis, cyber security, and social media—all affecting how CIOs deal with the legal complexities, business integration, and security challenges mentioned earlier. Cloud computing has established an entirely new service model that allows businesses to gain access to outside networks that store data and provide common software solutions at lower and more effective prices. This mobility requires IT executives to provide employees with the capacity to work wherever they are, without necessarily requiring them to use a laptop or desktop computer. Predictive analysis, a subset of data analytics, provides the ability of users to access reliable data and understand past transactions to effectively predict what will happen in the future. Finally, social media must optimize communication between companies and their customers and suppliers.

Oxford Economics recently surveyed C-suite executives and asked them to rate the impact of each of these areas on their businesses over the next five years. Almost 60% selected mobile technology, and over 35% selected predictive analysis and cloud computing, with slightly over 30% picking social media.

This leads to two important questions: (1) How will this new wave of "disruptive" technologies affect organizations, and (2) can CIOs establish a natural evolution in their organizations that will lead to a fundamental shift in the way IT is managed and measured?

The New Paradigm

Prahalad and Krishnan realized the effects of consumerization on IT in their book *The New Age of Innovation*. They established a model called the "New House of Innovation."[4]

At the core of this model is the proposition that there is a need for "flexible and resilient business processes and focused analytics."[5] The "pillars" of this need are represented by N = 1 and R = G. N = 1 is the consumer: Every business must serve each consumer as a unique individual. R = G, however, suggests that resources must be global. So the model essentially frames consumerization as being the ability to serve one customer's needs by using multiple resources from global sources. In other words, to successfully compete, organizations must be agile enough to provide specialized services; the only way to accomplish this is through a multitude of providers that can respond and deliver. For example, if a user needs service at an off-peak time, the organization that can provide such support using global resources will be the winning businesses of the future. A consumer needing something at midnight in New York perhaps will be serviced by someone in Singapore—it's "on-demand," specialized for the individual. An alternative analogy is the Burger King slogan: "Have it your way." The difference here is that consumers want it on demand. So Burger King would have to provide hamburgers at midnight and provide almost unlimited choices. Not an easy world, but the reality of what technology has created in the *new* world. So the message for the contemporary CIO is to treat every user as a unique entity and have dynamic resources that can deliver what they want and when they want it. To accomplish this feat, CIOs need multitudes of strategic alliances and new types of employees.

Consumerization of Technology: The Next Paradigm Shift

We continue to expand this idea of the paradigm shift expressed thus far. The need for new forces in organizations can be represented by four fundamental shifts in IT service requirements now also known as the key aspects of digital transformation:

1. Speed must be more important than cost.
2. The workforce must be empowered to respond to consumer and market needs.
3. Choice of devices over standardization and controls.
4. On-demand infrastructure (networks, computing power, and storage).

Much of these four shifts will serve to further the commoditization of many traditional IT roles and responsibilities. This will place greater emphasis on the ability of the CIO to lead. Thus, there must be emerging shifts in the way IT is used, led by the CIO, to construct this new consumerization:

- Information is more important than the technology used to deliver it.
- IT must be embedded in the business more significantly and in a much different way.
- Service deliveries must use internal and external resources through strategic alliances and partnerships.
- Knowledge within IT must be mapped into actual business responsibilities.
- The traditional role of IT must be openly diminished.

So the CIO dilemma ultimately is to figure out how to lead this transformation. The impact on the IT organization will be significant in five ways:

1. IT must completely overhaul its value services, transitioning them to areas like business intelligence to improve collaborations with users and customers.
2. Back-office operations will continue to be commoditized and outsourced where appropriate.
3. Business units will become increasingly capable of obtaining IT services directly from third-party service providers.
4. Business leaders must learn how to develop and drive their own technology strategies and seek leadership from the CIO.
5. Traditional IT roles such as project management and change management must be transitioned into more business-defined services.

The End of Planning

Accenture issued a report in February 2012 from its Institute for High Performance. The report, "Reimagining Enterprise IT for an Uncertain Future," discusses the complexity of being an IT executive, emphasizing the "uncertainty" of the future. More important was Accenture's finding that there are seven "'large-scale forces" that can make or break IT organizations:

1. The culture impact of consumer IT: Smartphones, social networks, and other consumer technologies are creating the need to change cultures, attitudes, and workplace practices.
2. Global, Internet-based competition: Companies with Internet-based models are challenging and overtaking traditional industry leaders from North America, Europe, and Japan.
3. Vulnerable technology and information—particularly security and reliability.
4. Increasing pressure for quality and efficiency—while keeping costs low.
5. Rise of data-driven decision making for critical systems.
6. New approaches to innovation—rethinking how to provide and control new products and services.
7. Disruptive disasters caused by man-made catastrophes and wars.

The report also states, "Executives are paid to anticipate what might go wrong and what might be different tomorrow than it is today." Ultimately, this means that CIOs cannot operate based on long-term plans because its assumptions are likely to be highly vulnerable to realities. As we will discuss later in the book, CIOs need to "sense" opportunity and "respond" in a dynamic fashion. This represents a huge leap in their thinking and doing.

The world of the CIO has changed. Some may view this change as the end of the role—others will see this transition as an opportunity to transform their organizations, evolve the culture, and build technology-based businesses with an emphasis on the following core concepts:

- Employees and consumers will demand special technologies and services, which will alter the "control" mindset of many IT organizations over their constituents.
- Historical CIO responses to change will not work this time—avoiding or ignoring the need to change will not be sufficient for the CIO to survive.

- CIOs must surround themselves with technology-proficient staffs who can handle the complexities of new IT innovations, which will continue to occur at an accelerated pace.

The CIO in the Organizational Context

Understanding the changes confronting CIOs is significant. But we must also address how these changes will affect the organization. The evolution of IT will change workplace operations dramatically and will continue to increase its relevance among all components of any business, including operations, accounting, and marketing.[6] Given this increasing relevance, the CIO needs to provide significance in relation to:

- The impact it bears on organizational structure.
- The role it can assume in business strategy and competitive advantage.
- The ways in which it can be evaluated.
- The ways of integrating IT with business-line leaders (non-IT executives).

The CIO and Organizational Structure

Sampler's original research explored the relationship between IT and organizational structure.[7] His study, at that time, indicated that there is no clear-cut relationship that has been established between the two. However, his conclusions were that there are five principal positions that IT can take in this relationship:

1. IT can lead to centralization of organizational control.
2. Conversely, IT can lead to decentralization of organizational control.
3. IT can bear no impact on organizational control, its significance being based on other factors.
4. Organizations and IT can interact in an unpredictable manner.
5. IT can enable new organizational arrangements, such as networked or virtual organizations.

According to Sampler, the pursuit of explanatory models for the relationship between IT and organizational structure is a challenge, especially since IT plays dual roles. It enhances and constrains the capabilities of workers within the organization, and because of this, it possesses the ability to create a unique cultural component. While both roles are active, their impact on the organization cannot be predicted; instead, they evolve as unique social norms within the organization. Because IT is changing so dramatically, it continues to be difficult to compare prior research on the relationship between IT and organizational structure. However, with the effect of consumerization, the five principles need to be readdressed as follows:

1. The centralization of IT over the organization will likely not occur, since it is important that IT be integrated into the business. Only commodity-related services like e-mail will be controlled through central services or outsourcing. We will categorize these functions as "supporter" IT functions in Chapter 2.
2. Because of the integration factors, decentralization can lead to tremendous inefficiencies and divergent efforts; rather, IT will become more "distributed."
3. As automation and technology in general increase in multiple facets of business, it will become more of a factor in organizational control. This will relate to security issues and control of data dissemination within and outside the organization.
4. Organizational interaction will need to become more formal, although it will continue to be unpredictable—that is, without planning due to consumerization.
5. IT will continue to enable new organizational arrangements, such as networked or virtual organizations.

Earl originally studied the effects of applying business process reengineering (BPR) to organizations.[8] BPR is a process that organizations undertake to determine how best to use technology to improve business performance. BPR is now an old term but was at the forefront of the need for true IT business integration. Earl concluded that BPR was "an unfortunate title: it does not reflect the complex nature of either the distinctive underpinning concept of BPR [i.e., to reevaluate methods and rules of business operations] or the essential practical challenges to make it happen [i.e., the reality of how one goes about doing that]."[9] In Langer's 2001 study of the Ravell Corporation, he found that BPR efforts require buy-in from business-line managers and that that such efforts inevitably require the adaptation by of individuals of different cultural norms and practices.[10] These reflective studies provided early key insights for where the current challenges are in IT leadership—simply that true integration does not occur by creating new IT positions that work with non-IT employees, but rather a more evolutionary approach to realignment of knowledge and application of technology among all those that exist in the organization. The CIO then becomes the logical leader of this transition.

Schein, as discussed earlier, also pioneered some of the human resource factors of how challenging the transformation of culture could be to traditional organizations.[11] He recognized that IT culture represented a subculture in collision with many others within an organization. He concluded that if organizations were to be successful in using new technologies, especially in a global context, they must cope with ceaseless flows of information to ensure organizational health and effectiveness. His research indicated that CEOs were reluctant to implement new systems of technology unless their organizations felt comfortable with it and were ready to use it. While many CEOs were aware of cost and efficiency implications in using IT, few were aware of the potential impact on organizational structure that could result from "adopting an IT view of their organizations."[12] Such results suggested that CEOs needed to be more active and more cognizant than they have been of potential shifts in organizational structure when adopting IT opportunities. Today, the lack of understanding and management of the CIO by the CEO is clearly part of the problem of integration to support consumerization.

IT's Role in Business Strategy

While many chief executives recognize the importance of IT in the day-to-day operations of the business, their experience with attempting to utilize IT as a *strategic* business tool has been frustrating and has not materially improved since the research completed by Bensaou and Earl.[13] Their research identified five problem areas. They cite:

1. A lack of correspondence between IT investments and business strategy.
2. Inadequate understanding of the payoff from IT investments.
3. The perception of too much "technology for technology's sake."
4. Poor relations between IT specialists and users.
5. The creation of system designs that fail to incorporate users' preferences and work habits.

While McFarlan created a strategic grid designed to assess the impact of IT on operations and strategy, for the most part we have not seen a material usage in many organizations.[14] The grid showed that IT had maximum value when it affects both operations and core business objectives—certainly no surprise. Based on McFarlan's hypothesis, Applegate and colleagues established five key questions about IT that may be used by executives to guide strategic decision making[15]:

1. Can IT be used to reengineer core value activities and change the basis of competition?

2. Can IT change the nature of the relationship and the balance of power between buyers and sellers?
3. Can IT build or reduce barriers to entry?
4. Can IT increase or decrease switching costs?
5. Can IT add value to existing products and services or create new ones?

The research and analysis conducted by McFarlan and Applegate, respectively, suggest that when operational strategy and its results are maximized, IT is given its highest valuation as a tool that can transform the organization; it then receives the maximum focus from senior management and board members. However, Applegate also focused on the risks of using technology. These risks increase when executives have a poor understanding of competitive dynamics, when they fail to understand the long-term implications of a strategic system that they have launched, or when they fail to account for the time, effort, and cost required to ensure user adoption, assimilation, and effective utilization. Applegate's conclusion underscores the need for IT management to educate senior management, so that the latter will understand the appropriate indicators for what can maximize or minimize their investments in technology.

Szulanski and Amin claim that while emerging technologies shrink the window in which any given strategy can be implemented, if the strategy is well thought out, it can remain viable.[16] Mintzberg's research suggested that it would be useful to think of strategy as an art, not a science.[17] This perspective is especially true in situations of uncertainty. The rapidly changing pace of emerging technologies, we know, puts a strain on established approaches to strategy—that is to say that it becomes increasingly difficult to find comfortable implementation of technological strategies in such times of fast-moving environments, requiring sophisticated organizational infrastructure and capabilities.

Ways of Evaluating IT

Firms have been challenged to find a way to best evaluate IT, particularly using traditional return-on-investment (ROI) approaches. Unfortunately, in this regard, many components of IT do not generate direct returns. Cost allocations based on overhead formulas (e.g., costs of IT as a percentage of revenues) are not applicable to most IT spending needs. Lucas establishes nonmonetary methods for evaluating IT.[18] His concept of conversion effectiveness places value on the ability of IT to complete its projects on time and within its budgets—this alone is a sufficient factor for providing ROI, assuming that the project was approved for valid business reasons. He called this overall process for evaluation the "Garbage Can" model. It allows organizations to present IT needs through a funneling pipeline of conversion effectiveness that filters out poor technology plans and that can determine what projects will render direct and indirect benefits to the organization. Indirect returns, according to Lucas, are those that do not provide directly measurable monetary returns, but which do provide significant value that can be measured by using his IT investment opportunities matrix. Utilizing statistical probabilities of returns, the opportunities matrix provides an effective tool for evaluating the impact of indirect returns. We will revisit these concepts in Chapter 2 when discussing Langer's theory of driver and supporter.[19]

Executive Knowledge and Management of IT

While much literature and research has been produced on how IT needs to participate in and bring value to an organization, there has been relatively little analysis conducted on what non-IT chief executives need to know about technology. Applegate and colleagues suggest that non-IT executives need to understand how to differentiate new technologies from older ones and how to gauge the expected impact of these technologies on the businesses in which the firm competes for market share.[20] This is to say that technology can change the relationship between customer and vendor and thus should be examined as a potential for providing competitive advantage. The authors state that non-IT business executives must become more comfortable with technology by actively participating in technology decisions rather than delegating them to others. They need to question experts as they would in the financial areas of their businesses. Lou Gerstner, former CEO of IBM, is a good example of a non-IT chief executive who acquired a sufficient knowledge and understanding of a technology firm; he was then able to form a team of executives who better understood how to develop the firm's products, services, and overall business strategy. This research could not have been more accurate, and the need for methods of evaluating technology maturity in non-IT executives and managers will be presented.

Allen and Percival also investigate the importance of non-IT executive knowledge and participation with IT: "If the firm lacks the necessary vision, insights, skills, or core competencies, it may be unwise to invest in the hottest [IT] growth market."[21] The authors point out that success in using emerging technologies is very different from success in other traditional areas of business. They conclude that non-IT managers need to carefully consider expected synergies to determine whether an IT investment can be realized and, especially, whether it is efficient to earn cost of capital.

Recent and historical studies have focused on four important components in the linking of technology and business: (1) Its relationship to organizational structure, (2) its role in business strategy, (3) the means of its evaluation, and (4) the extent of non-IT executive knowledge in technology. The challenge in determining the best organizational structure for IT is posed by the accelerating technological advances of the past four decades, and by the difficulty in comparing organizational models to consistent business cases. Consequently, there is no single organizational structure that has been adopted by businesses—and it appears that success of IT systems for strategic uses is more dependent on leadership skills than on structure. This belief is the basis of this book, that is, that leadership, especially using methods of strategic advocacy, is more directly connected with CIO success. Indeed, it is well documented that product and service realizations in industry depend more on combinations of the people associated with the project than of its structure.

While most chief executives understand the importance of using technology as part of their business strategy, they express frustration in determining how to effectively implement a technology-based strategic approach. This frustration results from difficulties in understanding how IT investments relate to other strategic business issues, from difficulty in assessing payoff and performance of IT, generally, and from perceived poor relations between IT and other departments.

Because most IT projects do not render direct monetary returns, executives find themselves challenged to understand technology investments. They have difficulty measuring value since traditional ROI formulas are not applicable. Thus, executives would do better to focus on valuing technology investments by using methods that can determine payback based on a matrix of indirect returns, which do not always include monetary sources. There is a lack of research on the question of what general knowledge non-IT executives need to have in order to manage effectively the strategic use of technology within their firms. Non-IT chief executives are often not engaged in day-to-day IT activities, and they often delegate dealing with strategic technology issues to other managers. The remainder of this chapter examines the issues raised by the IT dilemma in its various guises especially as they become relevant to, and are confronted from, the top management or chief executive point of view.

IT: A View from the CEO

To investigate further the critical issues facing IT, Langer conducted a study in which he personally interviewed more than 40 chief executives in various industries including finance-investment, publishing, insurance, wholesale/retail, and hotel management. Executives interviewed were either the CEO or president of their corporation. For this interview study, a population of New York–based mid-size corporations was canvassed. Mid-size firms, in this case, comprise businesses of between 200 and 500 employees. Face-to-face interviews were conducted to allow participants the opportunity to articulate their responses, in contrast to answering printed survey questions; executives were therefore allowed to expand and clarify their responses to questions. The interview discussions focused on three sections: (1) Chief executive perception of the role of IT, (2) management and strategic issues, and (3) measuring IT performance and activities.

The research revealed that the matter of defining a mission for the IT organization remains as unresolved as finding a way to reckon with the potential impact of IT on business strategy. Executives still seem to be at a loss on the question of *how to integrate IT into the workplace*—a human resource as well as strategic issue. There is uncertainty regarding the dependability of the technology information received. Most agree, however, in their need for software development departments to support their developed software, in their need to outsource certain parts of technology, and in their use of outside consultants to help them formulate the future activities of their IT departments.

While the amount of time that executives spend on IT issues varies, there is a positive correlation between a structure in which CIOs report directly to the chief executive and the degree of activity that executives state they have with IT matters. CEOs understand the potential value that technology can bring to the marketing and productivity of their firms. They do not believe, however, that technology can go unmeasured; spending needs some rationale for allotting a figure in the budget. For most of the firms in this study, the use of the Internet as a technological vehicle for future business is not determined by IT. This suggests that IT does not manage the marketing aspects of technology and that it has not achieved significant integration in strategic planning.

The variations found in our research of where IT reports, how it is measured, and how its mission is defined must lie as a core responsibility of the contemporary CIO. But the wide-ranging inconsistencies and uncertainties among CEOs described earlier leave many of them wondering whether or not they should be using information technology as part of their business strategy and operations. While this quandary does not in itself suggest an inadequacy, it does point to an absence of a "best practices" guideline for using technology strategically. Hence, most CIOs have not developed a clear plan on how to evolve IT contributions toward business development. Though a high majority of CEOs feel that IT is critical to the survival of their businesses, the degree of IT assimilation within the core culture of organizations still varies. This suggests that the effects of cultural assimilation lag behind the actual involvement of IT in the strategic direction of the company.

Of course, "best practices" always embodies the implicit notion of best principles, and the problems confronting executives—the need for practical guidelines—remains. For instance, our studies show that IT performance is measured in many different ways. It is this type of practical inconsistency that leaves chief executives with the difficult challenge of understanding how technology decisions can be managed.

This chapter has addressed the IT dilemma through two fundamental perspectives: The CIO's role and responsibilities to the organization; and the view from the CEO and organization at large. Ultimately, the purpose of this book is to provide practitioners, CEOs, and educators with remedies to the dilemmas that we have presented. Thus, the book is broken down into three components. First, it provides a grounded theory of how these executives position the role of technology within the business, the strategic advocacy practices they use, and how they adapt them. Second, it examines the organizational implications of these strategic relationships in terms of implications for organizational learning and innovation. Third, it looks at the learning process as a device for nurturing these strategies in high-potential technology professionals and managers.

Notes

1. A. M. Langer, *Information Technology and Organizational Learning: Managing Behavioral Change through Technology and Education*, 2nd ed. (Boca Raton, FL: Taylor & Francis, 2011); and E. H. Schein, *Organizational Culture and Leadership*, 2nd ed. (San Francisco: Jossey-Bass, 1992).
2. N. Carr, "IT Doesn't Matter," *Harvard Business Review* 81(5) (2003): 41–49.
3. Langer, *Information Technology and Organizational Learning*.
4. C. K. Prahalad and M. S. Krishnan, *The New Age of Innovation: Driving Cocreated Value through Global Networks* (New York: McGraw-Hill, 2008).
5. Ibid., p. 6.
6. E. H. Schein, *Organizational Culture and Leadership*; M. J. Earl, "Business Processing Engineering: A Phenomenon of Organizational Dimension." In M. J. Earl (Ed.), *Information Management: The Organizational Dimension* (New York: Oxford University Press, 1996), 53–76; and Langer, *Information Technology and Organizational Learning*.
7. J. L. Sampler, "Exploring the Relationship between Information Technology and Organizational Structure." In M. J. Earl (Ed.), *Information Management: The Organizational Dimension* (New York: Oxford University Press, 1996), 5–22.
8. Earl, *Information Management*.
9. Ibid., p. 54.
10. A. M. Langer, "Fixing Bad Habits: Integrating Technology Personnel in the Workplace Using Reflective Practice," *Reflective Practice* 2(1) (2001): 100–111.
11. Schein, *Organizational Culture and Leadership*.
12. Ibid., p. 293.
13. M. Bensaou and M. J. Earl, "The Right Mind-set for Managing Information Technology." In J. E. Garten (Ed.), *World View: Global Strategies for the New Economy* (Cambridge, MA: Harvard University Press, 1998), 109–125.
14. L. M. Applegate, R. D. Austin, and F. W. McFarlan, *Corporate Information Strategy and Management*, 2nd ed. (New York: McGraw-Hill, 2003).
15. Ibid.

16. G. Szulanski and K. Amin, "Disciplined Imagination: Strategy Making in Uncertain Environments." In G. S. Day and P. J. Schoemaker (Eds.), *Wharton on Managing Emerging Technologies* (New York: John Wiley & Sons, 2000), 187–205.

17. H. Mintzberg, "Crafting Strategy," *Harvard Business Review* 65(4) (1987): 72.

18. H. C. Lucas, *Information Technology and the Productivity Paradox* (New York: Oxford University Press, 1999).

19. A. M. Langer, *Information Technology and Organizational Learning: Managing Behavioral Change through Technology and Education*, 1st ed. (Boca Raton, FL: Taylor & Francis, 2005).

20. L. M. Applegate, R. D. Austin, and F. W. McFarlan, *Corporate Information Strategy and Management*, 2nd ed. (New York: McGraw-Hill, 2003).

21. F. Allen and J. Percival, "Financial Strategies and Venture Capital." In G. S. Day and P. J. Schoemaker (Eds.), *Wharton on Managing Emerging Technologies* (New York: John Wiley & Sons, 2000), p. 295.

CHAPTER 2

IT Drivers and Supporters

This chapter provides a perspective of why technology has a unique effect on corporate performance. Specifically, if we look at information technology (IT) from a layperson's point of view, we might better understand how to make technology a more integral part of strategic and competitive advantage. More important is to provide a template for how organizations respond to the generic catalysts for change brought on by technological innovations. Furthermore, how do we objectively view the role of technology in this context, and how should organizations adjust to its short- and long-term impacts?

Drivers and Supporters

According to Langer, there are essentially two types of generic functions performed by departments in organizations: "Driver" functions and "supporter" functions.[1] These functions relate to the essential behavior and nature of what a department contributes to the goals of the organization.

Drivers are defined as those units that engage in direct revenue or front-line generating activities. Supporters are units that do not generate obvious direct revenues but rather are focused on the support of front-line activities. Examples of support functions are operations such as internal accounting, purchasing, or office management. Support departments, due to their very nature, are evaluated on their effectiveness and efficiency or economies of scale. In contrast, driver organizations are expected to generate direct or indirect revenues for the firm. Drivers are also expected to take more risks—since they must inevitably generate returns for the business. As such, drivers engage in what Bradley and Nolan coined "sense and respond" behaviors and activities.[2] Let me explain.

19

Marketing departments often generate new business by investing or "sensing" an opportunity, quickly—because of competitive forces in the marketplace. As a result they must sense an opportunity and be allowed to respond to it timely. Furthermore, the process of sensing opportunity and responding with competitive products or services is a cycle undergoing more and more scrutiny—simply put there is less time to respond. Thus, failures in the cycles of sense and respond are expected. Langer's analogy of the launching of new fall television shows is an example. Each of the major stations goes through a process of "sensing" what shows might be interesting to the viewing audience.[3] They "respond" after research and review with a number of new shows. Inevitably, only a few of these selected shows are actually successful; some fail almost immediately. While relatively few shows succeed, the process is acceptable and is seen by management as the consequence of an appropriate set of steps for competing effectively—even though the percentage of successful new shows is very low. Therefore, it is required that today's driver organizations are expected to engage in high-risk oriented operations, of which many will fail for the sake of creating ultimately successful products or services.

The preceding example raises two questions: (1) How does "sense and respond" relate to the world of information technology, and (2) why is it important? Information technology is unique in that it is both a driver and a supporter, the latter being the generally accepted norm in most firms. Indeed, many IT functions are established to support a myriad of internal functions such as:

- Accounting and finance
- Data-center infrastructure (e-mail, desktop, etc.)
- Enterprise level application
- Customer support
- Web and e-commerce activities

As one would expect, the previous IT functions are typically viewed as overhead, as a commodity, and thus constantly managed on an economy-of-scale basis—that is, how can we make this operation more efficient, with a particular focus on cost containment?

So what then are IT driver functions? By definition they are those that engage in direct revenues and identifiable return on investment (ROI). How do we define such functions in IT, as most activities are sheltered under the umbrella of marketing organization domains? (Excluding, of course, software application development firms that engage in marketing for their actual application products.) Langer defines IT driver functions as those projects that if delivered would change the relationship between the organization and its customers, that is, those activities that directly affect the classic definition of a market: Forces of supply and demand, which are governed by the customer (demand) and the vendor (supplier) relationship.[4] Langer repeatedly uses the *Santander v. Citibank* case as an example.

Santander Bank, the major bank of Spain, had enjoyed a dominant market share in its home country. Citibank had attempted for years to penetrate Santander's dominance using traditional approaches (opening more branch offices, marketing, etc.) without success until, that is, they tried online banking. Using technology as a driver, Citibank made significant penetration into Santander's market share because it changed the customer-vendor relationship. Online banking, in general, has had a significant impact on how the banking industry has established new markets by changing this relationship. What is also interesting about this case is the way in which Citibank has accounted for its investment in online banking: It knows very little about its total investment, and essentially does not care about its direct payback. Rather, Citibank sees its ROI in a similar way that depicts driver/marketing behavior: The payback is seen in broader terms to affect not only revenue generation but also customer support and quality recognition.

Yet another example is Dana Deasy, when he was chief information officer (CIO) of the Americas for Siemens. At Siemens, Deasy was responsible for more than CIOs across separate and discrete businesses. His role was to promote e-business strategy. Essentially, the CIOs were challenged with the responsibility of rebranding their assets into clusters based on their generic business areas like hospitals, medical, and communications. The essence of this strategic driver was to use e-business strategy to provide multiple offerings to the same Siemens customer base.

Deasy engaged in an initiative to communicate with non-IT executives by using a process called "storyboarding." Storyboarding is the process of creating prototypes that allow users to actually see an example of how the technology will look and operate. Storyboarding tells a story and can quickly educate executives without being intimidating. Deasy was able to establish a unique life cycle for IT projects by creating excitement through animation— for example, what would Siemens be like if . . . ? He also was able to implement considerations about how IT as a business driver would be consistent with what the business was trying to accomplish. The concept resulted in a process where IT projects were reviewed every 90 days by an advisory board after products had experimental use with customers.

We see in this example that the biggest challenge is not necessarily keeping up with new technologies, but rather how technologies can be tested to determine exactly how they might impact the business. In order to address this dilemma, Deasy established the concept of "revalidation." Specifically, approved technology projects were reviewed every 90 days to determine whether they were indeed providing the planned outcomes, whether new outcomes needed to be established, or whether the technology was no longer useful. The concept of revalidation is an example of a "driver" technology that required a different method of evaluation. Specifically, it required that IT be given the ability to invest and experiment with technology in order to fully maximize the evaluation of the product to the business. This gave Deasy a way to evolve the culture at Siemens, that is, for management to recognize that not all approved technologies succeed. He also dramatically altered the ways in which software applications were to be evaluated by executive management.

After the technology is absorbed into operations, executives will seek to maximize the benefit by increased efficiency and effectiveness. Certain product enhancements may be pursued during this cycle; they can create "mini loops" of driver to supporter activities. Ultimately a technology, viewed in terms of its economies of scale and longevity, is considered for replacement or outsourcing. Figure 2.1 graphically shows the cycle.

The final stage of maturity of technology driver, therefore, is becoming a supporter, at which time it behaves as a commodity, meaning that it likely can be replaced or outsourced. Subsequent cases in this book explore methods that can be used to address many of the issues and challenges brought forth in this chapter. The concept of a driver becoming a supporter is analogous to the theory of an "S"-curve. According to Wideman, the S-curve is defined as "a display of cumulative costs, labour hours or other quantities plotted against time. The name derives from the S-like shape of the curve, flatter at the beginning and end and steeper in the middle, which is typical of most projects. The beginning represents a slow, deliberate but accelerating start, while the end represents a deceleration as the work runs out."[5] Such is the case with drivers and supporters. All initial IT projects should start as a driver and accelerate slowly up the S-curve. During this cycle, markets are evolving and very

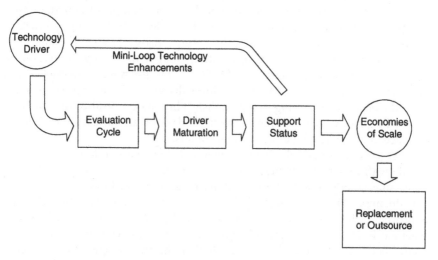

Figure 2.1   Driver to supporter life cycle.

uncertain or what Eisenhardt and Bourgeois coined as "high-velocity environments."[6] As a result of market uncertainty, IT requirements will evolve and thus CIOs need to continually react to changes in consumer preferences. This is where the IT "failure rate" needs to be established.

However, like all true S-curves, eventually the market will mature and products will become generic and sensitive to price. The commoditization of the product is inevitable. The question is: When? Thus, CIOs must be students of the S-curve—always thinking about where a product or service exists along the curve and how it affects the measurement of the IT organization.

Drivers: A Closer Look from the CIO

CIOs must step up to the challenge by putting this reality into perspective with their executive peers in the C-suite. Conversations about technology driver opportunities should never contain any technical jargon—it's communicating IT from a business perspective. While many CIOs admit this, not enough really practice how to articulate why IT is complex—or is it?

CIOs need to convey the essence that IT drivers must be more daring and engage in higher-risk oriented operations if they are to bring true value to the business. If you can get the business to understand that many aspects of IT are drivers, then the business can accept that there will be failure rates and changes needed along the way—especially given that the market is immature and changes are the norm. Think about this: If a baseball player gets a hit one out of three bats, he will bat over .300 and make the Hall of Fame. What then should be the batting average for driver IT projects? The CIO must define this in context of the business. So if you have an IT project and everyone understands that it is a driver, then the business cannot know what the overall costs might be—budgets likely mean little—yet so many projects fall into a trap in volatile markets.

Supporters: Managing with Efficiency

Supporter functions, as we defined, are units that do not generate obvious direct revenues, but rather, are designed to support front-line activities. Supporters must live and die on their efficiency and should never fail to provide service. So if you are implementing a supporter project, costs must be low, performance must be high, and failure rate nonexistent. An example of a supporter is e-mail—it better not fail. CIOs need to be careful, though; we do not suggest the supporters are not important. Being on the driver side has lots of glamour, but make no mistake: If the supporter functions are not working, a CIO will have a short life! Another way of saying this is that the lights need to be kept on, and don't underestimate the importance of the supporter side of the business.

Unfortunately, many CIOs spend too much of their own individual time on supporter functions. Perhaps this is due to the fact that CIOs feel comfortable with that side of the business. However, allocating too much of their individual time on supporter functions will ultimately detract from time spent with other executives regarding their driver needs. Effective CIOs will surround themselves with capable supporter personnel, so that they can free up time for the driver activities. Thus, the message to CIOs is to surround themselves with the talent that can run the day-to-day business. This does not suggest that CIOs should not be active in supporter functions; having regular updates from their management team is certainly necessary.

In some instances, a supporter can transform itself into a driver, almost like a reverse life cycle. This would mean that some feature or function of the supporter technology was enhanced in such a way that it could be used competitively. Examples of this kind of transformation relate to help desk activities that can be used to create new business opportunities while working on solving technology-related problems. Another interesting supporter to driver evolution is Web sites to social media, where new features could actually initiate revenue opportunities, as opposed to just supporting users.

Yet another example of an IT product going from supporter to driver occurred at Grey Healthcare Group. Grey, like many agencies, provides services to assist its clients to help market its product and services. During our conversation with CEO Lynn O'Connor-Vos, we discussed a product that initially was used to determine project costs for clients. It was a typical project management product that tracked usage for billing and accounting functions—an internal support product, for sure. Well, Lynn saw a driver function—by creating a more robust "Dashboard," customers could be much more aware of where they were with their budgets, and could make more dynamic decisions of how to better spend their advertising dollars. It was good for Grey and good for their clients. The Dashboard became a driver and interacted socially, if you will, in a way that prior Internet products could not be effectively implemented.

IT: A Driver or a Supporter?

The sheer fact that drivers become supporters, as shown in Figure 2.1, actually provides an interesting way for CIOs to communicate with their peers. Here is the business case:

- IT is unique in that it is both a driver and a supporter.
- IT drivers are those activities that can change the relationship with the customer. Stay away from trying to determine how much—the fact that it changes the market balance is most important.

- All initial IT initiatives should start out as drivers, and then become supporters over time. This is the S-curve of IT, and every CIO should have a sense of where their products fall. If your product is nearing support status, you must be more efficient and perhaps consider outsourcing.

The overall message is that IT can drive business strategy and yet support it at the same time. CIOs must know where they are with every project initiative. If you are a driver, be strategic and attend executive meetings. If you have a supporter, hire the best people or companies to run them and manage them effectively, but do not spend too much executive time with these projects. Most important, both drivers and supporters are important—you can't do one without the other. You must be strategic but the lights must stay on at all times.

Technological Dynamism

Langer introduced technology dynamism as "the unpredictable and accelerated ways in which technology, specifically, can change organizational behavior and culture."[7] Perhaps if we look at IT as a variable, independent of others, we can examine the contribution to the life of a business operation. It is capable of producing an overall totalizing, yet distinctive effect on organizations: It has the unique capacity to create accelerations of corporate events in an unpredictable way. IT, in its many aspects of unpredictability, is necessarily a variable; and in its capacity as accelerator—its tendency to produce change or advance—it is dynamic. As a dynamic kind of variable, IT, via a responsive handling or management, can be tapped to play a special role in organizational development. It can be pressed into service as the dynamic catalyst that helps bring organizations to maturity in dealing not only with new technological quandaries but with other agents of change as well. Change generates new knowledge, which in turn requires a structure of learning that should, if managed properly, result in transformative behavior, supporting the continued evolution of organizational culture. Specifically, technology speeds up events, such as the expectation of getting a response to an e-mail, and requires organizations to respond to them in ever-quickening time frames. Such events are not as predictable as what individuals in organizations have experienced prior to the advent of new technologies—particularly with the meteoric advance of the Internet. In viewing technology then as a *dynamic* variable, as one that requires of organizations systemic and cultural change, we may regard it as an inherent, internal driving force—a form of technological dynamism.

"Dynamism" is defined as a process or mechanism responsible for the development or motion of a system. "Technology dynamism," therefore, is based on the acceleration of events and interactions within organizations and which in turn create the need to better empower individuals and departments. Another way of understanding technological dynamism is to think of it as an internal drive recognized by the symptoms it produces. The new events and interactions brought about by technology are symptoms of the dynamism that technology manifests. The next section discusses how CIOs can begin to make this inherent dynamism work in its favor on different levels.

Responsive Organizational Dynamism

The technological dynamism at work in organizations has the power to disrupt any antecedent sense of comfortable equilibrium, or an unwelcome sense of stasis. It also upsets the balance among the various factors and relationships that pertain to the question of how we might integrate new technologies into the business—a question of what Langer called "strategic integration"—and how we assimilate the cultural changes they bring about organizationally—a question of what he called "cultural assimilation."[8] Managing the dynamism therefore is a way of managing the effects of technology. Langer proposed that these organizational ripples, these precipitous events and interactions can be addressed in specific ways at the organizational management level. The set of integrative responses to the challenges raised by technology is what Langer called "responsive organizational dynamism" (ROD). There are two distinct categories that present themselves in response to technological dynamism: Strategic integration and cultural assimilation.[9]

Strategic Integration

Strategic integration is a process that firms need to use to address the business impact of technology on its organizational processes. That is to say, the business *strategic* impact of technology requires immediate organizational responses and in some instances zero latency. Strategic integration therefore is the concept of how to recognize the need to scale resources across traditional business geographic boundaries, to redefine the value chain in the life cycle of a product or service line and generally to foster more agile business processes.[10] Strategic integration, then, is a way to address the need to change business processes caused by new technology innovations. Evolving technologies are now catalysts for competitive initiatives that create new and different ways to determine successful business investment. As a result, organizations need to see how the technology specifically provides opportunities to compete, and in many cases survive.

Historically, organizational experiences with IT investments have resulted in two distinct steps of measured returns. The first step often shows negative or declining productivity as a result of the investment; in the second step we experience a lagging of, though eventual return to, productivity. The lack of returns in the first step or phase has been attributed to the nature of the early stages of technology exploration and experimentation, which tend to slow down the process of organizational adaptation to technology. The production phase then lags behind the organization's ability to integrate new technologies with its existing processes. Another complication posed by technological dynamism via the process of strategic integration is a phenomenon called "factors of multiplicity"—essentially what happens when several new technology opportunities overlap and create a myriad of projects that are in various phases of their developmental life cycle. Furthermore, the problem is compounded by lagging returns in productivity, which are complicated to track and to represent to management. Thus, it is important that organizations find ways to shorten the period between investment and technology's effective deployment. Murphy identifies five factors that are critical to bridging this delta:

1. Identifying the processes that can provide acceptable business returns
2. Establishing methodologies that can determine these processes
3. Finding ways to actually perform and realize expected benefits
4. Integrating IT projects with other projects
5. Adjusting project objectives when changes in the business require them[11]

Technology complicates these actions, making them more difficult to resolve—hence the need to manage the complications. To address these compounded concerns, strategic integration can shorten life cycle maturation by focusing on the following integrating factors:

- Addressing the weaknesses in management organizations in terms of how to deal with new technologies and how to better realize business benefits
- Providing a mechanism that both enables organizations to deal with accelerated change caused by technological innovations and that integrates them into a new cycle of processing and handling change
- Providing a strategic framework whereby every new technology variable adds to organizational evolution, particularly using strategic advocacy (Chapter 3)

- Establishing an integrated approach that ties IT accountability to other measurable outcomes integrating acceptable methods of the organization

In order to realize these objectives, executives must be able to:

- Create dynamic internal processes that can function on a daily basis to deal with understanding the potential fit of new technologies and its overall value to the local department within the business, that is, to provide for change at the grass roots level of the organization.
- Provide the discourse to bridge the gaps between IT and non-IT-related investments and uses into an integrated system.
- Monitor investments and determine modifications to the current life cycle of idea-to-reality.
- Implement proven techniques that can be used by CIOs that allows them to bring about evolutionary change at the executive level, blending IT with the business.

Another important aspect of strategic integration is what Murphy calls "consequential interoperability," in which "the consequences of a business process" are understood to "dynamically trigger integration."[12] This integration occurs in what he calls the "Five Pillars of Benefits Realization":

1. **Strategic alignment:** The alignment of IT strategically with business goals and objectives
2. **Business process impact:** The impact on the need for the organization to redesign business processes and integrate them with new technologies
3. **Architecture:** The actual technological integration of applications, databases, and networks to facilitate and support implementation
4. **Payback:** The basis for computing ROI from both direct and indirect perspectives
5. **Risk:** Identifying the exposure for underachievement or failure in the technology investment

Murphy's Pillars are useful in helping us understand how technology can engender the need for strategic integration. They also help us understand what becomes the strategic integration component of ROD. His theory on strategic alignment and business process impact supports the notion that IT will increasingly serve as an undergirding force, one that will drive enterprise growth by identifying the initiators (such as e-business on the Internet) that best fits business goals. Many of these initiators will be accelerated by the growing use of e-business, which becomes the very *driver* of many new market realignments. This e-business realignment will require the ongoing involvement of executives, business managers, and IT managers. Indeed, the Gartner Group's original forecast that 70% of new software application investments and 50% of new infrastructure expenditures by 2005 would be driven by e-business was very accurate.

The combination of evolving business drivers with accelerated and changing customer demands has created a business revolution that best defines the imperative of the strategic integration component of ROD. The changing and accelerated way businesses deal with their customers and vendors requires a new strategic integration to become a reality, rather than remain a concept given discussion to but affecting little action. Without action directed toward new strategic integration, organizations would lose competitive advantage, which would ultimately affect profits. Most experts see e-business as the mechanism that will ultimately require the integrated business processes to be realigned, thus providing value to customers and modifying the customer/vendor relationship. The driving force behind this realignment emanates from the Internet, which serves as the principle accelerator of the change in transactions across all businesses. The general need to optimize resources forces organizations to rethink and to realign business processes in order to gain access to new business markets.

Murphy's "Pillar of Architecture" brings out yet another aspect of Responsive Organizational Dynamism. By "architecture" we mean the focus on the effects that technology has on existing computer applications, or legacy systems (old existing systems). Technology requires existing IT systems to be modified or replacement systems to be created that will mirror the new business realignments. These changes respond to the forces of strategic integration and require business process reengineering (BPR) activities, which represent the reevaluation of existing systems based on changing business requirements. It is important to keep in mind the acceleration factors of technology, and to recognize the amount of organizational effort and time that such projects take to complete. We must ask: How might organizations respond to these continual requirements to modify existing processes? We shall see in later chapters how ROD represents the answer to this question and an important strategic weapon for the CIO to use to support change.

However, Murphy's "Pillar of Direct Return" is somewhat limited and narrow because not all IT value can be associated with direct returns, but it is important to discuss. Technology acceleration is forcing organizations to deal with broader issues surrounding what represents a return from an investment. The value of strategic integration relies heavily on the ability of technology to encapsulate itself within other departments where it ultimately provides the value. CIOs need to steer their executive colleagues away from IT direct returns; rather, the real IT value can be best determined within individual business units at the micro level. That is, let the appropriate level business unit(s) establish the case for why certain IT investments need to be pursued. Most important is to educate executives that most IT paybacks are indirect: For example, Lucas demonstrates that many technology investments are nonmonetary in nature.[13] The IT department is one among others that becomes susceptible to great scrutiny and is subject to budgetary cutbacks during economically difficult times. This does not suggest that IT "hide" itself, but rather that its investment be integrated within the unit where it provides the most benefit—this would be then the driver side of the front-line IT project. Notwithstanding the challenge to map IT expenditures to its related unit, there are always expenses that are central to all departments, such as e-mail and network infrastructure. These types of expenses can rarely provide direct returns and are typically allocated across departments as a "cost of doing business."

Because of the increased number of technology opportunities, Murphy's "Risk" pillar must be a key part of CIOs' strategic integration approach. The concept of risk assessment is not new to an organization; however, it is somewhat misunderstood as it relates to technology assessment. Technology assessment must, because of the acceleration factor, be embedded within the strategic decision-making process. This can be accomplished only by having an understanding of how to align technology opportunities for business change and by understanding the cost of forgoing the opportunity, as well as the cost of delays in delivery. Many organizations use risk assessment in a very unstructured way, which does not provide a consistent framework to dynamically deal with emerging technologies. Furthermore, such assessment needs to be managed throughout the organization as opposed to being event-driven activities controlled by executives.

Strategic integration represents the objective of dealing with emerging technologies on a regular basis. It is an outcome of ROD, and it requires organizations to deal with a variable that forces acceleration of decisions in an unpredictable fashion. Strategic integration would require businesses to realign the ways in which they include technology in strategic decision making. CIOs need to create appropriate infrastructures to support the ongoing examination of innovations and how they provide customer value at the business unit level.

Cultural Assimilation

Cultural assimilation is a process that addresses the organizational aspects of how technology is internally organized, including the role of the IT department, and how it is assimilated within the organization as a whole. The inherent, contemporary reality of technological dynamism is not limited only to strategic issues, but *cultural* change as well. This reality requires that IT organizations connect to all aspects of the business. Such affiliation would foster a more interactive culture rather than one that is regimented and linear, as is too often the case. An interactive culture is one that can respond to emerging technology decisions in an optimally informed way, one that understands the impact on business performance.

The kind of cultural assimilation elicited by technological dynamism and formalized in ROD is divided into two subcategories: The study of how the IT organization relates and communicates with "others" and the actual displacement or movement of traditional IT staff from an isolated "core" structure to a firm-wide, integrated framework.[14]

IT Organization Communications with "Others"

Langer's case study called "Ravell" showed the limitations and consequences of an isolated operating IT department within an organization.[15] The case study showed that the isolation of a group by a CIO can lead to IT marginalization, which results in the kind of organization where not all individuals can participate in decision making and implementation, even though such individuals have important knowledge and value. Technological dynamism is forcing IT departments to rethink their strategic position within their firm's organizational structure. No longer can IT be a stand-alone unit designed just to service outside departments while maintaining its own separate identity. The acceleration factors of technology require more dynamic activity within and among departments, which cannot be accomplished through discrete communications between groups. Instead, the need for diverse groups to engage in more integrated discourse and to share varying levels of technological knowledge as well as business-end perspectives requires new organizational structures that will of necessity give birth to a new and evolving business social culture. Indeed, the need to assimilate technology creates a *transformative* effect on organizational cultures, the way they are formed and reformed, and what they will need from IT personnel.

Movement of Traditional IT Staff

In order to facilitate cultural assimilation from an IT perspective, CIOs must have their IT staffs better integrated with non-IT management than is currently the case. This form of integration can require the actual movement of IT staff personnel into other departments, which begins the process of a true assimilation of resources among business units. While this may seem like the elimination of IT's integrity or identity, such loss is far from being the case.

The elimination of the IT department is not at all what is called for here; on the contrary, the IT department is critical to the function of cultural assimilation. However, the IT department may need to be structured differently from the way it has been, so that it can deal primarily with generic infrastructure and support issues such as e-mail, network architecture, and security. IT personnel who focus on business-specific issues need to become closely aligned with the appropriate units so that ROD can be successfully implemented.

Furthermore, we must acknowledge that, given the wide range of available knowledge about technology, not all technological knowledge emanates from the IT department. The question becomes one of finding the best structure to support a broad assimilation of knowledge about any given technology; then we should ask how that knowledge can best be utilized by the organization. There is a pitfall in attempting to find a "standard" IT organizational structure that will address the cultural assimilation of technology. Sampler's research and Langer's studies with chief executives confirm that no such standard structure exists.[16] Organizations must find their own unique blend using organizational learning constructs. This simply means that that the cultural assimilation of IT may be unique to the organization. What is then more important for the success of organizational development is the process of assimilation as opposed to the transplanting of the structure itself.

Today, many departments still operate within "silos" where they are unable to meet the requirements of the dynamic and unpredictable nature of technology in the business environment. Traditional organizations do not often support the necessary communications needed to implement cultural assimilation across business units. However, business managers can no longer make decisions without considering technology; they will find themselves needing to include IT staff in their decision-making processes. However, CIOs can no longer make technology-based decisions without concerted efforts toward assimilation (in contrast to occasional partnering or project-driven participation) with other business units. This assimilation becomes mature when new cultures evolve synergistically as opposed to just having multiple cultures that attempt to work in conjunction (partner) with one another.

Without appropriate cultural assimilation, organizations tend to have staff that "take shortcuts, [then] the loudest voice will win the day, ad hoc decisions will be made, accountabilities lost, and lessons from successes and failures will not become part of . . . wisdom."[17] It is essential then for the CIO to provide for consistent governance, one that fits the profile of the existing culture or that can establish the need for a new culture. While many scholars and managers suggest the need to have a specific entity responsible for IT governance, one that is to be placed within the organization's operating structure, such an approach creates a fundamental problem. It does not allow staff and managers the opportunity to assimilate technologically driven change and understand how to design a culture that can operate under ROD. In other words, the issue of governance is misinterpreted as a problem of structural positioning or hierarchy when it is really one of cultural assimilation. As a result, many business solutions to technology issues often lean toward the prescriptive instead of the analytical in addressing the real problem.

Murphy's Risk Pillar theory offers us another important component relevant to cultural assimilation. This approach addresses well the concerns that relate to the creation of risk cultures formed to deal with the impact of new systems. New technologies can actually cause changes in cultural assimilation by establishing the need to make certain changes in job descriptions, power structures, career prospects, degree of job security, departmental influence, or ownership of data. Each of these potential risks needs to be factored in as an important part of considering how best to organize and assimilate technology through ROD.

Technology Business Cycle

To better understand technology dynamism or how technology acts as a dynamic variable, it is necessary to define the specific steps that occur during its evolution in an organization. The evolution or business cycle depicts the sequential steps during the maturation of a new technology from feasibility to implementation and through subsequent evolution. Table 2.1 shows the five components that comprise the cycle.

Feasibility

The stage of feasibility focuses on a number of issues surrounding the practicality of implementing a specific technology. Feasibility addresses the ability to deliver a product when it is needed in comparison to the time it takes to develop it. Risk also plays a role in feasibility assessment; of specific concern is the question: Is it possible or probable that the product will become obsolete before completion? Cost is certainly a huge factor but viewed at a "high level" (i.e., at a general cost range), and it is usually geared toward meeting a firm's expected returns from its investments. The feasibility process must be one that incorporates individuals in a way that allows them to respond to the accelerated and dynamic process brought forth by technological innovations.

Table 2.1   Technology business cycle.

Cycle Component	Component Description
Feasibility	Understanding how to view and evaluate emerging technologies from a technical and business perspectives.
Measurement	Dealing with both the direct monetary returns and indirect nonmonetary returns; establishing *driver* and *support* life cycles.
Planning	Understanding how to set up projects; establishing participation across multiple layers of management including operations and departments
Implementation	Working with the realities of project management; operating with political factions, constraints, meeting milestones, dealing with setbacks; ability to go live with new systems.
Evolution	Understanding how acceptance of new technologies affects cultural change and how uses of technology will change as individuals and organizations become more knowledgeable about technology and generate new ideas about how it can be used; this objective is established through organizational dynamism, creating new knowledge, and an evolving organization,

Measurement

Measurement is the process of understanding how an investment in technology is calculated, particularly in relation to an organization's ROI. The complication with technology and measurement is that it is simply not that easy to determine how to calculate such a return. This problem comes up in many of the issues discussed by Lucas in his book, *Information Technology and the Productivity Paradox*.[18] His work addresses many comprehensive issues surrounding both monetary and nonmonetary ROI, as well as direct versus indirect allocation of IT costs. Aside from these issues, there is also the fact that, for many investments in technology, the attempt to compute ROI may be an inappropriate approach. Lucas offers a "Garbage Can" model that advocates trust in the operational management of the business and the formation of IT representatives into productive teams that can assess new technologies as a regular part of business operations. The Garbage Can is an abstract concept for allowing individuals a place to suggest innovations brought about by technology. The inventory of technology opportunities needs regular evaluation. Lucas does not really offer an explanation of exactly how this process should work internally. ROD, however, provides the strategic processes and organizational-cultural needs that can provide the infrastructure to better understand and evaluate the potential benefits from technological innovations using the Garbage Can model. The graphic depiction of the model is shown in Figure 2.2.

Garbage Can Model of IT Value

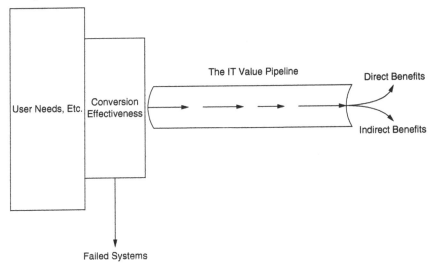

Figure 2.2   Garbage Can model of IT value.
Source: H. C. Lucas, Information Technology and the Productivity Paradox *(New York: Oxford University Press, 1999).*

Planning

Planning requires a defined team of user and IT representatives. This appears to be a simple task, but is more challenging to understand how such teams should operate, from whom it needs support, and what resources it requires. Let me be specific. There are a number of varying types of "users" of technology. They typically exist in three tiers: Executives, business-line managers, and operations. Each of these individuals offers valuable yet different views of the benefits of technology.[19] These user tiers are defined as follows:

1. **Executives:** These individuals are often referred to as executive sponsors. Their role is twofold. First, they provide input into the system, specifically from the perspective of productivity, ROI, and competitive edge. Second, and perhaps more important, their responsibility is to ensure that users are participating in the requisite manner (i.e., made to be available and in the right place, etc.) This area can be problematic because internal users are typically busy doing their jobs and sometimes neglect to provide input or to attend project meetings. Furthermore, executive sponsors can help control political agendas that can hurt the success of the project.

2. **Business-line managers:** This interface provides the most information from a business-unit perspective. These individuals are responsible for two aspects of management. First, they are responsible for the day-to-day productivity of their unit, and therefore they understand the importance of productive teams and how software can assist in this endeavor. Second, they are responsible for their staffs. Thus, line managers need to know how software will affect their operational staffs.

3. **Functional users:** These are the individuals in the trenches who understand exactly how processing needs to get done. While their purview of the benefits of the system is relatively narrower than the executives and managers, they provide the concrete information that is required to create the feature/functions that make the system usable.

The planning process becomes challenging when attempting to get the three user communities to integrate their needs and "agree to agree" on how a technology project needs to be designed and managed.

Implementation

Implementation is the process of actually using a technology. Implementation of technology systems requires wider integration within the various departments than other systems in an organization because they usually affect multiple business units. Implementation must combine traditional methods of IT processes of development yet integrate them within the constraints, assumptions, and cultural (perhaps political) environments of different departments. Cultural assimilation is therefore required at this stage because it delves into the internal organization's structure and requires individual participation in every phase of the development and implementation cycle. The following are nine of the unique challenges facing the implementation of technological projects:

1. **Project managers as complex managers:** Technology projects require multiple interfaces that often lie outside the traditional user community. They can include interfacing with writers, editors, marketing personnel, customers, and consumers, all of whom are stakeholders in the success of the system.

2. **Shorter and dynamic development schedules:** Due to the dynamic nature of technology, its process of development is less linear than that of others. Because there is less experience in the general user community and there are more stakeholders, there is a tendency by IT and executives to underestimate the time and cost to complete the project.

3. **New untested technologies:** There is so much new technology offered to organizations that there is a tendency by IT organizations

to implement technologies that have not yet matured—that are not yet the best product they will eventually be.

4. **Degree of scope changes:** Technology, because of its dynamic nature, tends to be very prone to "scope-creep"—the scope of the original project expanding during development.

5. **Project management:** Project managers need to work closely with internal users, customers, and consumers to advise them on the impact of changes to the project schedule. Unfortunately, scope changes that are influenced by changes in market trends may not be avoidable. Thus, part of a good strategy is to manage scope changes rather than attempt to stop them, which might not be realistic.

6. **Estimating completion time:** IT has always had difficulties in knowing how long it will take to implement a technology. Application systems are even more difficult because of the number of variables, unknowns.

7. **Lack of standards:** The technology industry continues to be a profession that does not have a governing body. Thus, it is impossible to have real enforced standards as other professions enjoy. While there are suggestions for best practices, many of them are unproven and not kept current with changing developments. Because of the lack of successful application projects, there are few success stories to create a new and better set of "best practices."

8. **Less specialized roles and responsibilities:** The IT team tends to have staff members that have varying responsibilities. Unlike traditional new technology driven projects, separation of roles and responsibilities is more difficult when operating in more dynamic environments. The reality is that many roles have not been formalized and integrated using something like ROD.

9. **Broad project management responsibilities:** Project management responsibilities need to go beyond those of the traditional IT manager. Project managers are required to provide management services outside the traditional software staff. They need to interact more with internal and external individuals as well as with nontraditional members of the development team, such as Web text and content staff. Therefore, there are many more obstacles that can cause implementation problems.

Evolution

Many of the needs to form a technological organization with the natural capacity to evolve have been discussed from an IT perspective in this chapter. However, another important factor is the changing nature of application systems, particularly those that involve e-businesses. E-business systems are those that utilize the Internet and engage in e-commerce activities among vendors, clients, and internal users in the organization. The ways in which e-business systems are built and deployed suggest that they are evolving systems. This means that they have a long life cycle involving ongoing maintenance and enhancement. They are, if you will, "living systems" that evolve in a similar manner in which organizational cultures have developed. So the traditional beginning-to-end life cycle does not apply to an e-business project that must be implemented in inherently ongoing and evolving phases. The important focus is that technology and organizational development have parallel evolutionary processes that need to be in balance with each other. This philosophy will be developed further in Chapter 3.

Information Technology Roles and Responsibilities

The preceding sections focused on how IT can be divided into two distinct kinds of business operations. As such, the rules and responsibilities within IT need to change accordingly and be designed under the auspices of driver and support theory. Most traditional IT departments are designed to be supporters, so that they have a close-knit organization that is secure from outside intervention and geared to respond to user needs based on their requests. While in many instances this type of formation is acceptable, it is very limited in providing the IT department with the proper understanding of the kind of business objectives that require driver-type activities. This was certainly the experience in the Ravell case study. In that instance, making the effort to get IT support personnel "out from their comfortable shells" made a huge difference in providing better service to the organization at large. Because more and more technology is becoming driver essential, this development will require of CIOs an increasing ability to communicate to managers and executives and to assimilate within other departments.

Another aspect of driver-and-support functions is the concept of a "life cycle." A life cycle in this respect refers to the stages that occur before a product or service becomes obsolete. Technology products have a life cycle of value just as any other product or service. It is important not to confuse this life cycle with processes during development as discussed earlier in this chapter.

Many technical products are adopted because they are able to deliver value—value that is typically determined based on ROI calculations. However, as products mature within an organization, they tend to become more of a commodity; and as they are normalized, they tend to become support oriented. Once they reach the stage of support, the rules of economies of scale become more important and relevant to evaluation. As a product enters the support stage, replacement based on economies of scale can be maximized by outsourcing to an outside vendor who can provide the service cheaper. New technological innovations then can be expected to follow this life cycle, where their initial investment requires some level of risk in order to provide returns to the business. This initial investment is accomplished in ROD using strategic integration. Once the evaluations are completed, driver activities will prevail during the technology's maturation process, which will also require cultural assimilation, and inevitably technology will change organizational behavior and structure. However, once the technology is "assimilated" and organizational behavior and structures are normalized, individuals will use it as a permanent part of their day-to-day operations. Thus, driver activities give way to those of support. Senior managers become less involved, and line managers then become the more important group that completes the transition from driver to supporter.

Conclusion

Throughout this chapter we have emphasized a perspective that IT has multitudes of uses within an organization. We divided these multiple value points into two major categories, drivers and supporters. CIOs must be able to provide a mechanism that both enables the organization to deal with accelerated change caused by technological innovations for driver applications and that integrates them into a new cycle of processing and handling consistent with the theories of S-curve life cycle. CIOs must also recognize that the supporter side of their responsibility is equally important but measured for success very differently than its corresponding driver approaches.

Notes

1. A. M. Langer, *Information Technology and Organizational Learning: Managing Behavioral Change through Technology and Education*, 1st ed. (Boca Raton, FL: Taylor & Francis, 2005).
2. S. P. Bradley, and R. L. Nolan, *Sense and Respond: Capturing Value in the Network Era* (Boston: Harvard Business School Press, 1998).
3. A. M. Langer, *Information Technology and Organizational Learning: Managing Behavioral Change through Technology and Education*, 2nd ed. (Boca Raton, FL: Taylor & Francis, 2011).
4. Ibid.
5. Wideman Comparative Glossary of Common Project Management Terms, v2.1. Copyright © R. Max Wideman, May 2001.
6. K. M. Eisenhardt, and L. J. Bourgeois, "Politics of Strategic Decision Making in High-Velocity Environments: Toward a Midrange Theory," *Academy of Management Journal* 31 (1988): 737–770.
7. Langer, *Information Technology and Organizational Learning*, 1st. ed., p. 44.

8. Ibid.
9. Ibid.
10. T. Murphy, *Achieving Business Practice from Technology: A Practical Guide for Today's Executive* (Hoboken, NJ: John Wiley & Sons, 2002).
11. Ibid.
12. Murphy, *Achieving Business Practice from Technology*, p. 31.
13. H. C. Lucas, *Information Technology and the Productivity Paradox* (New York: Oxford University Press, 1999).
14. Langer, *Information Technology and Organizational Learning*, 1st ed.
15. Ibid.
16. J. L. Sampler, "Exploring the Relationship between Information Technology and Organizational Structure." In M. J. Earl (Ed.), *Information Management: The Organizational Dimension* (New York: Oxford University Press, 1996), 5–22.
17. Murphy, *Achieving Business Practice from Technology*, p. 152.
18. Lucas, *Information Technology and the Productivity Paradox*.
19. A. M. Langer, "Reflecting on Practice: Using Learning Journals in Higher and Continuing Education," *Teaching in Higher Education* 7 (2002): 337–351.

CHAPTER 3

The Strategic Advocacy Mindset

Chapters 1 and 2 established the core challenge confronting chief information officers (CIOs)—namely, effectively engaging with senior executives in the strategic conversations taking place and integrating technology as a driver into these conversations. In the words of Chris Scalet, the former CIO at Merck for many years, "I would always start the conversation in terms of what is the meaning for the business. They are never IT conversations or IT projects; they are always business enabler projects." As noted in Chapter 1, the CIO usually does not get visibility at an enterprise level. Chris Scalet and other successful CIOs get their seat at the table because they understand the business model and strategy of the organization and bring valuable insights for shaping strategy going forward.

According to Scalet, the CIO needs to be perceived as a businessperson who understands information technology (IT) and aligning it with the business—what we have argued in Chapter 2 as integrating IT as a driver of the business. The CIO needs to be stimulating dialogues with other senior executives. As also noted by Scalet, "Being around matters." Communicating and building strategic relationships with other senior executives is the most important key for success as a CIO. However, establishing and leveraging these relationships requires overcoming the widely held perception noted in Chapter 1 of IT executives and managers as "techies." This entails bringing a particular kind of mindset to these relationships, namely a strategic advocacy mindset.

What Is Strategic Advocacy?

By strategic advocacy we mean adding value to either the top or bottom line by cultivating alliances and establishing personal and functional influence through helping to define and respond to the adaptive and generative challenges that confront the organization and the possibilities they provide.

Adaptive challenges are created by extensions and new applications of existing technologies and practices. Generative challenges emerge when new technologies transform the existing competitive landscape. In the case of the CIO, strategic advocacy involves connecting technology and the agenda of the technology function to widely ranging trends in the political economy of the organization within the context of shifting agendas among senior executives in the organization, each of whom has his or her own perspective on the shifting business interests confronting their part of the organization and the organization as a whole. Strategic advocacy is a process of consciously working within the patterns of power and influence in the organization to develop a sustainable base of support and credibility by being seen as aligned with both the strategic performance (drivers) and maintenance (support) requirements of the organization. This chapter presents a framework and sets of tools for developing and putting strategic advocacy into practice. A strategic advocacy is a way of thinking and acting.

Strategic advocacy involves drawing on two sets of competencies:

1. Engaging in strategic learning and acting strategically[1]
2. Having political savvy[2] for building social capital and effectively influencing others without relying on formal authority[3]

While these competencies have always been at the core of effective leadership initiatives around innovation, particularly for leaders of what have traditionally been viewed as support functions, in today's world of rapid emergent and innovative changes being driven by technology, they have become even more critical for CIOs transitioning to the C-suite.

Broad technological innovations provide opportunities for strategic organizational change since such innovation plays an "unfreezing" function within the business environment and the organization. However, these innovations also generate initial resistance to change. Most people, including senior executives, respond to change with a focus on what they will lose, not on what they might gain or the collective benefits of the change. Fear of potential loss goes beyond attachment to tangible benefits and includes:

- A personal sense of identity as one has socially constructed it.
- The "known and tried" in terms of established skills and ways of working and coping.
- The established informal relationships on which one has come to depend.
- The existing sociopolitical context one has learned to navigate.[4]

This experience of loss is true of most people, including technology professionals, which explains why they initially resist abrupt transitions or transformational change. In a talk before students and faculty of the Executive Master of Science in Technology Management program at Columbia University, Chris Scalet described the history of technological innovation over the past 50 years, from mainframes to desktops to personal computers to the cloud. In each case, these innovations were initially resisted by leaders and experienced professionals within the technology function. The innovative advocates at one phase of the cycle became initial resisters at the next phase.

When significant change occurs, a sense of loss is experienced immediately, while the benefits—assuming there are benefits—will be experienced in the future. Every technology professional has had the experience of making additions to an existing support system that users have grown comfortable with and experiencing reactions of frustrations from the users when they encounter the change, even though, from a technology perspective, new benefits have been added. Additionally, strategic changes at the C-suite level involve making choices with the outcome uncertain: There can be both a perceived "optimistic" and a "pessimistic" outcome of the process. Critical assumptions need to be made regarding:

- Market response from investors and customers.
- Responses from the competitors.
- Tangential events such as global political changes that impact the supply/distribution channels and regulations.
- The threat of new innovations or replacement products that will make the strategy obsolete even while it is being implemented.

In short, both the conversations prior to and shaping strategic choices and the subsequent action taken can produce unanticipated consequences that are complex. There are multiple interacting feedback loops working across sectors of the organizational context that make precise prediction of results impossible.[5]

This complexity takes place both in the external institutional environment and in the internal political dynamics of the organization. For example, conversations about possible challenges to the organization and the opportunities that may accompany them are part of informal interactions in the hallways, over dinner, while traveling, and in individual offices. Often, these informal conversations set the stage for what happens in formal meetings. These informal meetings become even more frequent and important when the organization is confronted with significant strategic threats. In the words of one senior executive, "When we finally acknowledge that major changes are happening in the marketplace is when suddenly there are a lot of informal, off-site after hour dinner meetings that take place among members of our executive committee." All this complexity make the two skill sets that comprise strategic advocacy (again, engaging in strategic learning and action, and having political savvy for building social capital and effectively influencing others without relying on formal authority) key for effective engagement with other members of the senior executive team. Together, they comprise a particular type of mindset, one that is focused on the dynamic political economy of the organization.

The next section describes a political economy framework that encapsulates the scope of the necessary mindset for robust strategic advocacy. We then proceed to develop the practices for developing and exercising strategic learning and political savvy. First, however, we note that while we are making reference to senior executive teams and the C-suite, this framework and the practice of strategic advocacy applies to thinking and acting strategically throughout one's career in technology management, from individual contributor to midlevel manager positioning his or her function and new projects in the organization.

A few years back, Ram Charan, the globally recognized consultant and scholar on strategy and effective CEO actions, was addressing the Columbia Senior Executive Program. His presentation included a discussion on the importance of CEOs' recognizing the most significant potential threat to their business model and the common mistakes versus the most effective ways for CEOs to address the threat. As his presentation came to a close, he made the following comment: "The most effective CEOs don't begin thinking this way when they become appointed to the CEO position or the C-suite. They have been essentially thinking this way throughout their careers. It's the scope and nature of the threat to their business model that changes, not their way of thinking." The lesson was "begin developing this way of thinking now—you don't start thinking that way when you become a CEO." In fact, developing a strategic way of thinking can enhance both immediate effectiveness and the likelihood of eventually joining the senior team. The same principle applies to the next section. One doesn't develop a mindset for strategic advocacy when one becomes a CIO, as evidenced by the short retention spans of many new CIOs. The most effective CIOs have developed their way of engaging strategically throughout their career.

A Political Economy Framework for Contextualizing Strategic Advocacy

Organizations are open systems that are simultaneously both economic and political entities existing in a state of power dependency with other such entities that comprise a broader socioeconomic system. While these entities generally conform to the norms, values, and practices that comprise the institutional logics of their particular institutional sectors, they also must change in response to the disruptive actions of key competitors, the potential and threats of new technologies for their business model, and changes in their broader socioeconomic context. For these changes to happen and the organization to continue to thrive, the individuals embedded in them must act as agents stimulating and initiating innovation. In other words, engage in effective strategic advocacy.

This is easier said than done, particularly in organizations that have been highly successful, even by market leaders who have been innovators (consider the experience of Microsoft and Yahoo! over the past couple of decades), or are themselves embedded in deeply rooted institutional logics (e.g., higher education). The successful people comprising these organizations have internalized the practices that have made them and the organization successful (which explains the aforementioned resistance of technology managers to transformative changes in their field).

As previously noted, strategic advocacy on the part of CIOs and the technology professionals that work for them involves connecting technology and the agenda of the technology function to widely ranging trends in the political economy of the organization within the context of shifting agendas among senior executives. Strategic advocacy is a process through which CIOs and the professionals who work for them engage in political economy agency. A political economy framework maps key divisions, functions, and sectors within which actors in an organization need to track trends and interactions among these trends, and respond to the opportunities created and constraints imposed by the fluid interdependencies among them (these processes are mapped in Figure 3.1).[6] The word "trends" is an important one; looking for patterns as opposed to thinking in terms of specific data points in time is the essence of strategic thinking.[7] Remember the words of the cyberpunk novelist William Gibson: "The future is already here. It's just not evenly distributed yet."[8]

There has been a productive tradition of using a political economy (P-E) perspective as a conceptual lens for the understanding and analysis of organizational dynamics.[9] This perspective argues for the need to have a simultaneous focus on the interdependencies between the "polity" and the "economy" of the organization.[10] This dual focus explicitly considers the relationship between the external and internal polities and economies.[11] The strategic response to the opportunities and constraints afforded by the external political economy is determined through the interactions of a coalition of dominant actors in an organization's internal political economy.[12]

The term polity refers to the patterned use of influence within an organization and between the organization and social institutions.[13] The economy is the productive exchange system of the organization and how it organizes

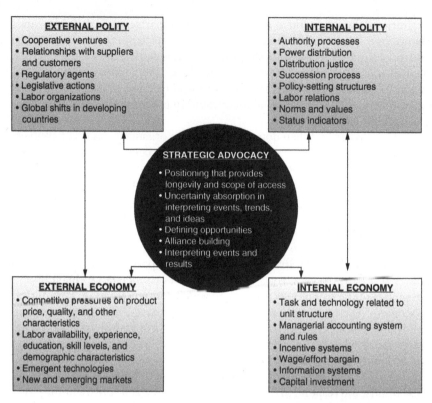

Figure 3.1   A strategic advocacy–focused political economy model.

work, generates value from its markets, and deals with innovation in terms of its relationships with customers and new product lines. Aligning the polity (internal and external) with the economy (internal and external) is a core function of strategy, and strategy formation is in part political,[14] as is the process of dealing with the external strategic context—hence the necessity of CIOs' engaging in strategic advocacy given that technology is a critical strategic driver.

Although the model presented in Figure 3.1 is described in relationship to the senior executive's scope of responsibilities, it applies at any level of the organization. Organizations are complex and fluid systems inclusive of strategic business units, divisions, functions, departments, and groups. The boundaries at any level are arbitrary constructions open to redefinition as evidenced by current trends such as transferring tasks to customers and increasingly relying on "part-time" employees, contract workers, and outsourcing arrangements. The point of strategic advocacy is helping to shape the direction of this evolution through adding strategic value. At the middle levels of the organization technology managers need to think strategically as they advocate for changes in the existing support system.

Two analytical tools that are central to the literature on strategic planning that structure and formalize thinking about the political economy of an organization are:

1. **PEST analysis: P**olitical factors, **E**conomic factors, **S**ocial factors, and **T**echnological factors.
2. **SWOT analysis:** Organization's **S**trengths, **W**eaknesses, **O**pportunities, and **T**hreats in the external environment.

The constraint in using these analytical tools is the potential for thinking to be constrained by the taken-for-granted assumptions and frames of reference that have become embedded in one's perspectives on their environment. To quote Albert Szent-Gyorgyi, 1937 Nobel Prize winner in biochemistry, "Discovery consists of seeing what everyone else is seeing and thinking what nobody else has thought."[15] We turn now to the specific sets of practices and competencies associated with strategic advocacy: Strategic learning and political savvy.

Strategic Thinking: A Particular Kind of Mindset

Increasingly, strategy theorists and researchers make a distinction between strategic thinking and strategic planning.[16] Willie Pietersen, a former CEO and currently Professor of Practice in Executive Education at the Columbia Business School, summarized the fundamental distinction between strategy and planning very well.[17] Strategic thinking starts from the context of the broader environment. It is:

- Outside-in, focusing on what is happening outside the organization.
- Noticing trends and patterns and seeking opportunities they will generate.
- Focusing on ideas and insights.
- Playing with divergent perspectives and thinking.
- Learning from diverse settings.
- Testing the viability of emerging opportunities through critical assessment of assumptions.

In contrast, planning is:

- Inside-out.
- Focusing on numbers.
- Convergent thinking.
- Allocating resources in support of execution of strategy and supporting programs.

Both are critical, but, in the words of Pietersen, "mixing them can be toxic."[18] Pietersen is making the point that in planning there is typically no divergent thinking that challenges existing assumptions and mental models of the world, no radically new insights into possible futures.

As Kings College Professor Lawrence Freedman has written ". . . strategy is much more than a plan. A plan supposes a sequence of events that allows one to move with confidence from one state of affairs to another. Strategy is required when others might frustrate one's plans because they have different and possibly opposing interests and concerns." (p. xi)

The distinction between strategic thinking and planning is increasingly important in the world of increasing complexity in which technology is not only intensifying competition among traditional competitors but also enabling new entrants who transform the competitive landscape. Obvious examples are the rise of Amazon, Uber, and Airbnb and how they have transformed the competitive landscape for brick and mortar stores, taxis, and the hospitality industry. While change has always been part of the competitive landscape of business, the rates of change are growing more and more rapidly.

In addition to the rising pace of change, the wider ecosystem of the strategic landscape is also changing. The first two decades of the 21st century saw the emergence and growth of what Van Alstyne, Parker & Choudary describe as platform business providing an entirely new strategic framework and a new source of competition for businesses operating within the traditional pipeline framework. Platform businesses provide for high-value exchanges through bringing together producers and consumers, where as value is created in pipeline businesses through controlling a linear series of activities. Again, Uber and Airbnb are textbook examples of not only disruptors of particular industries but operating in a disruptive ecosystem.

In the platform ecosystem (Figure 3.2):

- Owners of platforms control their intellectual property and governance;
- Providers serve as the platforms' interface with users;
- Producers create their offerings, and;
- Consumers use those offerings.

THE PLAYERS IN A PLATFORM ECOSYSTEM

A platform provides the infrastructure and rules for a marketplace that brings together producers and consumers. The players in the ecosystem fill four main roles but may shift rapidly from one role to another. Understanding the relationships both within and outside the ecosystem is central to platform strategy.

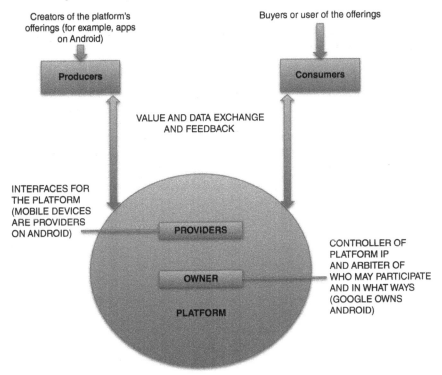

Figure 3.2   The platform ecosystem.
Source: Van Alstyne, Parker & Choudary, "Platforms and the New Rules of Strategy," Harvard Business Review, *April, 2016, p.58.*

Platforms are very dynamic systems. For example, a person or family can be both producers and customers at different points in time; an owner of an Airbnb may also stay in another Airbnb when traveling. An Uber driver may also use Uber services. Providers or producers who interconnect with other members in a platform's ecosystem may subsequently partner and withdraw to create their own platform.

In summary, pipelines are grounded in resource control with a focus on internal optimization and providing customer value while platforms are focused on resource orchestration for external interaction with a focus on ecosystem value.

As technology continues to change the strategic landscape, strategic insight is a necessary competency for CIOs and other technology executives and professionals.

Strategic Insight and Expert Knowing—Complimentary but Distinct Mindsets

Strategic thinking and planning involve distinct mindsets. Planning involves an expert mindset, starting from the content of one's expertise. Methods and skills are applied to solve problems, provide answers, and focus on "facts." Expertise works within structured boundaries. Strategic thinking involves robust imagination by valuing one's experience and expertise while seeking insight through observing new trends, pursuing diverse possibilities, and challenging one's assumptions. One of the authors often asks participants in his executive education workshops and strategy development classes, "Where does strategy come from?" The answers called out typically are "goals," "the organization's mission," and "its purpose." The next question asked is "Where do goals, mission, and purpose come from?" Confused looks frequently follow. The answer is learning: Strategic learning that challenges embedded assumptions, perspectives, and logics that block out new possibilities. We define strategic learning as a process of robust imagination, involving generating new insights, combined with learning through one's experience and the diverse experiences of others.

Strategic learning is easier said than done, as evidenced by the dominant companies who were once the innovators creating and driving their markets, but now find themselves behind the curve and even potentially becoming obsolete. While these dominant incumbents in an industry succeed in adapting and extending existing technologies, products, or services, they find it difficult to create something new. The reason is the struggle to let go of the past.[19] Strategic thinking is a learning process seeking insights that emerge from raising provocative questions and framing new opportunities. Expert thinking focuses on logic and meeting predetermined goals as traditionally framed by self and others. Strategic thinking focuses on transforming the organization through framing new opportunities and challenging existing frameworks of thinking and activities associated with leadership; planning involves control and accountability, and is at the core of effective management.

Professional training involves cultivating expert thinking. Like many professions, IT professionals have developed an expert mindset reinforced by their intrinsic interest in working with and applying technology and technological innovation. The challenge that confronts them is complementing this expert mindset by also cultivating a strategic mindset. Returning to the previously cited observation of Ram Charan, one cannot wait until he or she is in the C-suite to begin developing this capability. If one enters the C-suite as CIO with only an expert mindset, it is too late.

As noted earlier, the key to developing a strategic mindset is focusing on the trends and patterns in different sectors and talking to people who hold diverse viewpoints. When Ram Charan was addressing the Columbia Senior Executive Program in the presentation previously mentioned, he asked the class, "How many of you are familiar with the Dell case?" They all raised their hands, which Charan knew would happen because the class had discussed the Dell case the previous week. "Fine," he said. "Today I want you to consider a different question. If you are Michael Dell, what's the biggest emerging threat to your business model?" The class broke into their teams for discussions. When they came back to the main classroom, Charan processed their thinking. While a range of interesting answers were reported by the various teams, only one group mentioned the emerging devices that could make laptops increasingly less dominant in the technology marketplace.

That's the critical question. What trend is on the horizon that is a potential threat to our business model, and what opportunities does it provide? The same question is relevant at the function and department levels as well. Speaking to the Executive Master of Science in Technology Management students at Columbia University in 2011, Chris Scalet stated, "In five years, the technology function as we know it will cease to exist." He was trying to get the students to focus on making meaning of existing trends and the implications for strategically positioning themselves in the future. Successfully doing this involves engaging in a learning process that generates and leads to implementing breakthrough strategies.

In today's world of continuous dramatic change, this learning process involves a continuing course of action by pursuing adaptive (extending existing technologies, products, and services) and generative (creating something new) change. We will argue in Chapter 7 that one's ability to engage in robust strategic learning requires a tolerance for ambiguity and for dealing with incomplete, and even contradictory, information. This is a developmental move from the structured thinking of the expert. There are specific practices that can facilitate this developmental move, while also enhancing one's strategic thinking.

This kind of mindset involves utilizing analytical tools such as PEST and SWOT as a classification system for capturing insights and a bridge between strategic learning and planning:

- Dialogue for considering diverse viewpoints
- Reasoning through analogies both for envisioning new market possibilities and bringing into awareness how prior experience is shaping one's thinking
- Scenario learning for generating new options and moving from divergent to convergent thinking and planning

Yorks and Nicolaides argue that insight is the foundation of strategic learning.[20] Strategic insight involves an increased awareness of new possibilities derived through engaging diverse perspectives, assessing trends in the various components of the political economy, and challenging assumptions. The challenge is surfacing and testing assumptions and ideas, synthesizing trends and patterns across the political economy context into a plausible future storyline.

Engaging in Dialogic Processes

Dialogic processes can be defined as seeking to suspend assumptions and engage in genuine learning and thinking with others, as opposed to arguing for preferred outcomes.[21] This involves asking open probing questions and listening without responding immediately with a reaction, further probing the points being made. This is particularly true when engaging with people holding different viewpoints or who have different experiences. The tendency is to think of and respond with a counterargument or to state why an idea won't work, rather than explore more deeply that other person's rationale.

In team or group meetings, dialogue can involve brainstorming ideas and proposals, picking the most radical ones for which a substantive argument has been made, and then collectively listing the possible benefits *before* considering the downsides.[22] As the process unfolds, this often leads to seeing the advantage of what initially seemed to be an idea not worth pursuing. Even when the group then turns to considering the problems or downsides of an idea whose benefits had become clearer, if an insurmountable problem emerges for using the idea as stated, there is a possibility of exploring alternative ways of achieving the same benefits.

Reasoning Through Analogies

In their *Harvard Business Review* article "How Strategists Really Think: Tapping the Power of Analogy," Gavitte and Rivkin demonstrate how reasoning from analogy is often the basis for innovative thinking.[23] Gavitte and Rivkin note how Charles Lazarus, the founder of Toys 'R' Us, used the analogy of the supermarket as inspiration for his idea for a new kind of toy store. Another is Andy Grove of Intel, who learned from how the U.S. steel industry ceded the low end of the business to mini-mills only to see them move into higher-end products. He "seized on the steel analogy, referring to the cheap PC as 'digital rebar,'" changing Intel's resistance to providing cheap microprocessors for inexpensive PCs, and arguing that if they conceded the low end today, they can lose the high end tomorrow. Returning to the strategic ecosystem of platforms, one can already see how new producers are creating services analogous to existing ones.

Gavitte and Rivkin define reasoning through analogy as the process through which persons ". . . faced with an unfamiliar problem or opportunity . . . think back to some similar situation they have seen or heard about, draw lessons from it, and apply these lessons to the current situation."[24] When used properly, analogies can generate new insights for strategic opportunities. However, analogies can be dangerous when the persons using them act "on an analogy on the basis of superficial similarity" and fail to carefully assess it.[25]

Gavitte and Rivkin offer a process of mapping analogies in order to test the insight being offered:

- Actively searching for differences by first thoroughly assessing the factors that comprised the causal traits or characteristics that made the source analogy successful.
- Carefully testing similarities between the above and the situation it is being applied to, testing for similarities between the two situations and identifying key differences.
- Surfacing the presumptions behind asserted crucial correspondences between the two situations, by asking critical questions around what is known, what are the maybes, what is unclear, and how maybes can be turned into either known or unclear. Also, asking what emerges if the presumptions are reframed.
- Modeling the landscape.

The testing of presumptions can be carried out by utilizing what we call the learning window (see Figure 3.3):

- Cell one, *what do we know and why we know it* because we have solid data that has been confirmed and its interpretation is widely accepted.
- Cell two, *what do we think we know and what we need to discover in order to know it* because there are some data, but it is inconclusive.
- Cell three, *what do we know we do not know*, and is it possible to get information or data that would move us to cell one or cell two?
- Cell four, *staying open to the unexpected* as we continue to explore the analogy.

Yorks and Nicolaides argue an explicit focus on mapping analogies has another potential benefit, especially under conditions of uncertainty and complexity.[26] Analogies, whether consciously used or not, are a primary way in which informal and incidental learning from experience[27] is subsequently enacted. Under conditions of uncertainty and complexity, experience is a double-edged sword, having value but also potentially not being applicable in the new situation. Seeking to make explicit these analogies that comprise

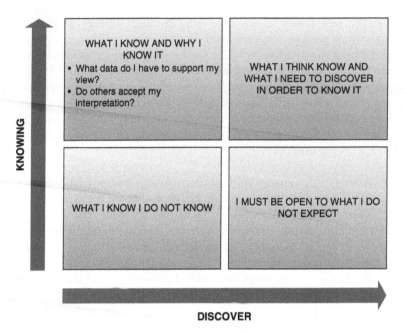

Figure 3.3   The learning window.

one's experiences that are being subconsciously drawn upon is a way of valuing experience and being aware of its potential barriers to new insights or adopting new courses of action. Often, questioning by others during strategic dialogues brings awareness of how one is drawing on one's experience and provides a way of reflexively assessing its value in the current situation. Listening to questions from others, answering, and then inviting them to share what they think one is assuming (I believe you are assuming that . . .) is one way of structuring such a dialogue.

Scenario Learning

Unlike problem solving, one never really knows how a strategic decision is likely to play out. Indeed, ongoing adjustments during a strategy's implementation are almost always necessary. Given this reality, the idea behind scenario learning is learning from the range of possible futures and then taking into account the level of risk that is acceptable and making a decision. Scenario learning is a form of vicariously "learning from the future."[28] As such, it can also prepare one for the uncertainties that might emerge once the strategy is being implemented. Scenario learning is a process that can generate new insights while moving the strategic conversation toward convergence and making decisions.

Consistent with the distinction between strategic thinking and planning, Fahey and Randall "prefer scenario learning to the more common term 'scenario planning' for a number of reasons."[29] Among them is the reality that to be truly effective in addressing conformation bias (seeking only supportive evidence for an idea) managers must be willing to "suspend their beliefs, assumptions and preconceptions." For Fahey and Randall the term "learning implies . . . dialogue . . . . Managers and others . . . must engage each other in a free ranging exchange of ideas" provoking "some degree of tension . . . . Such tension is the essence of collective learning."[30]

While computer-driven simulations are useful for modeling potential scenarios, the higher the degree of uncertainty in the environmental context being simulated, the greater is the level of incompressibility on the reliability of the simulation.[31] Incompressibility refers to the fact that in building such simulations of open systems we are forced to leave things out. Since the effects of these omissions are nonlinear, we cannot predict their scale of impact. While simulations are often the only way to get a feel for the dynamics of complex systems, it is important to avoid the expert mindset tendency of seeing them as providing predictable answers. Rather they are part of the data base for learning.

Again the importance of dialogue for the strategic learning process has been raised by Fahey and Randall. Chantell Ilbury and Clem Sunter[32] have provided a thinking framework that is both a way of fostering one's strategic mindset and structuring a dialog around possible scenarios. It involves four cells, moving from relative certainty, through an absence of control, high uncertainty, to relative control:

- The first step is to identify the rules of the game, meaning *what are the given boundaries of the context within which one would be taking action.* These might include laws, regulations, financial givens, and the like. There are constraints that are taken for granted. In some instances, they need to be verified.
- The second step involves brainstorming the key uncertainties that exist and might significantly alter the outcome.
- A third step is translating how these uncertainties would play out in terms of possible scenarios.
- Focusing on three or four scenarios that provide a range of possible outcomes will lay out what options exist in terms of possible actions.
- Based on analysis of the options and level of risk tolerance, a decision regarding taking action can be made.
- Once a decision for action is made, lay out plans B and C for adjusting the action.

In thinking strategically at the organization level, the focus is on implications for the business model. In addition to being practices that can be used in formal strategy conversations, they can also be used as informal ways of framing hallway, lunch, or dinner conversations that are the basis for stimulating thinking about the strategic context. The tools don't even have to be mentioned by name. "You know this is like . . ." is one way of informally initiating informal strategic conversations using reasoning by analogy. "Thinking about the action we are considering, three things come to mind as possible events that could mediate what we want to do . . . . A couple of different scenarios come to mind." In both cases, the models are held in one's head as a way of thinking.

Strategic thinking is one aspect of strategic advocacy, arriving at insights that can be the basis for strategies that add value to the organization. Political savvy is the other. We turn now to this critical competency.

Political Savvy as the Underpinning of Effective Strategic Advocacy

We have taken the term "political savvy" from Joel DeLuca, who defines it as "ethically building a critical mass of support for an idea you care about."[33] Although in popular culture the word "politics" carries negative connotations, in practice little significance, positive or otherwise, occurs within complex organizations without political initiatives.[34] When things go right, we refer to who effectively applied *influence*; when they go poorly, we use the term *politics* to express negative experiences. Straightforwardly, defined organizational politics are "how power and interests play out in the organization,"[35] and political agency in the context of the organizational political economy is the process of participating in this "play." As DeLuca notes, organizational politics is a double-edged sword, with one edge representing the actions of those who pursue self-interest through Machiavellian and deceitful methods and the other edge seeking to use influence that links multiple agendas to broader organizational interests. The first is dysfunctional politics; the second, functional.

At the heart of strategic advocacy is seeking to see in the patterns of an organization's political economy opportunities for both adding value and developing the relationships that will make this possible. Any executive or manager who considers how to effectively advance a proposal and says to a colleague, "Let's think strategically about this" is moving into the realm of politics. DeLuca notes that, "Political savvy is not about acquiring power; it is about making an impact in specific situations." Likewise it is not about proper exercise of authority, but influencing those with authority to make the decision. "Political savvy has little to do with one's place in the hierarchy. The clerk who automates the mail room despite resistance may have more political savvy then the CEO who makes things happen by giving orders."[36]

Political savvy, as used here, does not imply "pushing through" one's ideas intact. Rather, the goal is to have an open and useful conversation that gives the idea a hearing and thorough assessment, sometimes resulting in modification or even a decision not to pursue. It involves taking into account the legitimate agendas of other stakeholders, seeking to develop a win-win that really does provide value to the organization. Politically savvy executives and professionals align their interests and others' to the collective interests of the organization. Strategic advocacy requires thinking strategically across multiple sectors of the organization's political economy. As discussed earlier, this includes thinking strategically in terms of opportunities at the societal, organizational, group, and personal level for adding value to the organization. It also includes thinking strategically in the political context of the key stakeholders. What does this mean in practice? The following are six strategic actions for developing and practicing political savvy:

1. Mapping the political territory
2. Assessing the trust/agreement matrix
3. Linking agendas
4. Utilizing currencies
5. Following the credibility path
6. Developing social capital through networks and coalitions

Mapping the Political Territory

Developed by DeLuca, mapping the political territory provides an overview of the key stakeholders, the perceived potential supporters and opponents of one's proposed plan or project along with the relationships among them. More important, the map provides focus for reflecting on the assumptions one is holding and strategizing a course of action. In creating the map, five questions are asked (see Figure 3.4):

1. Who are the key stakeholders or players?
2. What is their power or influence in the organization, particularly in reference to the project or initiative in question?
3. To what extent are they applying, or likely to apply, their influence for or against the initiative?
4. How easily can their position be changed?
5. What significant relationship exists between the key stakeholders (both positive and negative relationships)?

The answers to these questions can be placed on the analytical tool illustrated in Figure 3.5. Ranking their power/influence involves relative judgments

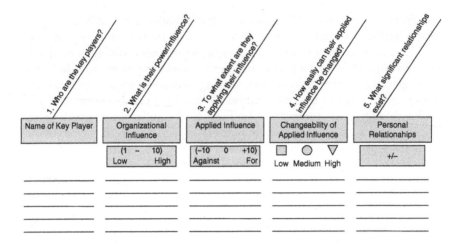

Figure 3.4 The political data sheet.
Source: J. DeLuca, Political Savvy: Systematic Approaches to Leadership Behind-the-Scenes *(Berwyn, PA: EBG, 1999).*

for thinking and discussion purposes among team members. It is important to consider the particular project since some stakeholders have a relatively stable degree of influence on the key decision maker; others may have more or less influence, depending on the topic and their expertise. The assessment of how they are likely to apply their influence is a relative, subjective ranking ranging from positive 10 through neutral to negative 10. Again, these are relative judgments.

Their assumed changeably is depicted as either a circle, meaning possibly changeable; a square, representing an assumed fixed position; and an upside down triangle, meaning not a fixed position and highly changeable one way or the other. Relationship connections should be reserved for consistently strong ones, either positive (represented by a +) or negative (represented by a –). When placed on the map (Figure 3.5), the result is a map that can begin to trigger strategic thinking regarding political advocacy. This is particularly powerful when the map is used for dialogue among team members preparing to propose an innovative project.

It is important to remember that the map is not the territory itself. Positions will change. Some important initial questions include: What is one's "data" for the assessments made? and What assumptions is one holding about the key stakeholders and how can they be tested? It is actually useful to begin developing the map when assuming a new position to begin building a critical understanding of the context. For the new CIO, senior management meetings are opportunities for engaging in what researchers would call field observation.

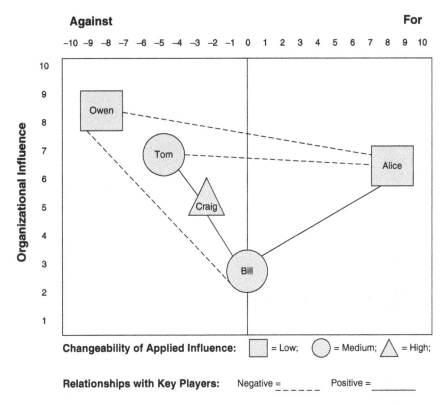

Figure 3.5 Organization politics map.
Source: J. DeLuca, Political Savvy: Systematic Approaches to Leadership Behind-the-Scenes *(Berwyn, PA: EBG, 1999).*

Considerable learning can take place during informal conversations. A midlevel IT manager, mapping the territory in preparing to strategically advocate for what he believed was a necessary project, found the range of stakeholders to be included expanded beyond his initial mapping. The more he considered the map and reflected, the more he realized he had limited his interactions in the organization.

The map is a tool that raises questions for thinking about how to exercise leadership through strategic advocacy. The most effective executives intuitively consider the variables in the map when deciding on a course of influencing action. In the case of very important initiatives, making the process explicit can lead to a more thorough assessment and a more robust strategy-making process. In the case of CIOs and others in the IT function, they need to have several maps in their heads—one that indicates the position that key senior executives hold regarding technology in general and others linked to particular initiatives that are being proposed.

Assessing the Trust/Agreement Matrix

An important initial assessment is to impose the trust agreement matrix (see Figure 3.6) on the map of the territory, making critical distinctions between allies, opponents, and adversaries.[37] Opponents are those who may generally disagree with you but can be trusted. Adversaries are those who disagree with you and can't be trusted. For example, they may be friendly face to face but act behind your back. On particular projects, opponents may be bedfellows on a particular issue because they agree with the need for the particular initiative or strategic move being advocated because it aligns with their interests. What other allies might be cultivated who are not on the initial map is another critical question.

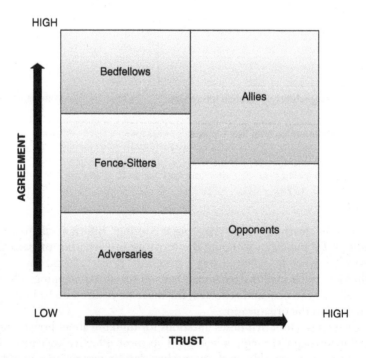

Figure 3.6   The trust/agreement matrix.
Source: Peter Block, The Empowered Manager: Positive Political Skills at Work *(San Francisco: Josey-Bass, 1987), p. 132.*

Linking Agendas

Thinking through how the initiative can be modified, the technical design adapted, or new components added to meet the diverse agendas of key stakeholders can often both result in more value for the organization and create more support. Particular consideration should be given the agendas of stakeholders who are somewhat resistant (0 to –5 on the map), but linking agendas can change the position of even a negative 9 or 10, perhaps turning an opponent or fence-sitter into a bedfellow on this initiative. Also, linking agendas might minimize resistance coming from a reaction to the sense of loss that might be experienced.

Utilizing Currencies

Cohen and Bradford describe several types of currencies that can be used when exercising influence.[38] Currencies are resources that are useful to others in the organization and therefore have an exchange value in building and sustaining alliances. Some currencies are relatively tangible, such as information, time, or task support. Other currencies are more intangible but often just as valuable, such as lending personal support, recognition, or visibility to others. CIOs and IT managers and professionals need to build reservoirs of currencies that can become the lifeblood of their work within the organization.

Following the Credibility Path

Looking at the relationships on the map and alliances in the CIO's social capital network provides insight into the credibility path.[39] The credibility path rests on the principle that influencing someone about a decision often turns on who is the messenger making the proposal. Convincing others of the value of a proposed idea frequently depends on who communicates the idea. Sometimes it makes sense to let others take the lead, particularly when advocating to a key stakeholder with whom the CIO or technology professional does not have a positive relationship. This is a good use of allies. Actually, the term "credibility path" was used by a highly successful CIO during one of our interviews:

> The (business unit) CEO has for a number of years been a very strong supporter of technology. He recognizes how technology can be an enabler for his business and be a driver for his business. We have built a lot of proprietary forums for him . . . . So we have a CEO who is a strong supporter of the function and we have people embedded in that service line. We use the success there to demonstrate how we can enable other service (business) lines. It's following the credibility path.

Effective influencers often follow the credibility path letting whoever has the most credibility carry the idea forward.

Developing Social Capital Through Networks and Coalitions

Another critical strategic action is pursuing opportunities for cultivating informal networks that can be used for developing coalitions in support of particular projects. Such networks are a form of social capital, which are networks that provide executives with access to a variety of resources. Social capital can be seen as actual and potential resources from network and coalition relationships developed by individuals or organizational units. Social capital networks are social structures made of nodes (individuals or groups)[40] that are joined by various interactions such as business and personal relationships. Positioning oneself as the "node" that can provide connections between otherwise separate networks is a way of leveraging one's ideas and also establishing new credibility paths.

Social networks are an avenue for raising awareness and cultivating understanding. Coalitions provide for maneuverability by enhancing options through multiple credibility paths, taking coordinated action, and increasing the range of possible currencies. They also provide opportunity for surfacing potential objections and shaping perceptions. This is why being out in the organization is so critical.

Conclusion

Use of the tools and practices presented throughout this chapter requires bringing a strategic mindset to one's thinking. The same kind of thinking is necessary for arriving at:

- New, generative strategic insight about how technology can be integrated into the business model to enhance its value as a driver.
- Insights regarding how to best navigate the political system and build effective relationships.

Like practitioners in other professions, many IT professionals have an expert mindset that often works well with other IT professionals when they are engaging in technical advocacy. When dealing with executives outside the IT profession, this mindset fails to build effective relationships. The impact from an influencing perspective can be summarized as:

$$Expertise \& Facts \times 0 = 0$$
$$(Technical\ advocacy)$$

Building strategic relationships through strategic advocacy can be summarized as:

Strategic insight × Expertise & Facts × Political savvy = Strategic relationships

While this chapter focuses on the individual, the same logics apply among groups and other organizations. Noticing what trends and shifts are taking place in the broader context and the emerging ideas and innovations that potentially impact the strategic positioning of one's organization provides the substance for strategic advocacy (see Figure 3.7). This is the true complexity of the organization's political economy and the need for strategic learning.

Of course, another challenge is moving from divergent to convergent thinking testing insights through one's social network. Integrating the strategic insights gleaned from assessing trends in the institutional context with trends in the political dynamics of the organization is key to establishing influence in the organization as one participates in the business conversation.

The continuing development of AI will bring new opportunities and threats to the strategic positioning of businesses and by extension how traditionally distinct functions are aligned and contribute to the strategic direction of the organization. AI changes the talent needs of the business, not just eliminating jobs, but changing the skills required in the roles being impacted. Acquiring new talent being actively recruited across various industries makes both recruiting and retaining the sought-after talent a strategic challenge. For example, John Deere builds agricultural equipment that plants seeds at the proper depth following landscape measures from other automated

Figure 3.7 The complex strategic advocacy context.

equipment. The company is developing drones to coordinate the two pieces of equipment, which requires successfully recruiting talent in competition with companies like Amazon and Google. This strategically driven talent management challenge involves collaboration between the IT functions with other functions in the company. Companies in virtually every industry are facing this need. As a consequence, IT, HR, and Operations must work together as a "golden triangle" requiring both business acumen and strategic advocacy competencies on the part of technology executives. Strategic advocacy involves working effectively through the strategic workplace complexities of the 21st century as well as effectively positioning innovative technologies in the organization.

This chapter has presented key frameworks for meeting the CIO challenge. In Chapter 7, we present a more thorough discussion of the process for developing the strategic advocacy mindset. In Chapter 4, we turn our attention to cases derived from successful CIOs that illustrate the way this mindset emerges in practice.

Notes

1. W. Pietersen, *Reinventing Strategy: Using Strategic Learning to Create and Sustain Breakthrough Performance* (Hoboken, NJ: John Wiley & Sons, 2002).
2. J. DeLuca, *Political Savvy: Systematic Approaches to Leadership Behind-the-Scenes* (Berwyn, PA: EBG, 1999).
3. A. R. Cohen and D. L. Bradford, *Influence without Authority*, 2nd ed. (Hoboken, NJ: John Wiley & Sons, 2005).
4. W. W. Burke, *Organization Development: Principles and Practices* (Boston: Little Brown, 1982).
5. K. A. Richardson and A. Tait, "The Death of the Expert?" In A. Tait and K. A. Richardson (Eds.), *Complexity and Knowledge Management: Understanding the Role of Knowledge in the Management of Social Networks* (Charlotte, NC: Information Age Publishing, 2010), 23–39.
6. L. Yorks, "Toward a Political Economy Model for Comparative Analysis of the Role of Strategic Human Resource Development Leadership," *Human Resource Development Review* 3 (2004): 189–208.
7. W. Pietersen, *Strategic Learning* (Hoboken, NJ: John Wiley & Sons, 2010).
8. Quoted in Pietersen, *Reinventing Strategy*.
9. J. K. Benson, "The Interorganizational Network as a Political Economy," *Administrative Science Quarterly* 20 (1975): 229–249; R. E. Cole, "The Macropolitics of Organizational Change," *Administrative Science Quarterly* 30 (1985): 560–585; L. W. Stern and T. Reve, "Distribution Channels as Political Economies: A Framework for Analysis," *Journal of Marketing* 44 (1980): 52–64; D. R. Van Houten, "The Political Economy and Technical Control of Work Humanization in Sweden during the 1970s and 1980s," *Work and Occupations* 14 (1987): 483–513; G. L. Wamsley and M. N. Zald, *The Political Economy of Public Organization* (Bloomington: Indiana University Press, 1976); L. Yorks and D. A. Whitsett, *Scenarios of Change: Advocacy and the Diffusion of Job Redesign in Organizations* (New York: Praeger, 1989); L. Yorks, "Toward a Political Economy Model for Comparative Analysis of the Role of Strategic Human Resource

Development Leadership," *Human Resource Development Review* 3 (2004): 189–208; M. N. Zald, *Organizational Change: The Political Economy of the YMCA*. Chicago: University of Chicago Press, 1970); M. N. Zald, "Political Economy: A Framework for Comparative Analysis." In M. N. Zald (Ed.), *Power in Organizations* (Nashville, TN: Vanderbilt University Press, 1970), 221–261).

10. J. Arndt, "The Political Economy Paradigm: Foundation for Theory Building in Marketing," *Journal of Marketing* 47 (1983): 44–54.

11. Zald, *Organizational Change.*

12. R. E. Miles and C. C. Snow, *Organizational Strategy, Structure, and Process* (New York: McGraw-Hill, 1978); A. M. Pettigrew, *The Awaking Giant: Continuity and Change in ICI* (Oxford, UK: Basil Blackwell, 1985); J. Storey, "Management Control as a Bridging Concept," *Journal of Management Studies* 22 (1985): 269–291.

13. Zald, "Political Economy."

14. I. C. MacMillan, *Strategy Formulation: Political Concepts* (New York: West, 1978); I. Palmer and C. Hardy, *Thinking About Management: Implications of Organizational Debates for Practice* (London: Sage, 2000); A. M. Pettigrew, *The Politics of Organizational Decision-Making* (London: Tavistock, 1973); Pettigrew, *The Awaking Giant.*

15. Pietersen, *Reinventing Strategy.*

16. See, for example, E. D. Beinhocker and S. Kaplan, "Tired of Strategic Planning?" *McKinsey Quarterly* (August 3, 2007); V. Govindarajan and C. Trimble, "Strategic Innovation and the Science of Learning," *MIT Sloan Management Review* 45(2) (2004): 67–75; B. Leavy, "The Concept of Learning in the Strategy Field," *Management Learning* 29 (1998): 447–466; D. P. Lovallo and L. T. Mendonca, "Strategy's Strategist: An Interview with Richard Rumelt," *McKinsey Quarterly* (2007), www.mckinseyquarterly.com/Strategys_strategist_An_interview_with_Richard_Rumelt_2039.

17. Pietersen, W. *Reinventing Strategy.*

18. Ibid.

19. H. Penton, Material from conversation and presentation at a Saudi business school, 2011.

20. L. Yorks and A. Nicolaides, "A Conceptual Model for Developing Mindsets for Strategic Insight under Conditions of Complexity and High Uncertainty." *Human Resource Development Review*, 11 (2012): 182–202.

21. Ibid.

22. G. M. Prince, *The Practice of Creativity* (New York: Collier Books, 1970); Yorks and Nicolaides, "A Conceptual Model for Developing Mindsets for Strategic Insight."

23. G. Gavitte and J. W. Rivkin, "How Strategists Really Think: Tapping the Power of Analogy,"*Harvard Business Review* (April 2005): 54–63.

24. Ibid., p. 54.

25. Ibid., p. 57.

26. Yorks and Nicolaides, "A Conceptual Model for Developing Mindsets for Strategic Insight."

27. V. J. Marsick and K. E. Watkins, *Informal and Incidental Learning in the Workplace* (London: Routledge, 1990).

28. Yorks and Nicolaides, "A Conceptual Model for Developing Mindsets for Strategic Insight."

29. L. Fahey and R. M. Randall, "What Is Scenario Learning?" (Ch. 1), and "Integrating Strategy and Scenarios (Ch. 2). In L. Fahey and R. M. Randall (Eds.), *Learning from the Future* (New York: John Wiley & Sons, 1998), 3–38.

30. Ibid., p. 5.

31. P. Cillers, "Knowing Complex Systems." In K. A. Richardson (Ed.), *Managing Organizational Complexity: Philosophy, Theory, and Application* (Greenwich, CT: Information Age Publishing, 2005), 7–19.

32. C. Illbury and C. Sunter, *The Mind of a Fox* (Cape Town, South Africa: Human & Rousseau/ Tafelberg, 2001), 36–43.

33. DeLuca, *Political Savvy*, p. 112.
34. Pfeffer, J. *Managing with Power: Politics and Influence in Organizations* (Boston: Harvard Business School Press, 1994).
35. DeLuca, J. *Political Savvy*, p. 44.
36. Ibid., pp. 112–113.
37. P. Block, *The Empowered Manager: Positive Political Skills at Work* (San Francisco: Jossey-Bass, 1987).
38. A. R. Cohen and D. L. Bradford, *Influence without Authority*, 2nd ed. (Hoboken, NJ: John Wiley & Sons, 2005).
39. Ibid.
40. J. Nahapiet and S. Ghoshal, "Social Capital, Intellectual Capital, and the Organizational Advantage," *Academy of Management Review* 23 (1998): 242–266; N. M. Tichy, M. L. Tushman, and C. Fombrum, "Social Network Analysis for Organizations," *Academy of Management Review* 4 (1979): 507–519.

CHAPTER 4

Real-World
Case Studies

his chapter presents case studies that exemplify chief information officers (CIOs) that have enabled their organizations to truly use information technology (IT) as a strategic driver while at the same time providing the necessary supporter functions. Thus, these cases represent stories of how these CIOs have approached the challenges of the job and have sustained a successful track record. The cases were conducted using personal one-on-one interviews; in one case (Cushman & Wakefield) we were able to interview other C-suite colleagues, which provided a view from those at the same level as the CIO.

The interview protocol was made up of nine major questions:

1. History of how the CIO obtained the position with his/her company.
2. What critical ways do they add value to their organization?
3. How is the way they add value in their current position different from their previous roles or jobs?
4. How were their approaches different in lesser roles?
5. Articulation of two or three critical roles and what triggered changes in management strategy.
6. What is the most important competency for a CIO?
7. Attributes of the most successful CIO they know.
8. Attributes of the most ineffective CIO they know.
9. Insights of the future.

Our case studies covered six different types of corporate CIOs:

1. BP (oil and gas)
2. Covance (drug development services)
3. Cushman & Wakefield (real estate)

4. Merck (pharmaceutical)
5. Procter & Gamble (branded products and services)
6. Prudential (financial services)

BP: Dana Deasy, Global CIO

Dana Deasy has been global CIO of BP for five years. Prior to this, he held CIO roles at Tyco International, Siemens, and GM. His decision to join BP relates to his belief that "you don't know how the world and management really work until you get out of your comfort zone."

For Deasy, working for Siemens was the first step—venturing into a multinational conglomerate—and he attributes the attraction that BP had for him to his international experience. Part of the value proposition he brought to BP was his experience in working with different organizational models. By models he means centralized, decentralized, or as in BP, what is known as a federated model. This means that the firm uses both forms of centralized and decentralized designs. Most important, he attributes his cross-industry experience as the reason BP had confidence in his ability to relate to the oil and gas business. Deasy also explains that not having experience in that particular business might have been seen as a disadvantage, but during his interview he explained why his prior experience could be very beneficial to BP.

Deasy feels the most important trait that supports his success is his ability to communicate. As he stated to us, "If you can't communicate, you can't create vision, and if you can't create vision, you can't get an organization to move." Deasy relates the ability to establish vision with the emotion of excitement—visions become reality when people get excited about what you are saying. Deasy's method of creating excitement has always been through storytelling—stories that vary depending on whom you are talking to. Deasy will speak in technology-specific terms when he is engaged with his organization, but is careful not to speak too much technical jargon in front of executives or the business. In other words, to be a successful CIO, you need to be able to dynamically switch from technical to business speak on demand, depending on your audience.

Deasy also discussed the importance of balancing the counsel you receive from others with your own sense of what is the right decision. Thus, successful CIOs need to know when to listen and when to act on their own. This is especially true when you need to deal with difficult issues that otherwise you would defer to your management team. To a large extent, Deasy suggests that you must know when to get involved in the details, but at the same time allow others to make decisions.

Another important factor for CIO success is the ability to deal with ambiguity. Looking back on Deasy's career, it is clear that in each of his CIO roles, there was not a clear road map that defined his position. Indeed, in each job he was the first to hold the role as a corporate or global CIO, so there was no history for the position. While this creates great opportunity, it also puts pressure on the new CIO to clearly develop a road map to demonstrate how they can bring value to the business.

Deasy explained that his role at BP is substantially different from others because of the complex federated model. This means that his team, while they report to him, also has close ties and responsibilities to the business units for which they support. So, he uses a different set of skills that are more focused on influencing people to get on board, as opposed to setting the direction: What he labels "purposeful direction." Therefore, leading without the real authority is a true challenge for him.

Earlier in his career, Deasy admitted that he depended much more on the superiority of his technical skills. Technical skills were the basis of authority in the IT world, which was further supported by the fact that IT was segregated from business decisions. This resulted in a mentality that allowed him to feel that he could control outcomes through his technical expertise. This obviously changed as he became more engaged as a CIO.

One of the most salient triggers for Deasy's evolution and change was his experience at Rockwell, supporting the space program. During his tenure there, Deasy was involved with the *Challenger* disaster. He was responsible for the IT that supported the help desk. As he explains, "It was the first time in my life that I ever had to deal with a real crisis." Deasy had to step up and really understand what it meant to live through a crisis. The experience pushed him to have the confidence that he could make a difference.

According to Deasy, the most successful CIOs constantly challenge themselves as well as their own IT organization, whereas the least effective IT leaders are those who feel they know everything. These individuals tend to alienate others and are rarely open-minded enough to deliver what the business needs.

Perhaps the most important part of our interview with Dana was his final takeaway—what he calls the "four *P*'s." These four *P*'s are the characteristics that CIOs must have to be successful. The first *P* is *patience* because CIOs will be told often that their plans will not work—you will be challenged for sure. CIOs also need *perseverance*, because you will have setbacks — projects that will not work out the way you expected. The third *P* is *performance*. CIOs must get results, or eventually management will lose confidence in them. Finally, successful CIOs are *passionate* about their jobs. With all the pressures and complexity of his job, Deasy made it clear to us that he loved being a CIO. Note: Dean Deasy left BP to become Global CIO of JPMorgan Chase. He is currently CIO of the US Department of Defense.

Merck & Co.: Chris Scalet, Senior Vice President and CIO

Chris Scalet was CIO at Merck for almost 10 years. He was responsible for a number of operations within the company. His original team started with 50 people but eventually grew to over 600 staff members that run facilities around the world. Scalet's CIO functions expanded outside IT to also include shared service responsibilities in human resources, travel, credit card, real estate, corporate security, and aviation. In effect, Scalet's organization that had operations responsibilities became part of his domain.

Scalet attributed his expanded role to his experience in the manufacturing sector, which influenced his appreciation for how IT functions could also help with automating other areas. Additionally, like Scalet, the CEO was a huge advocate of Six Sigma, so it was logical for the CIO to be selected to expand best practices in other domains. When Scalet joined Merck in 2003, the IT function was decentralized and had little governance. Sixty percent of IT reported to their respective division president. As a result, there was huge duplication of functions, so Scalet set out to create various shared services functions, which made the IT organization more cost effective and optimized performance. The effort resulted in closing 85 data centers, for example.

Scalet feels that he had an unusual opportunity with Merck to get visibility at the enterprise level—that is, he had a "seat at the table (the executive team)," which catapulted him into executive conversations pertaining to how IT could add strategic value to the organization. Also, by being given responsibility outside IT as well, Scalet was able to better align with business needs. An ideal CIO, according to Scalet, is one who is a businessperson first with a great understanding of IT issues. CIOs also need to understand IT architecture because this skill will allow them to adjust IT infrastructures to meet the needs of the business as well as the dynamics of the market. Scalet feels strongly that "CIOs should understand that IT is really about information." CIOs need to put information where users can get to it quickly, which will allow them to make better decisions. Application software continues to become more of a commodity; thus, it will be how you provide the information that will set CIOs apart in the value that they bring to their organizations. Indeed, Scalet believes that providing data faster not only saves time but speeds up decision making by 30 to 40%.

Scalet's relationship with his CEO was excellent, but his conversations with board members were very different. "Topics at the board are almost always about general business," says Scalet, "so CIOs need to always keep this in mind." Inevitably, Scalet realizes that an effective CIO must report to a CEO that appreciates the complexities of IT as well as the role in general. Furthermore, successful CIOs must realize that 80 to 90% of their job is people related, and they need to comfortably interact with all levels of management. IT decisions also need to be made in the context of the broader interests of the company, and as a result CIOs must respect the input and feedback they get from their peers.

Scalet also feels that good CIOs gauge the industry and anticipate scenarios that can benefit the company. They must bring these issues to the other executives or the board and present it in a way that helps the team make informed decisions. For example, in Scalet's world at Merck, he needed to constantly think about the effects of mobility on the pharmaceutical industry, the impact of cloud computing, and the IT capabilities that could reshape information back to customers.

Covance: John Repko, CIO

John Repko had been CIO for Covance for over eight years when we interviewed him. Covance is one of the world's largest and most comprehensive drug development services companies with more than 12,000 employees in 65 countries. He has since become senior vice president and CIO of Tyco. Repko is unique in that he also had been a practicing certified public accountant (CPA) for nine years and a Six Sigma Master Black Belt prior to moving into the IT leader position at GE. We've found that very few CIOs have that financial process background and dual capability. Repko's IT organization consists of about 800+ resources worldwide, of which 300 were employees, with the remainder being outsourced contract labor. Repko's role as CIO was not limited to IT, but also included the interface to Laboratory Technology, which is especially mission critical given Covance's leading position in the drug development services sector.

What was also unique about Repko's success was that he initially joined Covance in 2003 as vice president of global applications, and from June 2005 until January 2006 served as interim CIO before being appointed as permanent SVP and CIO.

Repko stated that his time at Covance could be broken down into three major "chapters": Chapter 1 was the challenges of getting out of the existing third-party IT contracts that were hurting the company and limiting IT's effectiveness. Chapter 2 involved the transformation of the IT management team and specific systems that were not working properly. Chapter 3 was to initiate more effective IT projects, including a data center consolidation and a key clinical application.

His focus was to transform the organization, and this required the replacement of many staff positions. Repko moved to Covance from GE and brought a number of his prior GE colleagues over to Covance to assist with the transformation. Repko's new IT organization was more centralized and was able to prematurely terminate an expensive outsource contract with a major Tier 1 provider. Thus, Repko's initial plan was to bring more of IT back under in-house control. There was also little IT governance at Covance at the time, so Repko had to initiate controls that served to bring "order" within IT at the company.

Repko believes strongly in hiring people that he knows and trusts and then building a team around a known management team. By bringing in the right talent, Repko was able to launch five major system transformations involving a new enterprise resource planning (ERP) system as well as providing the right technology to support Covance's toxicology business. Repko worked to ensure effective outsource partnerships with HCL and Accenture, feeling that these particular companies were leaders in project implementation that were relevant to Covance's needs. This relationship also allowed the IT management team to spend more time on business matters as they partnered with these providers to drive successful outcomes. Repko was as active with Covance's board. The Covance board meets five times annually, and Repko has attended four of those five meetings for the past several years. Furthermore, Repko had two directors from the board who had IT backgrounds and acted as advisers to him between meetings. He met privately with them before presenting to the board, so this process really allowed him to be prepared to discuss complex business issues with the remaining board members.

In terms of Repko's relationship with his C-suite members, he iterated the importance of leveraging one's relationships. In particular, it was the CEO who recruited him, and thus it gave Repko access to the key people in the firm. It also gave Repko the ability to get his CEO to understand the salient issues for him to be successful at Covance. Repko has a philosophy to be direct with his colleagues and likes to bring value quickly—and "with a lot of supporting data." At Covance, this meant speaking directly with the leadership and scientists in the company, requiring Repko to do several world tours in his first three years on the job! Winning support from the other executive members requires a one-at-a-time philosophy with a straight-shooter mentality. As a result, no one thought of Repko as a yes-man—something that was very important to his C-suite colleagues.

Repko's prior experience at GE was the critical part of his career growth. At GE, Repko assumed more than 10 different roles. Although Repko never had direct dealings with the GE board, the interrelationships with the GE management teams prepared him well to deal with senior management at Covance and at the board level. Indeed, GE was excellent training for developing your career. The bottom line for Repko is that GE taught him much about how to get things done.

Repko feels that one of the biggest mistakes made by other CIOs is their lack of self-confidence and fear of hiring really good talent—in some cases more experienced than themselves—below them. For example, in Repko's organization, five members were former CIOs. "It is hard to focus on key things if you do not have the right talent in place." Another concern offered by Repko is to not accept mediocrity in performance of staff. He recalled a time when he waited too long to take action on a key staff member, which he later regretted. As he stated, "If someone is detracting from your objectives, they should not be on the team." Repko suggests that up-and-coming CIOs surround themselves with lots of partners. The CIO should ensure they develop a relationship with all of the C-suite members, especially the CEO and the CFO. Another key suggestion he offered to us was the importance of building talent and loyalty within the organization. Finally, CIOs must always have detailed knowledge of the numbers, so having solid training in budgeting and accounting is critical. As Repko explained, "A CIO has to be in total command of his/her numbers."

Cushman & Wakefield: Craig Cuyar, CIO

Craig Cuyar was CIO of Cushman & Wakefield (C&W) for over five years. The company is a global commercial property and real estate services firm. When Cuyar came to C&W, IT was at the bottom of the pyramid, so his main focus was to get IT at the strategic level—as an enabler. Cuyar compares this concept to Maslow's hierarchy of need theory, in which one cannot reach self-actualization until you satisfy one's basic needs first. Therefore, the IT organization cannot become an enabler if it cannot provide the basic support functions like e-mail, or as we say, "keeping the lights on." The challenge at C&W was to rethink the core values, which was that IT was limited to support services, and transforming that into a strategic mission as well. Unlike the other CIOs we interviewed, Cuyar reports directly to the CFO, which is a controversial issue in the CIO community. However, Cuyar has direct access to the CEO and other board members.

Unfortunately, when the economic crisis hit in 2008, much of Cuyar's strategic desires had to be put on hold, simply because of constraints faced by the meltdown of real estate globally. Cuyar has spent that time reviewing the overall IT architecture and has now begun executing his original strategic plan. Cuyar enlisted Ernst & Young to help formulate their IT strategy. Cuyar designed his strategy to first address the implementation process. He began by moving to a global outsourcing of the service desk and the desktop support functions. Other IT functions are going to IBM and Tata Consultancy Services (TCS). Currently, the IT function has 200 employees and an equal number of outsourced resources, which represents about 1.5% of C&W's worldwide 14,500 employees.

Cuyar sees a huge amount of work evolving into a shared services model and to perhaps use this to differentiate C&W in the market. While C&W is not the largest firm in the business, they seek to be known as the highest in quality and as such the IT function must be consistent with that mission.

Cuyar has quarterly meetings with the other members of the executive management team. These meetings are mostly focused on ensuring that the IT department continues to be aligned with the goals of the business units. As Cuyar states, "These meetings are designed to ensure that we are aware of past performance and [that] we are equally cognizant of the wants and activities of the services and functions required of IT."

Cuyar sees the major strength of IT is that it cuts across multiple disciplines of the firm. As a result, IT always has a good pulse of what is driving profitability in the company. The only other organization that has a lot of information about the organization is finance, but not at the same level of detail, so when you think about it, "IT really has the best overall understanding of the business and its drivers of revenue and net income," according to Cuyar. The weakness that Cuyar sees is the reporting structure he has to the CFO—for which he feels identifies his organization too much as a back office operation. Fortunately, Cuyar went through a review process with Ernst & Young, which ultimately allowed IT to describe how the operation could help transform the business. The result of that study allowed the business units to see the driver aspects of IT, which otherwise would not have been disclosed within the finance function. However, it is important to note that Cuyar does not criticize his CFO and apparently there is a dual objective to get both IT and Finance in better positions to drive business value; from this perspective, IT and Finance have a common objective. In terms of his relationship with his CEO, Cuyar paraphrases it as "budding." This is simply because the CIO is a relatively new role in the C-suite. Cuyar's exposure to the board is limited at this time and he hopes that the role of the CIO will continue to evolve at the company. Cuyar's organization does have multiple "line" CIOs around the world who have dotted reporting lines to their business CEOs. This allows those relationships to become closer aligned to the driver factions that have an effect on the day-to-day challenges of those local businesses. However, Cuyar's role in New York deals more with the global heads of the firm.

Cuyar felt the most important part of his success relied heavily on his communication ability and feels it is at the center of his leadership style. As he pointed out, "It's not about doing things right but doing the right things and knowing what they are." Cuyar feels that another important trait of a successful CIO is to be a good listener, which ultimately helps with a person's communications skills. Having benchmarks are also critical, the most important ones being time, headcount, and sound financials.

CIOs, according to Cuyar, have three core areas of responsibilities: Operational, transformative, and business strategy. Those CIOs that tend to struggle have trouble with doing all three. Lesser CIOs tend to gravitate to an operational focus and fail to lead their organizations strategically. As a result these CIOs never transform the IT role and ultimately fail. Furthermore, the three variables are complex — to some extent Cuyar feels they tend to exist in economic cycles. For example, what he experienced during the downturn in the economy resulted in his need to refocus how IT could drive operational excellence to reduce costs. Craig Cuyar is currently Global CIO for Omnicom.

Prudential: Barbara Koster, SVP and CIO

Barbara Koster is a senior vice president and global chief information officer at Prudential Financial, Inc.

She joined Prudential in 1995 as CIO of the company's individual life insurance business after a 20-year career at Chase Manhattan Bank. She became global CIO in 2004 and was promoted to senior vice president and head of Global Business & Technology Solutions at Prudential and a member of the company's Senior Management Committee in 2010.

One of the most important projects Koster has worked on at Prudential was establishing Pramerica Systems Ireland, Limited, a software development subsidiary located in Ireland that develops software and other systems solutions and provides client contact services to Prudential's businesses around the world. Most recently, she launched a data center in Japan that provides cost-effective and enhanced technology services to the company's businesses in Japan and around the world.

Koster has won many awards for excellence and innovation in business and technology. In 2011, she was named one of the "Fifty Best Women in Business" by NJBIZ. In 2008, she was listed among the top Executive Women of New Jersey and named CIO of the Year by the Executive Council. She also has been named a Premier IT Leader by Computerworld magazine, a Top Twenty Financial Management Technologist by the CIO Forum, and one of the Elite Eight by Insurance & Technology magazine.

Koster's recipe for success is to deliver business-driven technology solutions that are developed through strong business partnerships and a thorough understanding of business needs. The underlying philosophy she follows is to find creative ways to integrate technology into business to support its strategy and goals. And Koster firmly believes the best way to understand business goals is to be an attentive listener.

What we found unique about Koster's management style is her commitment to talent management to ensure that her staff is properly trained and is given opportunities for continual professional development. She also leverages technology to promote work-life balance and alternative working arrangements— giving employees flexibility to do their best work. Indeed, one of the shortfalls in most IT organizations today is that they have failed to implement appropriate plans to replace their retiring talent. However, at Prudential, where the turnover rate for IT specialists is relatively low, succession planning strategies have been developed and managers are attentive to making sure IT specialists have a broad range of technology experiences. Koster also encourages her leadership team to develop partnerships with colleges, universities, and nonprofit organizations to attract diverse new IT talent into the organization and encourage young people to pursue careers in IT.

Koster reports directly to the Prudential vice chair and works in close association with the chairman and CEO. As a member of the executive management team, Koster is uniquely positioned to integrate IT with business strategy.

"Being able to take risks and feel confident about your convictions is crucial to the CIO role," advises Koster. "The time has never been more right for CIOs to be strategic, but we must always remain aligned with the business and aware of its challenges and opportunities."

Procter & Gamble: Filippo Passerini, Group President and CIO

Filippo Passerini has been with Procter & Gamble (P&G) for over 30 years, working his way up from the initial position of systems analyst in 1981. Passerini, originally from Italy, has truly worked for the company in a global capacity, having roles and responsibilities in the United Kingdom, Latin America, Europe, and the United States. Today, Passerini is not only the CIO, but holds a unique senior position as group president of Global Business Services. The role represents the integration that Passerini has accomplished with the business—an extraordinary partnership that has created a natural process of solving business challenges through constantly evolving innovation that is closely aligned with the business.

Passerini's philosophy on the role of IT is very clear: IT must assist the business to transform, and as such must go beyond just enabling IT; rather, IT must help the business to *maximize* its performance. The success of this transformation is accomplished through Passerini's leadership model that starts with the ability to collaborate effectively with internal business partners. The vision that Passerini presents to his team is simple: Transform the way business is done at P&G. Specifically, the goal is to create a competitive advantage for the company via progressive business models. Passerini feels strongly that you cannot adopt technology just for technology's sake: "You have to start with the end in mind—what's in it for the business? It's about creating distinctive, breakthrough business models and then using technology to enable them. It's not about technologies; it's about how you use them to drive value for the business." Simply put, technologies are really only a means to an end.

Passerini's use of personnel is consistent with Langer's driver theory, implementing a process that moves IT personnel into the actual business units. He calls such IT staff "service managers." Passerini expressed his philosophy about achieving success, believing strongly that CIOs should not be afraid to make mistakes; rather, they should focus more on what they learn from their setbacks. Passerini shared a setback he had in the United Kingdom early on in his career that taught him "it is always possible to turn an issue into an opportunity." Indeed, that setback created a huge opportunity because he demonstrated his ability to weather the storm and ultimately achieve success. The concept fits the analogy of "lots of people can sail a ship in calm waters, but you're not a true captain until you navigate through a storm." Our takeaway here is simple: Being impressive during pressure periods conveys a sense of confidence from your colleagues. It certainly paid off for Passerini. However, he notes that you cannot make the same mistake multiple times, for sure.

Passerini also discussed some of the "soft" yet important attributes for the successful CIO, which he defined as passion for the job, ability to closely track progress, anticipation of changes in the market, and effectively utilizing Big Data to guide the business. Passerini's close relationship with his business peers reflects the importance of these soft skills. His business colleagues often reach out to him to help solve market challenges and seek the creation of new business models in a joint effort with IT, so it's not about IT's providing a technology to enable the business, but having IT as a true partner to drive the transformation of the business. Passerini provided an example of the success of this collaboration. P&G used traditional focus groups to determine consumer needs IT (enabled virtual technologies for these focus groups), which help to reduce cycle time and speed innovations to market, while resulting in a significant cost savings.

Passerini believes that there has never been a better time for CIOs: "I feel that we're at a unique point where the stars (business needs) and the moon (enabling technology) are aligned for the CIO to play an unprecedented leadership role in the business."

Cushman & Wakefield: A View from Another Perspective

At Cushman & Wakefield we had the opportunity to speak with two of Craig Cuyar's colleagues in the C-suite, the CFO and the senior VP of human resources (HR). The questions we asked them related to the following six areas:

1. Major contributions and assessment of the CIO
2. What they see as important actions performed by the function
3. Value of technology in general

4. Disappointments and common errors that CIOs make during their tenure
5. Controlling cost issues
6. Importance of the CIO relationship with the CEO

The CFO

The chief financial officer (CFO) of C&W had prior experience with hiring and managing a CIO. When he came to C&W he realized that the current CIO of 25 years could not drive IT globally. He stated that there were many things wrong and Cuyar had to realign IT and create a platform that could drive strategy. It is important, according to the CFO, that CIOs focus on practical things and stay away from the IT "gizmos." He also recommends that CIOs speak "plain English." Much of this advice relates to his past experiences with IT leadership and their organizations. So the CFO was clear that most CIOs need to overcome the history of poor experiences that many executives have had with IT organizations.

As a result, the CFO feels that the most important thing for a "transitional" CIO to accomplish is "do things," that is, get as many little things done as possible. In this way the CIO can begin to create his/her reputation of getting things done as opposed to just talking about it. The CFO also recognizes the importance of the CEO's buy-in. As previously stated, the CIO at C&W reports directly to the CFO, so working together to determine how best to bring value to the CEO is critical for success. The strategy in this case then is for the CFO to be an advocate for the CIO position.

According to the CFO, it is best for the CIO to first ensure that his/her strategy is in line with the CEO, but also to be consistent with the rest of the business heads. As he states, "You know you can talk to the CEO and get the overall strategy, but it is equally important that the [CIO] go into each of the businesses." The CFO also feels that the CIO needs to clearly define the "key drivers" that are impacting change at the firm. His comment reminded us how the word "driver" is a common phrase used among CFOs. CFOs also need to see the existence of defined processes that need to comply with Sarbanes-Oxley. Indeed, CFOs are focused on governance, and it is helpful when CIOs present well-defined controls that satisfy the audit responsibilities of the CFO function. The CFO of C&W related his own experience with defining finance strategy to the board when he first came to C&W in 2008. As he stated to us, "I made it known [to the board] what my overall vision was and then how this defined my strategy." The CIO must develop those same skills. In cases like C&W, where the CIO reports to the CFO, both the IT and finance visions need to be integrated into one strategy, even if they have unrelated parts.

Interestingly, the CFO did not emphasize the importance of the CIO to put everything in a financial perspective. Rather, CIOs need to explain, whether discussing a driver or supporter, how IT participates with the business and what the related costs need to be to support it. However, the CFO did disclose his fears about how many CIOs get caught up with the technology itself and completely lose focus on the return on investment (ROI) of their projects, so he did not want to diminish the importance of the CIO's need to understand financial investments formulas.

At C&W, the board is very quantitative, so ideas are fine but they really do look at the details. The CFO explained to us that it was not unusual for the board sessions to cover multiple detailed spreadsheets that explain every financial aspect of the business. This differed from the CFO's experience with other boards—he found most of the past boards to be more concentrated more on qualitative measures than at C&W.

The CFO values his relationship with Cuyar. Notwithstanding the challenges and setbacks they have had in the business, ultimately the new uses and application of IT at C&W are beginning to take effect. This is best represented by renewed interests from other departments. The CFO stated that at the last board meeting, HR discussed plans to use the one source of data that had been devised by Cuyar for other departments.

The decision of what kind of CIO to hire is complex. It's like hiring a new CFO — there are all different types depending on what a firm desires. The CFO highlighted the importance of understanding the goals of the position: Do you need an operational CIO, a transformational CIO (support to strategy), a CIO that can complete a specific task or major project, or one that is strategic? This opens the conversation about the longevity of the CIO. If you hire a CIO for a specific reason, what happens when that objective is reached? The CFO stated simply, "This really needs to be determined up front."

We asked the CFO the question: "Does IT contribute to the overall business strategy?" The CFO responded, "We are not an organization that is at that point." The CFO believed the company is in "catch-up" mode because of how far they fell behind. Thus, the firm is not at the point where they can expect IT to provide realistic competitive advantage; rather, they first need the support side to operate efficiently.

The CFO feels strongly that one of Cuyar's greatest strengths is his patience, particularly in the way he handled the delays in the IT plan due to the downturn in the economy. Furthermore, Cuyar did an excellent job in assessing his staff and rethinking the skills sets that were necessary to bring the IT organization forward. Of course, he also established the right rapport with the business, which ultimately helped support the transformation that IT desperately needed. Ultimately, what Cuyar brought to the company was proper governance. He formed a council of businesspeople who assist IT in determining the next steps, as opposed to just making decisions on their own; it also sent the right message to the management team that IT could function in a vacuum. Thus, the council reviews many things and participates in many IT decisions. This resembles Lucas's Garbage Can model discussed in Chapter 2, where the organization devises a group that determines what IT projects are to be approved. It resembles an operating committee for IT projects. These committees should be composed of various operations personnel from each business concern, which is exactly the approach taken by Cuyar.

The CEO at C&W is not an "IT-savvy" executive, so while Cuyar communicates with him, the CEO does not attend many board meetings unless there is a very specific IT issue that needs to be discussed. Therefore, the CFO provides most of the communication of IT issues to the board. Because of this process, the CFO has to be sure he articulates IT needs as a separate entity, not to be confused with finance. Because the CEO is not IT-savvy, the CFO is careful to keep the conversations about IT at a basic dialogue. This does not suggest that the CEO is not approachable. The CFO has arranged quarterly sessions with Cuyar to ensure that IT has a seat at the CEO table, and they continually practice the "speak" that is necessary to relate a technology issue to the CEO.

The CFO believes that Cuyar's efforts will lead to a substantial IT transformation at C&W over the next three years. After that period, the newer technologies will begin to take hold and become productive tools for the field personnel. The CFO feels that "Craig is going to be involved in driving our business [and] making technology a business enabler." The CFO recognizes that the competition is way ahead. C&W is the third largest firm in their industry, and if they are to grow, it is essential that the driver side of IT emerge according to plan. He also relates the slow adoption of IT to the age group of the field personnel, citing that many of the field staff are engaged in a personal business, doing things the old way. Their staff ages range from 55 to 65, so there will be a turnover, which will require the business to adapt the needs of younger, more IT-savvy field personnel.

Human Resources

The HR executive discussed some pragmatic needs from the CIO position. Specifically this included the reliance on "platform" decisions to deliver much needed data on employment issues. By platform, the HR executive means the systems that need to deliver information. It also relates to the need to accumulate the necessary data from appropriate internal and external sources. During our discussion the HR executive used words such as "usability," "ease of data entry," and "sophisticated spreadsheet requirements."

To get this information, the HR executive admitted that the CIO function is more important than ever and certainly is a critical member of the C-suite. However, there is now a need for the CIOs to know more than just their own discipline; that is, they must understand the intricacies of the other functional areas as well. This is not a unique responsibility at the C-suite, according to the HR executive: "It is very similar for me as head of HR; I work with legal and finance [for example] in everything I do." So the CIO needs to be up to date on all of the contemporary technologies that can help each area and provide the right executive direction to the other C-suite members. In other words, the CIO needs to provide an inventory of opportunity and then present it to business heads in a way that "thinks about the market and the competitive frame, and thinking beyond the task at hand." As an HR executive, "I need to be a good listener and I think the CIO has the same challenges, serving multiple facets of the business in different ways." According to the HR executive, the CIO is still the leading technical adviser in the firm, and as such must present the vision of how IT can make a difference for the business and what the risks are for taking no action. Additionally, he feels that the CIO must be in tune with the market—what other firms in the industry are doing and what appears to provide a competitive advantage or as he says, "I think it is also being up to speed on all the different technologies that are critical and being used in other organizations."

The disappointments of IT typically occur when the technical aspects of the solution do not go smoothly, according to the HR executive. He provided an example that related to an electronic performance product that had "hiccups" in the database and lacked the necessary support from Oracle. Problems like these hurt IT because it leaves a poor impression on the IT brand. "It also hurts my reputation," explained the HR executive. "It's more to me than a platform; when the hiccups happen, or the deadlines are not met, it reflects on me as well." But the CIO also needs to be careful not to jump in too quickly or prematurely offer solutions without truly understanding the abilities of the organization to assimilate technology changes. This particularly resonated with the HR executive because he too wanted best practices in HR, but found that he needed to have realistic expectations on how staff transformed their use of technology. As he explained to us, "You should be able to gauge where the status of the organization is at that point and its appetite for change." Thus, there are ways of moving the organization along rather than pushing it especially when the organization is not ready for it. This, then, according to the HR executive, is crucial for CIO success and certainly fatal if mishandled. These comments from the HR executive resonated with us, as they are consistent with Langer's responsive organizational dynamism (ROD) theory, in which cultural assimilation is critical for absorbing new technology innovations.

The HR executive feels the most important thing for the CIO to do at the C-suite is to listen —listening in terms of priority and where the sense of urgency is in the business. In many ways, he stated, "Listening is being able to deliver, so you need to listen to where that low hanging is so people can see that you can execute." Furthermore, the executions must be done timely, and this above all will provide the CIO with early success stories that will inevitably build confidence from the other C-suite members.

The relationship the HR executive has with the CIO is excellent, clearly feeling that Cuyar is not one of these leaders that blame the problems on the technology or on others. The HR executive was clear on Cuyar's value: "Craig and I talk all the time. One thing I like about him which aligns with my thinking is that he never takes no for an answer, so for him there seems to always be a solution for me." So good is their relationship that both HR and IT leaders meet monthly and include select members from their staffs to attend, so from our perspective there is real integration between the two departments.

In terms of the department relationship with IT, the HR executive stated that supporting IT from a talent perspective was very much standard. He did not perceive IT staff as unusual or apart from how he supports other departments. He has an HR team that focuses on IT needs and did not foresee any changes in how HR supports the IT department.

The evolution of the CIO role will change for sure according to the HR executive: "It's getting tougher [especially] with the younger generation coming into the workforce with different needs and the challenge of accommodating them." And yet at the same time, per the HR executive, the organization must maintain controls and security. The clash of consumerization and controls will continue to be at the forefront of management challenges for the CIO, he explained. For example, just debating how effective an iPad can be for us is exciting until we start discussing the security challenges. The solutions here are not obvious, and many times the CIO bears the bad news, explained the HR executive. The other area of conflict highlighted by the HR executive was the policy on saving data, which inevitably relates to access of information for employees and customers. This became a huge issue especially for departments that did not understand the legal ramifications (confidentiality, for example). And with the technology ever changing, the CIO needs to constantly be up to date and must interact with every aspect of our business, so "yes, the role is evolving for sure," explained the HR executive. Another way he articulated the issue to us: "The uncertainty in the technology makes the organization want to protect itself." Most important though from the HR perspective is that the CIO cannot do this alone—it is not a sole IT responsibility. How disclaimers should work and the effects of this for example on each of our businesses can vary, thus "the evolution is really the broadening of communication across the company."

The HR executive feels overall that the IT evolutions will have positive impacts on further formalizing the CIO role at C&W. His advice for CEOs seeking a new CIO is to be aware of the importance for these individuals to have outstanding listening and communicating skills. His list of good CIO attributes also includes:

- Experience working with senior management teams.
- Worked at a public company.
- A good culture fit in general.
- Ability to see the whole picture.
- Someone who could likely report to the CEO.
- Is technically proficient.
- Possesses strategic vision.

Conclusion

The case studies in this chapter showed remarkable consistency in the way successful CIOs defined their success. Not surprisingly, these successful attributes are often defined as the "soft" skills, and often not the focus of up-and-coming IT managers. These necessary soft skills can be divided into two categories: (1) Personal attributes and (2) organizational philosophy. The next sections summarize the components of each of these categories based on the feedback presented in this chapter. The 24 components are further expanded in Chapter 5.

Personal Attributes

We define personal attributes as individual traits that appear to be keys for IT leadership. They include the following 11 traits:

1. **Push yourself outside your professional comfort zone:** Successful CIOs need to keep reinventing themselves and should strive for continual excellence at their jobs. Look for more responsibilities in different places outside the normal IT functions.
2. **Communication skills are at the forefront of leadership:** Without great communication skills, CIOs cannot influence the business or even imagine an integration strategy.

3. **Do not become too enamored with politics:** CIOs should not overplay the power of playing politics. Successful CIOs tend to be direct with their colleagues and staff.
4. **Do not shy away from tough decisions:** CIOs must do what is necessary, especially with their staffs and constituents. If someone is not performing, do the right thing and make the necessary changes.
5. **Get used to ambiguity:** If you need to be told exactly the problem, you will likely not bring much value. The life of most executives requires an existence in the uncertain and poorly defined.
6. **Take risks:** A strategic CIO cannot achieve success without engaging in projects that have risk factors — it's reality. The challenge for the CIO is to understand the extent of the challenge and the significance of the rewards to the business.
7. **Lead without authority:** Great leaders can influence the behaviors in others without using the power of their position. Influencing the change of behavior in others is far more sustainable.
8. **The importance of technical skills diminishes as you approach the CIO position:** CIOs should not confuse IT knowledge with skills. Skills relate to doing; knowledge better supports management of others.
9. **Have pride in ownership:** There is no better judge of excellence than your own. CIOs need to strive to be the best and take responsibility for their actions.
10. **Learn to listen:** CIOs must learn to listen to their feedback they receive and listen to what people really need. Too many CIOs think they know what people want, which often is not accurate.
11. **Do not accept mediocrity:** We live in a competitive world and expecting the very best from your staff is critical, especially from a global perspective.

Organization Philosophy

We relate organization philosophy to issues that represent the way the organization should operate. It should include the following 13 objectives:

1. **Integration of IT is a fundamental objective:** Successful CIOs understand that integration means that IT resources are truly embedded in the business. This requires CIOs to move their resources and ensure that they spend time with their colleagues in the business.
2. **CIOs must be knowledgeable about the business:** This somewhat relates to (1), but also suggests that spending time and integrating

resources is not enough. IT must be intimately familiar with the challenges of the business, the way the units operate, and their culture. Only with this knowledge can IT become an equal partner.

3. **Have a road map:** CIOs need to develop a plan of what they want to accomplish, why it is valuable to the business, and how they will accomplish the objectives. This includes the specifics of cost, ROI, and time to completion.

4. **Keep your pulse on costs:** CIOs still need to be fiscally responsible and must shed the reputation as big spenders. Where IT can be used to reduce costs and increase shareholder value is still an extremely important part of the role.

5. **Having a seat at the table does matter:** The argument that it does not matter where the CIO actually reports is bogus. CIOs need to report directly to the CEO and have a regular place of attendance at key board meetings. Perceptions are realities and if the CIO function does not get the top reporting line, then the message to the firm from the top is clear; IT is not important enough.

6. **Business comes first:** The CIO must always think about the value IT brings to the business. If that business value is not there, then the value of the IT is not relevant.

7. **Expand the role beyond traditional IT:** We saw from our cases that many successful CIOs are now taking on expanded roles outside of just IT issues. This includes operations, infrastructure, and shared services.

8. **Have the best people:** CIOs cannot accomplish their complex roles without surrounding themselves with the appropriate staff. In actuality, having the best IT staff is extremely important to securing an effective supporter function.

9. **Pay attention to Big Data:** Data analytics, as discussed earlier, has become an increasingly important conversation at the board level. Big Data are essential for competitive advantage and also understanding a firm's legal exposures and security coverage.

10. **Align with the business:** This somewhat relates to being knowledgeable about the business. But it is not enough to be knowledgeable. The CIO must be aligned with the aspirations of the business units, so that there is interdepartment harmony.

11. **Drive profitability:** The more the CIO can strategically support the organization to drive more profits, the more valuable the function. The more valuable a CIO is to the organization, the more capacities and power will be afforded to the role.

12. **Use benchmarks:** Having statistical analysis of the IT operations is still very important, certainly in supporter functions. CIOs need to show they use metrics to optimize the performance or their organizations.

13. **React to the dynamics of the market:** In Chapter 2, we discussed Bradley and Nolan's concept of "sense and respond." It is clear from our cases that successful CIOs understand that they cannot know the future and need to be very agile to changes in the market that affect the organization.

CHAPTER 5

Patterns of a Strategically Effective CIO

This chapter provides evidence of why certain chief information officers (CIOs) have attained success as a strategic driver of their businesses.

This evidence is presented from the case studies from Chapter 4 and integrates our findings based on our theories of why certain CIOs are more successful than others. As stated earlier, these results have led us to understand the patterns that suggest why certain CIOs obtain success in introducing IT strategy to their firms and how they build credibility among C-level peers in their organizations.

We concluded Chapter 4 with presenting 24 key attributes of successful CIOs. These skills were divided into two categories: (1) Personal attributes and (2) organizational philosophy. We expand each of these attributes further here to include more theory and practical guidance.

Personal Attributes

We defined personal attributes in Chapter 4 as "individual traits that appear to be keys for IT leadership." The following section provides an expanded description of these 11 attributes as they relate to the value it brings to the business.

1. Push Yourself Outside Your Professional Comfort Zone

Successful CIOs need to keep reinventing themselves and should strive for continual excellence at their jobs. Look for more responsibilities in different places outside the normal IT functions.

Much has been written about what makes certain individuals want to progress to higher stages of maturity. Kegan, in his book *In Over Our Heads*, described learning as being able to go beyond one's comfort zone.[1] He described the willingness to evolve as being directly correlated to a "value proposition." In other words, individuals learn because they have a reason to, an objective, to move to another level of sophistication. Kegan also recognized that transformation has its rewards but also losses—these losses are those that one gives up by moving to the next level. The loss can be what successful CIOs have called "the reinvention of themselves." When people reinvent themselves, they must be willing to move outside their comfort zone—a zone that they have previously mastered. So it requires an individual to have a certain drive to want to succeed at the next level, to give up their comfort for the rewards of that next level. The CIOs who achieve that success are the individuals who have now broadened their responsibilities in tangential areas of responsibilities, like operations and shared services. Indeed, business strategists have long realized that the ability of an executive to learn faster or "better" than his or her competitors may indeed be the key to long-term business success.[2]

Langer's case study, "Fixing Bad Habits," showed that the use of reflective practices was key to supporting individual learning and subsequent transformation.[3] Furthermore, this study found that such development greatly enhanced the adaption of new technologies, the understanding of strategic value, and the improved assimilation into the social norms of the business.

There is clearly a positive correlation of CIO development to theories of individual growth. This suggests that CIOs need to evolve their roles by developing a mindset that supports adapting new ideas, thinking processes, and the ultimate willingness to change. Those CIOs who continually defend old norms likely will be unsuccessful as change agents, which is what CEOs define as a critical attribute in today's technology leaders.

2. Communication Skills Are at the Forefront of Leadership

Without great communication skills CIOs cannot influence the business or even imagine an integration strategy.

Social discourse and the use of language are critical to creating and sustaining internal interactions. Technology dynamism and responsive organizational dynamism (ROD) show that the context of globalized forces has added to the complexity of understanding "the language and symbolic media we employ to describe, represent, interpret, and theorize what we take to be facticity or organizational life."[4] Langer translated this into the need to develop a "language of technology."[5] That is, how do we incorporate technology into the normal processes of discourse—ow can we make technology an "organized discourse," so that it can be integrated into the day-to-day speak of the business?

The importance of great communication skills, then, in accordance with our interviews, suggests that success lies with the CIO's ability to make the social connections with his/her colleagues and staff. These connections require

CIOs to use many different forms of communication including language, talk, stories, and conversations, all of which represent the heart of social life. These types of communication require learning because it involves sense-making and builds on the knowledge development of the organization. This becomes critical for CIOs to implement ROD, especially in dealing with change driven by technological innovations. Indeed, Dana Deasy stated in our interview that telling stories was a huge part of his strategy throughout his career. Simply put, those CIOs who understand the process of how technological concepts need to be delivered are those who will have more success at the C-suite.

The concept of converting learning to strategic benefit was pioneered by Willie Pietersen.[6] He established a learning cycle that can be used to transition learning concepts into better communication approaches. He created a strategic learning cycle that comprised component processes that contained four action verbs: Learn, focus, align, and execute. The explanation of each is as follows:

1. **Learn:** Conduct a situation analysis to generate insights into the competitive environment and into the company's own realities.
2. **Focus:** Translate insights into a winning proposition that outlines key priorities for success.
3. **Align:** Align the organization and energize the people behind the new strategic focus.
4. **Execute:** Implement strategy and experiment with new concepts. Interpret results and continue the cycle.

CIOs can use Pieterson's learning model as a template for preparing conversations with business partners. The Execute step, in particular, has significant relevance in communication success, specifically, its implication that interpretation is a cycle that requires multiple loops. Here, we translate this into the cycle of communication, where one idea could require multiple loops of communication until the community of participants reach agreement. It is important to note that the CIO is part of this community and thus may need to adjust and negotiate during the cycle of communication.

3. Do Not Become Too Enamored with Politics

CIOs should not overplay the power of playing politics. Successful CIOs tend to be direct with their colleagues and staff.

We do not suggest that politics is not an active part of organization life, rather that it is important to distinguish between what is *good* politics and *bad* politics. *Good* politics can be defined as the normal interactions of how things get done in organizations. It is often mistaken for *bad* politics, which are the destructive agendas and actions taken by people against others for unethical gain. The feedback we received from the interviews, particularly those made by Koster from Prudential, distinguishes the salient differences between the two and how often individuals misinterpret what is really strategic advocacy rather than bad politics.

Deluca provides five basic questions for mapping the political territory for purposes of strategic advocacy:

1. Who are the key players?
2. What is their power or influence in the organization?
3. To what extent are they applying their influence for or against the issue?
4. How easily can their applied influence be changed?
5. What significant relationships exist among the key players?[7]

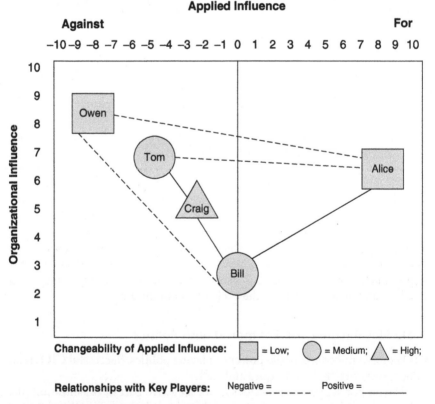

Figure 5.1   Organizational mapping grid.
Source: J. Deluca, Political Savvy: Systematic Approaches to Leadership Behind-the-Scenes (Berwyn, PA: EBG, 1999).

Deluca defines these advocacies as political savvy, which he describes as the "unofficial influence approaches occurring out of sight in most organizations."[8] As Deluca states:

> Political savvy entrepreneurs will know how to better cut across organizational, cultural, and geographical lines to put together strategic alliances. Not only among individuals within the organization, but across multiple businesses as well[9]

It is interesting that Deluca refers to entrepreneurs in this context. Indeed, we believe that CIOs need to perceive themselves and operate with an entrepreneurial mindset. Notwithstanding the cultural norms of whether strategic advocacy is cast as good politics in many organizations, Deluca provides a way of using politics in a positive way. Figure 5.1 provides a data sheet that can be used to determine the relative strengths of political relationships in the organization. This "political mapping" can be used to develop a strategic plan to influencing key players in the organization.

Using the grid, then, CIOs can develop the strategic goals using Figure 5.2.

Perhaps the most effective way to distinguish good politics from bad politics is the questions of *ethics*. Those who transform good politics into strategic advocacy using Deluca's approach do so by choosing to become an active and ethical participant as opposed to a destructive force for personal gain at all costs.

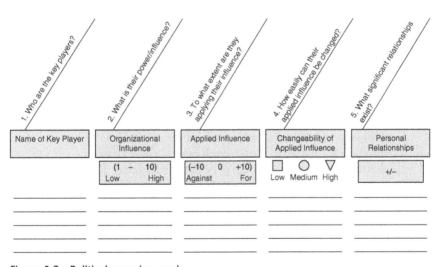

Figure 5.2   Political mapping goals.
Source: J. DeLuca, Political Savvy: Systematic Approaches to Leadership Behind-the-Scenes *(Berwyn, PA: EBG, 1999).*

4. Do Not Shy Away from Tough Decisions

CIOs must do what is necessary, especially with their staffs and constituents. If someone is not performing, do the right thing and make the necessary changes.

Having the ability to make tough decisions is an attribute of any good leader, certainly not limited to the role of a CIO. However, we find that many short tenure CIOs are not very good managers. The topic of tough decision making is a subset of a larger subject often referred to as "tough-minded management." Batten defined a tough-minded manager as one who would be impatient with the "unused potential" of the people working for him or her.[10] The essence of tough management is to develop the talent, to push your people to their maximum strengths and to see the value of the organization as the *sum* of all the strengths of each individual. So the goal for a CIO is to develop those strengths in each person. Batten offers a number of general guidelines:

- Individuals tend to be happier when they are pushed, stretched at work, and pulled into many different areas of responsibility.
- Managers need to develop a person's weakness as an underdeveloped strength—so it's like using a negative as a potential positive.
- Always expect high performance. Do not allow mediocrity in your staff.
- Care enough about individual strengths to emphasis it as part of all assessments of performance and organizational successes.

Ferrell and Gardiner provide seven distinct attributes of tough-minded managers:

1. Accepts that risks must often be taken and that conflict is inevitable in making tough choices.
2. Understands that short-run losses may be inevitable and unavoidable to achieve long-run success.
3. Believes that the best long-run approach to business is integrity.
4. Is aware that ethical problems may arise in the workplace, and of how ethical decisions are usually made in the workplace.
5. Has reached a level of moral development where economic self-interest is not paramount, and where personal ethical values are important.
6. Has learned that trust is the glue that holds business relationships together.
7. Believes strongly that maintaining self-esteem and self-respect outweighs material gain.[11]

Inferred in tough-minded managers are high degrees of ethical behavior. Thus, setting an example and working as hard as those around you are significant aspects of achieving excellence. The CIOs in our cases not only get the performance from their staffs, but also receive their admiration—they set an example, stretch themselves as much as they do their staffs, and always work on building their strengths.

The more difficult challenge for CIOs is dealing with those who either continually underperform or do not buy into the "sum of the parts" which ultimately defines the value of the whole. Indeed, Langer's study of Ravell showed that employees are not always authentic and some individuals will engage in political behavior that can be detrimental to any organizational learning effort.[12] Simply put, they are not interested in participating. In such cases, leaders must make the tough choice to eliminate such people from the organization. Thus, as much as a CIO should attempt to find the right place for an individual to contribute, acceptance of continual poor performance or a lack of enthusiasm for the objectives of the organization by any employee are detrimental to the success of the IT department.

5. Get Used to Ambiguity

If you need to be told exactly the problem, you will likely not bring much value. The life of most executives requires an existence in the uncertain and poorly defined.

Many of the students in our Executive IT Master's program at Columbia University are challenged with coursework that requires them to deal with ambiguous problems. They tend to ask us, "Can you tell me exactly what you want?" These students often have well over 10 years' experience and are at senior management positions. Yet they have lived in IT environments that are very requirements specific—learning that they need to understand the specifications in order to proceed. Furthermore, IT specialists tend to be developed in a learning environment that is scientific, which advocates the need for specifics and clarity. However, executive responsibilities are often vague, cloudy, and require creative methods of helping others understand what they really need. In fact, the higher you get, the more vague things are—typically goals are clear, like we need to cut the budget, we need to increase margin. However, such goals come without the specifics of how to attain them—that's where CIOs need to improvise and figure out how to get to the end point of what is needed. We always tell our students that those dealing with ambiguity are at the forefront for getting compensated well! Indeed, why do we require executives who need to be told what to do all the time?

Eichinger and Lombardo developed a model of dealing with ambiguity which is used as a Microsoft learning training tool. They define three essential "expert" qualities:

1. Anticipates impact of change, and directs self and others in smoothly shifting gears.

2. Uses ingenuity in dealing with ambiguous situations, and guides others to cope effectively.
3. Thrives on situations involving risk and uncertainty.[13]

They suggest using the following self-questions to help assess these skills:

- What decision must I make to minimize risk in spite of not having all the information?
- What new project can I undertake today, even though I have other things in the works?
- How can I prepare others right now for the impact of an anticipated change?
- What disjointed task or project can I organize?
- Is there someone with whom I must "clear the air" or make amends?
- What big task can I break down into smaller tasks to facilitate its completion?

Their research also provides additional suggestions for "overcompensating for ambiguity" or as they define "overdoing ambiguity":

- May move to conclusions without enough data.
- May fill in gaps by adding things that aren't there.
- May frustrate others by not getting specific enough.
- May undervalue orderly problem solving.
- May reject precedent and history.
- May err toward the new and risky at the expense of proven solutions.
- May overcomplicate things.

Unfortunately, there is much literature that trains managers how not to be ambiguous with their staffs! It is interesting that the way we develop managers tends to prepare them poorly for life at the C-suite.

6. Take Risks

A strategic CIO cannot achieve success without engaging in projects that have risk factors—it's reality. The challenge for the CIO is to understand the extent of the challenge and the significance of the rewards to the business.

The conversation surrounding risk taking is quite complex. Risks almost certainly support a level of failure; and failure, as we discussed earlier, is not generally accepted for IT initiatives. But IT risk and failure rate must become part of the reality for many firms. Langer defined this risk with driver projects by calling for the creation of a "batting average" defining this as the rate of failure for a new IT initiative.

It became apparent to us, especially during our interview with Passerini from Proctor & Gamble, that failures are essential components of achieving success. To always operate in an environment with low risk likely provides for little upward mobility, and likely will underprepare a young CIO for success at the C-suite. We learned that how one deals with the failures can be very advantageous because those at the C-suite have all experienced a "run rate." Indeed, most failures that are within the risk rate—or rate of failure, are not really failures!

However, this concept does not suggest that CIOs should feel free to fail. The point is that they must establish the rate of failure for driver projects within an acceptable rate. This rate must be consistent with the firm's acceptable ROI. We already defined that failure rates are not acceptable for supporter projects.

A supporting factor for establishing an IT batting average is to use benchmarks. Unfortunately, many CIOs use benchmarks from other IT projects, which in many cases is problematic because the C-suite executives are more interested in industry data that can foster competitive advantage. Therefore, it is more impressive to use industry data from operational or sales sources. For example, use sales risk factors in the industry and correlate them to risks of IT projects given that shifts in market needs will often change IT requirements.

Dana Deasy, when he was CIO of the Americas for Siemens Corporation, dealt with the challenge of establishing the viability of IT risks. The challenge at Siemens was how technologies could be tested to determine exactly how it might impact the business. In order to address this dilemma, Deasy established the concept of "revalidation." Specifically, approved technology projects were reviewed every 90 days to determine whether they were indeed providing the planned outcomes, whether new outcomes needed to be established, or whether the technology was no longer useful. This required that IT be given the ability to invest and experiment with technology in order to fully maximize the evaluation of IT in strategic integration. This was particularly useful to Deasy, who needed to evolve the culture at Siemens to recognize that not all approved technologies succeed, as well as to dramatically alter the expected life cycle of how software applications were evaluated by IT and senior management. This challenge was significant in that it had to be accepted by over 25 autonomous presidents, who were more focused on shorter and more precise outcomes from technology investments.

Deasy was able to address the challenges that many presidents had in understanding IT "jargon," specifically as it related to the benefits of using technology. He engaged in an initiative to communicate with non-IT executives by using a process called "storyboarding." Storyboarding is the process of creating prototypes that allow users to actually see an example of how the technology will look and operate. Storyboarding tells a story and can quickly educate executives without being intimidating. Deasy's process of revaluation has its own unique life cycle at Siemens:

- Create excitement through animation. What would Siemens be like if . . .
- Evaluate how the technology would be supported.
- Recognize implementation considerations about how the technology as a business driver is consistent with what the organization is doing and experiencing.
- Technology is reviewed every 90 days after experimental use with customers and presented to the C-suite on an "as-needed" basis.
- Establish ROD, that is, the reality of instability of technology and that there are no guarantees to planned outcomes; rather, promote business units to understand the concept of "forever prototyping."

7. Lead Without Authority

Great leaders can influence the behaviors in others without using the power of their position. Influencing the change of behavior in others is far more sustainable.

There has been much written about what represents leadership. There are many definitions, but most agree that true leadership starts with the ability to influence the behaviors of others without the use of power. As managers rise to executive levels of management, their power among their colleagues actually decreases—many have opinions at the C-suite, and anyone can be questioned. This is unlike the rise to management, which is typically based on individual performance rewards. Those individual performances are rewarded with promotions that require more responsibility. With more responsibility, one typically receives the power to lead. Such is no longer the case at the C-suite where influence becomes the more relevant factor for success.

Conger, a professor at London Business School, suggests that executives must use more lateral styles of leadership.[14] His article in *Harvard Management Update* titled "Exerting Influence without Authority" states that lateral leadership provides a "constellation of capabilities." The constellation comprises four intertwined capabilities:

1. **Networking:** Having strong networks of people inside and outside the organization who can carry out your initiatives. As Conger states, "Certain people are portals to other people—they can connect you to more and bigger networks." As they say, "You are only as good as

those you surround yourself with," and networking is the infrastructure to getting the resources you need to get quick answers to executive problems.

2. **Constructive persuasion and negotiation:** Too often, according to Conger, people view persuasion and negotiation as manipulation; however, it's proven to enhance one's influence.

3. **Consultation:** Develop relationships with people you need. Do not feel asking for advice is a sign of weakness—getting someone's input on an idea you have constitutes their support. Don't try to impose your will on those who you cannot control. Of course, seeking input means that you need to negotiate what you want, but that is the way most organizations get things done.

4. **Coalition building:** Numbers matter, and the more people you have supporting your idea, the better. Without question, coalitions have the most positive impact on lateral leadership.

While lateral leadership makes sense it is difficult to train managers to exercise it. The problem stems from those executives who might seek advice and support from other colleagues and then do not receive it. However, there is no question that the successful CIOs have mastered the practice. Their success, we believe, can be attributed to high levels of individual perseverance and passion. Remember, "No only means no now!"[15]

8. The Importance of Technical Skills Diminishes as You Approach the CIO Position

CIOs should not confuse IT knowledge with skills. Skills relate to doing; knowledge better supports management of others.

Still today, most CIOs come from IT technical backgrounds. It is very difficult to let go of one's reliance on their technical expertise, which has served to catapult their careers. However, the importance of technical skills becomes less important as one climbs the ladder into the C-suite. Actually, the technical experience is assumed at the C-suite, but not used in discourse. Indeed, being too technical might work against an executive manager, who might be seen as unable to transition to the broader management challenges of their area of responsibility.

At the CIO level, human skills and conceptual skills become more important. The human skills involve a manager's ability to work with people and in particular motivate others. Ultimately, the human factor helps executives establish effective teams that can get things done. Conceptual skills can be related to the abilities presented in the later stages of Langer's CIO Arc. It allows CIOs to think abstractly and thus provides the ability for them to formulate long-term plans, policies, and overall business direction.

One's technical expertise is still important however—as it provides the basis to build human and conceptual actions.

CIOs must always remember that many see them as techs and geeks and must be very sensitive to stay away from using technical jargon at business meetings. Unfortunately, we have seen time and time again that IT people tend to gravitate back to technical terms, especially when they are under stress. It takes practice to lose that reliance, but those who are successful have mastered the balance and the slogan: "Talk business above and technical below!"

9. Have Pride of Ownership

There is no better judge of excellence than your own. CIOs need to strive to be the best and take responsibility for their actions.

Those who are successful at what they do love their jobs and take great pride in what they do. Our successful CIOs are no different and want very much to leave something behind in the organizations they manage. Part of striving for the best is having someone to look up to. All of our case study subjects discussed people who made a difference in their professional lives and influenced certain of their behavior patterns. This does raise the question of whether a manager has had the opportunity to be mentored or developed by a senior person during their professional development. A number of CIOs we have met have hired coaches to personally assist them in developing what they see as weaknesses.

CIOs who have pride of ownership are great models for their staffs as well. They are the executives who others strive to be like and who motivate their people simply by displaying the dedication to excellence that they expect from themselves. It has been proven that most employees want to excel at their jobs, but less and less staff, particularly middle managers, receive the necessary attention they require to develop further. Current CIOs should be cognizant of this trend and attempt to provide formal and informal structures to help develop the next generation. Indeed, Sarbanes- Oxley requires that CIOs have the appropriate personnel to replace key positions in their IT organization. Furthermore, those CIOs who have been promoted into more senior operations positions have typically selected and nurtured their replacement before moving on.

10. Learn to Listen

CIOs must learn to listen to the feedback they receive and listen to what people really need. Too many CIOs think they know what people want, which often is not accurate.

We are continually amazed how well leaders listen. They listen to issues, what their staffs are saying to them, and especially listen to their customers.

Most important, they must listen to what their superiors and peers are saying. Too often, we have seen failed CIOs who tell us that they simply had no idea they were in trouble. The signs of dissatisfaction, upon review by these CIOs, typically reveal that messages were sent to them, but because they did not reflect on what was really being said, they missed the opportunity to address their shortfalls.

Research has shown that only 25% of people listen efficiently even though most feel they listen extremely well to their staff and supervisors. Effective listening executives need to help their people to solve important problems but must first truly understand the problem. How often we hear that peers complain that the CIO does not understand the issues. Likely, it's because the CIO is not listening to them in detail.

Ultimately, great executive listeners better match their responses to the situation at hand. They also reflect more on what is being said and have the ability to "reflect-on-action," which is the process of thinking about what has occurred and what might be effective actions to change the situation. At the CIO level, these reflections often require a change in behavior—that is, the actions and processes that a CIO uses to deal with interactions.

11. Do Not Accept Mediocrity

We live in a competitive world and expecting the very best from your staff is critical, especially from a global perspective.

Thomas L. Friedman and Michael Mandelbaum's book, *That Used to Be Us*, discusses the problems with accepting mediocrity.[16] Simply put, they state that global competition has made mediocrity unacceptable. Those executives who are mediocre will likely disappear. The concept of seeking excellence is not just an individual desire, but one who effects the entire organization. Thus, CEOs and boards expect the best from the least. The notion of rejecting mediocrity can be aligned with Prahalad and Krishnan's notion of N = 1 and R = G discussed in Chapter 1.[17] With consumers in control of what they want and when they want it, resources must provide the very best support and deliver products and services on demand. Thus, organizations today regularly examine global resources to meet those consumer demands in a just-in-time (JIT) delivery manner. As a result, the process of where to hire people, the percent of outsourced resources at lower prices you use, and where to get the best services are an ongoing challenge to remain competitive in a global economy.

The result of the consumerization substantially fostered by IT innovations will continue to challenge CIOs to think broader and to constantly investigate new ways of providing JIT products and services. However, providing the resources is no longer enough; the services must be the best or someone else will take the business away from you. CIOs must therefore be

JIT in thinking; they must react quickly and have global resources around the world that can provide answers—answers that provide actions to respond to new market needs.

Organization Philosophy

We defined organization philosophy in Chapter 4 as issues that represent the way the organization should operate. The following sections are an expansion of each of the 12 critical issues cited in our CIO interviews.

1. Integration of IT Is a Fundamental Objective

Successful CIOs understand that integration means that IT resources are truly embedded in the business. This requires CIOs to move their resources and ensure that they spend time with their colleagues in the business.

As stated earlier, Schein was the first scholar to see the IT and non-IT personnel collision between what he called "two cultures."[18] That collision must now be resolved and full integration must prevail. The question is how best to do that. Obviously, the CIO, being the most senior executive in IT, must lead the way to figuring out the best way to accomplish full integration. Using Einstein's ongoing quest to find a unified theory to deal with quantum physics, CIOs too need to find a unified method to complete IT and business integration.

Langer offered first steps to providing a concrete way of completing a unified integration by dividing IT into two groups: Drivers and supporters. The supporters would remain as separate entities, with drivers being absorbed into their respective business units. A unified integration, however, requires both sides to become active. CEOs can no longer sit in the background and hope that their executive team will figure it out. There must be an agenda of unification and a decision to how best to migrate resources for optimized performance throughout the businesses.

Some CIOs might see unification with the business as an approach that could lead to their becoming "disenfranchised," worrying that they will ultimately lose their value to the business. Warren Kudman, CIO of Sealed Air, offers interesting insights to this dilemma. While he agrees that CIOs need to work closely with their business units and maintain great flexibility, Kudman's IT organization is centralized and decentralized—so he provides maximum flexibility to provide many of those strategic driver needs that the business requires to survive, but at the same time centralizes those supporters. As Kudman stated, "I am in a model where IT is very centralized but my team is decentralized globally." Kudman brings up an important point: Do we just give away the resources or attempt to provide maximum flexibility with "just enough governance to maintain control while avoiding a lot of non-value-added bureaucracy and overhead?"

Ultimately, Kudman feels that the business must make the decisions and IT needs to be there to provide the guidance and best operating practices. He fears that business units that manage IT people directly may not have the appropriate career perspectives for IT staff—so it can be a dead-end move for IT professionals. There certainly is justification in these concerns. However, "just making an organization shift may not solve the real problem," as he puts it.

Perhaps there is middle ground to this dilemma. We discussed the notion of allowing IT personnel to "move" to a business unit, but not permanently. This might provide the best of both worlds—true integration without hurting long-term career growth. Such a strategy is not new. Japanese firms actually would assign their business managers to work in IT organizations to better understand their strategic potential. Why not do this with IT personnel in reverse? Our critique though still remains: Controlling IT budgets across the business can be problematic, so while your IT resources are operating inside a business unit, why not let them be responsible for the cost? Passerini found actually spending the time in the business invaluable. He transformed his operation by establishing the "service manager" position in an effort to create true unification. Ultimately, we believe that true integration can only be accomplished by taking more drastic measures. Indeed, history has shown that almost all CIOs agree with integration but few have accomplished it.

2. CIOs Must Be Knowledgeable about the Business

This somewhat relates to (1), but also suggests that spending time and integrating resources is not enough. IT must be intimately familiar with the challenges of the business, the way the units operate and their culture. Only with this knowledge can IT become an equal partner.

Another portion of integration is the knowledge challenge. Spending time is one thing, and it certainly improves knowledge transfer, but it does not provide the immediate value that is required today in businesses. Furthermore, how do we educate businesspeople to have them better understand the needs of IT—so that their expectations are more in line with the realities of how innovations mature? So many CIOs at conferences complain that their CEO and C-suite colleagues simply don't get it and that they fail to ever understand how technology works and why it costs so much and takes so long.

Education is always an option. Sending IT and non-IT people to training programs will provide some leverage for integration, but frankly, it takes too long, costs too much, and often does not embellish the realities of what is occurring in practice. More IT organizations need to embrace the concept of communities of practice, a way of integrating staff who have common goals and expected outcomes in business units.

Communities of practice are based on the assumption that learning starts with engagement in social practice and that this practice is the fundamental construct by which individuals learn.[19] Communities of practice are formed to get things done by using a shared way of pursuing interest. For individuals this means that learning is a way of engaging in, and contributing to, the practices of their communities. For specific communities, on the other hand, it means that learning is a way of refining its distinctive practices and ensuring new generations of members. For entire organizations it means that learning is an issue of sustaining interconnected communities of practice, which define what an organization knows and contributes to the business. The notion of communities of practice supports the idea that learning is an "inevitable part of participating in social life and practice."[20] Communities of practice also include assisting members of the community with the particular focus on improving their skills. This is also known as "situated learning." Thus, communities of practice are very much a social learning theory as opposed to one that is based solely on the individual. Communities of practice have been called "learning-in-working," where learning is an inevitable part of working together in a social setting. Much of this concept implies that learning in some form or another will occur and that it is accomplished within a framework of social participation, not solely or simply in the individual mind. In a world that is changing significantly due to technological innovations, we should recognize the need for organizations, communities, and individuals to embrace the complexities of being interconnected at an accelerated pace.

Furthermore, communities-of-practice theory justifies its use in ROD. Indeed, the size and complexity of technology innovations requires a community focus, which can be mapped to a business unit. This would be especially useful within the confines of specific departments that are in need of understanding how to deal with technological dynamism. Specifically, this means that through the infrastructure of a community, individuals can determine how they will operate with emerging technologies, what education they will need, and what potential strategic integration they will need to prepare for changes brought on by technology. Action in this context can be viewed as a continuous process much in the same way that Langer presented technology as an ongoing accelerating variable. The important thing to recognize here is the business unit becomes intimately involved with goal attainment and that IT personnel must be legitimately part of the community. Education occurs both formally and informally to then help create new identities of the unit and ultimately an evolving culture.

3. Have a Road Map

CIOs need to develop a plan of what they want to accomplish, why it is valuable to the business, and how they will accomplish the objectives. This includes the specifics of cost, ROI, and time to completion.

Having objectives is the first part of any plan. But providing the mechanics of how one will execute that plan and determining the costs associated with any product realization is the major challenge. CIOs do not have a great track record. The IT industry as a whole has not improved its conversion effectiveness. Late projects are the cause for most project overruns. We believe that telling stories, as suggested by Dana Deasy, is one very effective way of getting executive support. Deasy used storyboarding as a vehicle to articulate what the technology could do for the business.

Perhaps an effective framework for assisting CIOs to articulate their strategic plans is Marchand's Strategic Information Alignment (SIA). This framework asks three vital questions that can lead CIOs to know the relevance of their plans to business alignment:

1. Why is information important to competing in business today and in the future?
2. What priorities for information use and management are appropriate?
3. How should managers implement their strategic priorities and achieve improved business performance through people, information, and IT?

SIA has four major components that determine the focus of any business strategy:

1. **Manage risks:** Market, financial, legal, operational
2. **Reduce costs:** Transactions and processes
3. **Add value:** Customers and markets
4. **Create new reality:** New products, services, business issues

The model examines the relative importance of each of these components. Figure 5.3 is a graphical representation that depicts the relative consistency between IT and company objectives.

The solid line reflects where IT operates across the four sectors as compared to the dotted line, which is where the company wants to operate. Using SIA, CIOs can reconcile their IT efforts and understand where they stand. It also provides a graphical tool to represent why an IT initiative, if supported, will better align with the desired business objectives of the firm.

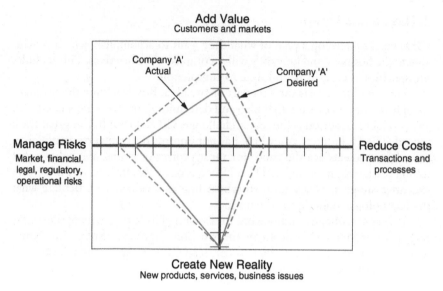

Figure 5.3   Strategy information alignment framework.
Source: D. A. Marchand, Competing with Information: A Manager's Guide to Creating Business Value with Information Content *(New York: John Wiley & Sons, 2000).*

4. Keep Your Pulse on Costs

CIOs still need to be fiscally responsible and must shed the reputation as big spenders. Where IT can be used to reduce costs and increase shareholder value is still an extremely important part of the role.

As they say, all evaluations of projects ultimately lead to an understanding of their costs. Because of the history of overruns, it is important that CIOs establish themselves as cost-conscious partners with their C-suite colleagues. The biggest challenge, however, is explaining why some costs cannot be easily associated with returns from the IT investment itself. We already noted the nonmonetary valuations theory advocated by Lucas's work, where he established ways of articulating the value of indirect or hybrid benefits of IT investments.[21] We still advocate that Langer's driver-supporter model is at the center of addressing this dilemma. Specifically, if all driver IT activities are directly incorporated in the business unit, including staff, then the explanation of the value of any such investment is clearer and more succinct because all the costs are associated with the business effort. This simply leaves the supporter side, which then becomes the center of how to use IT to reduce costs by using outsourcing alternatives, and/or by increasing business unit margins through efficiency.

The most important part of being cost-conscious is to behave cost-conscious. That is, to represent at meetings that all IT investments must correspond to business value and that the IT organization forever seeks to reduce its supporter expenses in line with the competition. CIOs must make it part of their repertoire of communications, and this alone will help diminish what can be false generalizations about IT as not being cost-conscious.

5. Having a Seat at the Table Does Matter

The argument that it does not matter where the CIO actually reports is bogus. CIOs need to report directly to the CEO and have a regular place of attendance at key board meetings. Perceptions are realities, and if the CIO function does not get the top reporting line, then the message to the firm from the top is clear: IT is not important enough.

The ongoing debate on where a CIO reports is serious. We find that where one reports really does matter and advocate that the CIO position should report to the CEO. Under some circumstances where all C-suite positions report up through a chief operating officer (COO), it can be reasonable for the CIO to report that way as well. However, this kind of reporting structure is often relevant in only very large organizations, and even in those cases there are exceptions. For example, it is not unusual for the chief legal counsel or even HR executive to report directly to the CEO. In most cases, the chief financial officer (CFO) will also have a direct reporting line to the CEO unless the COO is actually a former CFO.

The question for the CIO is how to influence that reporting structure. In our case interviews, almost half the subjects did not report to the CEO, yet they were successful CIOs. However, all of them did have direct access to the CEO. The reality is that a direct report to the CEO is likely something that needs to be negotiated prior to starting the job, unless, as in Passerini's and Koster's case, you are promoted into the position from within the organization. The most effective assistance for CIOs reporting to the CEO is probably through a third-party advocacy—something like a professional body like the American Institute of Certified Public Accountants (AICPA), who can issue standards on reporting structure or support certain policies that affect the CIO role. For example, CFOs must sign the financial statements—this places the CFO at a very important position not only with the CEO but also with the board. We believe the most important advocacy is simply the value the CIO brings, and our research supports the notion that the more the CIO positively affects strategic goals, the more likely the CEO would want them as a direct report.

6. Business Comes First

The CIO must always think about the value IT brings to the business. If that business value is not there, then the value of the IT is not relevant.

This concept is certainly consistent with the rest of our support for how IT can bring value to the business. The uniqueness of this issue, in this context, goes beyond just understanding or supporting what the business knows and wants. It opens the door for the CIO to drive business opportunities from a technology perspective. An example of this is what Passerini did to reduce costs of focus groups while improving penetration to the consumer. Another example involves the innovations used by the banks to allow consumers to make direct deposits by taking a picture of a person's check. These examples show how IT can lead the way, certainly not most of the time. But the opportunities are there to lead sometimes if, and only if, the CIO understands the business and has the creative ability to abstractly see where IT can make a difference.

7. Expand the Role Beyond Traditional IT

We saw from our cases that many successful CIOs are now taking on expanded roles outside of just IT issues. This includes operations, infrastructure, and shared services.

The ultimate reward for contemporary CIOs is their advancement beyond the role itself. We have seen this occur in many industries and in special cases. Indeed, Passerinni has risen to the level of a group president; Koster is on the executive management team at Prudential; and Scalet is taking on related operating responsibilities for shared services and real estate. Banks have also promoted their top CIOs to the role of chief of operations and technology. Given that technology can affect many aspects of the business, there is increasing opportunity to evolve and reinvent the position.

History has shown us that CIOs who fail to expand their roles may very well endanger their longevity on the job. The formidable threat usually occurs when someone else takes the responsibility away from you, that is, another peer will take the initiative of providing services that require IT. Should this occur it conveys a negative message to your peer executives that you may lack the necessary business skills to evolve the CIO position.

One of the potential career paths for CIOs is to take on a more chief administrative officer (CAO) role. This position would include the overall traditional CIO functions, but also include operations, certainly not in the same context of the COO, but a position that expands the use of technology into all operational areas in a firm. The advent of the CIO as an operating executive is certainly under way in many industries, as previously noted. We expect to see this continue to grow in consideration among CEOs because it allows the CIOs to improve automation benefits throughout the firm.

8. Have the Best People

CIOs cannot accomplish their complex roles without surrounding themselves with the appropriate staff. In actuality having the best IT staff is extremely important to securing an effective supporter function.

It is becoming increasingly important for the CIO profession to start thinking about the next generation of talented CIO leaders. That responsibility lies with our existing leaders—leaders who need to prepare for the education and development of their most talented staff.

Yet we do not see enough of such investments. Corporations have continued to cut their education budgets, and new CIOs cannot learn their jobs from experience alone. As faculty who manage a CIO leadership program, we see little increase in applications for master's degrees in technology management. Further, there is a lack of diversity in the application pool, especially with women.

Thus, not enough future stars are investing in their education and may be "ill-prepared" for the challenges that lay before them. Far more concerning is the lack of interest in becoming a CIO. There are too many negative discussions that occur at CIO conferences—if CIOs are not excited about the role, then few will venture to take it on.

Simply put, our CIO leaders need to accelerate the search for their successors. They need to create a pool of potential future stars, which requires future CIOs to have field experience with the businesses and an education program that broadens their knowledge beyond what current managers are experiencing at their jobs.

The following are some of the issues to consider:

- **Rotational programs:** Put star managers in six-month roles in the business units. This allows them to become much more knowledgeable about the business. More important, it gives them exposure, so they become known across the business.
- **Education:** Continuing education and conferences are fine, but allow IT managers to enroll in a part-time degree program where they get exposed to a broader education and get to meet other executives. A committed degree program also establishes a more critical and reflective person and one who can think in the abstract, beyond just the concrete needs of the business today.
- **Diversity:** This issue is of paramount importance to our future generations. Diversity goes beyond the legal and corporate requirements. The world is flat, as they say, and having a pool of diverse candidates

provides a company with broader knowledge and better decisions—so promote more women and more ethnicities in your organization.

- **Up and out:** Do not worry about losing those who you invest in. It happens and should happen. Great companies develop talent and lose some of them—indeed, there are only so many positions at the top. If you provide the program, those who leave will always remember it and some will return. Remember, talent development is a responsibility as much as an investment. Finally, it will add to the prestige of your company—that you invest in your people.
- **College graduates are not the only entry-level candidates:** In fact, they may not be the best solution, given the costs. We have seen great success in creating a competitive workforce using high school graduates who complete technical certifications and complete their college degrees part-time. Germany has had amazing results with apprentice programs to fill certain skill jobs, and they have set an example to fill needed talent.

Not all of the resources will be employees. Selecting the right outsource providers are equally important. The CIO must be careful with the outsource firms they select, especially since many of them suffer from high turnover. However, balancing employees with outsource talent is a reality, and CIOs need to have strategic relationships to accomplish R = G! Furthermore, good firms always compete on talent—just like Microsoft and Google tend to seek the same talent, so too must the CIO in their related industry.

9. Pay Attention to Big Data

Data analytics, as discussed earlier, has become an increasingly important conversation at the board level. Big Data is essential for competitive advantage and also understanding a firm's legal exposures and security coverage.

Data analytics is the quickest growing area of concern at the board level. Understanding what data tells us and how it adds to knowledge are critical needs for global organizations, especially those that deal directly with consumers. Big Data is somewhat a subset of a larger topic called knowledge management—the ability of a firm to manage its data and maximize its utilization for competitive advantage as well as protection of its assets.

This increasing recognition that the competitive advantage of organizations depends on its "ability to create, transfer, utilize, and protect difficult-to-intimate knowledge assets" has given birth to the value of Big Data.[22] Indeed, according to Bertels and Savage, the dominant logic of the industrial era imposes the challenges of understanding how to break the learning barrier of understanding the information era.[23] While we have developed powerful solutions to change internal processes and organizational structures, most organizations have failed to address the cultural dimensions of the information era. Organizational knowledge creation is a result of organizational learning through strategic processes. Nonaka defines organizational knowledge as "the capability of a company as a whole to create new knowledge, disseminate it throughout the organization, and embody it in products, services, and systems."[24] Nonaka used the steps shown in Figure 5.4 to assess the value and chain of events surrounding the valuation of organizational knowledge. This organizational knowledge feeds Big Data needs, which ultimately provide an understanding of the data both inside and outside the firm.

According to Nonaka, to create new knowledge means to recreate the company and everyone in it in an ongoing process that requires personal and organizational self-renewal. That is to say, knowledge creation is the responsibility of everyone in the organization. The viability of this definition, however, must be questioned. Can organizations create personnel that will adhere to such parameters, and under what conditions will senior management support such an endeavor? Once again, the CIO has a remarkable role to play in substantiating the need for knowledge management, Big Data, and the competitive advantage it brings to the firm.

10. Align with the Business

This somewhat relates to being knowledgeable about the business. But it is not enough to be knowledgeable. The CIO must be aligned with the aspirations of the business units, so that there is interdepartment harmony.

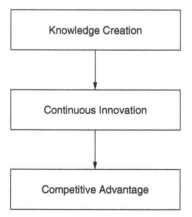

Figure 5.4   Assessing organizational knowledge.
Source: I. Nonaka and H. Takeuchi, The Knowledge-Creating Company: How Japanese Companies Create the Dynamics of Innovation *(New York: Oxford University Press, 1995).*

There is much written about the importance of relationship building. So many CIOs miss this and pay dearly for the lack of having an integrated relationship strategy. At the heart of relationship building is bringing value—but not from your perspective; rather, the perspective of the "other." The question to ask is: Who are the others?

Well, the first "other" is the C-level colleagues, including the CEO, of course. As previously stated, a relationship with C-level colleagues goes beyond a meeting, even a drink; it's really about understanding their needs and what brings value to them. This is accomplished through formal and informal meetings and discussions.

Formal meetings are ones that should be initiated by you and typically allow the CIO to assess how IT can bring value—it also allows CIOs to meet the key players in these departments. So, it is important that meetings involve the other managers who report up to the C-level colleagues.

Informal meetings are actually far more important. They occur in hallways, telephone chats, lunches, and business trips—the off-the-record conversations that enable people to really understand how to create important relationships. If a C-level partner can count on the CIO—and sense that he or she understands the challenges they have in the organization, it really helps. Informal meetings cannot occur every six months. They occur all the time and are typically event driven, that is, initiated by the CIO based on something that is going on inside the organization. If there is an opportunity to bring value, then a CIO should act on it—informally first! Informal discussions often lead to lasting relationships and even friendships, personal and business. These friendships do matter—remember that.

CIOs often err in thinking that all they need is a C-level partner to support them—it's not enough. Line managers, which we define as those managers who have daily production responsibilities, can be very influential and powerful within their own business domains. Knowing and working with line managers is critical—and thus forming relationships with them is equally as important. Furthermore, if line managers support IT, it only strengthens the relationship with the CIO's other C-level colleagues. So how does one do this? Work with a business C-level partner and get his or her authorization to start working directly with that person's direct managers. Do not do it alone; CIOs should enlist their line managers as well. Getting staff in line with their counterpart business manager shows that the IT organization has the depth and breadth to implement commitments to the business. Having strong IT line managers also affects how others view the CIO—lousy IT line managers equates to a lousy CIO. Remember the old cliché´ : "You're only as good as your people."

Our final recommendation to CIOs is to always try to be helpful—people appreciate it. CIOs should engrain this concept within their staff and make it a vital part of the IT way of doing business.

11. Drive Profitability

The more the CIO can strategically support the organization to drive more profits, the more valuable the function. The more valuable a CIO is to the organization, the more capacities and power will be afforded to the role.

We discussed the importance of having a seat at the table. This usually means reporting to the CEO directly and being engaged at all key meetings in the firm. But it also means presenting to their board of directors, the ultimate "seat" of exposure. Driving profits starts with delivering ideas and getting support to implement them. We are not advocating that CIOs become overnight marketing gurus. So profits for CIOs are generating related solutions like what Passerini offered at Procter & Gamble or Koster at Prudential. Most of what they accomplished was how they delivered their ideas at senior management meetings or at board events.

So what are the key issues that CIOs need to think about before and at a board meeting? What are boards interested in discussing? After a number of conversations with leading CIOs and with board members, the current consensus is as follows:

- Boards are less interested in reviewing the budget as they are about ideas and ways the CIO can assist the organization's growth, both operationally and strategically.
- Boards are concerned about security—how the CIO is providing protection against security risks and exposures of confidential information.
- Boards are now aware of the dangers and risks of the data the organization stores. A new and emerging area of CIO responsibility is known as "e-discovery." This involves the understanding of how much data is available and the legal exposures of saving such information.
- Boards need to understand the data they have. The CIO needs to do more with "data analytics," the interpretation of the information that an organization has and what it means.

How, then, do CIOs present these issues to their board? Here are some tips:

- Do research about all board members. What is their background? What do they tend to focus on? Speak with other executives who have presented to the board in the past; they may be able to provide tips and suggestions about how the board meeting tends to be conducted.
- Try to get to know your board members and attempt to speak and meet with them before the actual board meets. This will allow you to ascertain what they are thinking and what issues appear to be at the top

of their individual agendas. They may also help you to "sell" your ideas to other board members.

- Board meetings tend to run longer than scheduled, and the presentation time may be significantly reduced. Therefore, CIOs need to ensure that they have multiple versions of their presentation, that is, one that can be presented within time limits.
- Tell stories and keep it simple. Try to express your needs through a story of how the organization can excel as a result of your efforts and operations. Stories that show how success can be attained are very attractive to getting broad attention.

CIOs should be direct with their board. Do not speak in vague terms, and take responsibility for problem areas. Always articulate the plans designed to fix the problems and do not blame IT staff for what is ultimately the CIO's responsibility.

In our experience, many CIOs think their boards of directors want them to focus on costs and budgets. If they want a better understanding of board expectations, they should take some guidance from Virginia Gambale, who has long experience on both sides of the fence.

What directors really value in a CIO is sound strategic thinking and a great ability to execute, says Gambale, a former CIO at Merrill Lynch, Bankers Trust, and Alex Brown, and former partner at Deutsche Bank Capital. Gambale said boards expect the CIO to provide guidance on how technology can improve the firm's growth and market strength, help the company better reach customers, and develop innovations that boost market share. CIOs should practice "using the language of the board," she said. CIOs must talk about things like asset allocation, distribution channels, not technology itself. "Encase yourself in corporate strategy," she said. "Stay away from talking about the plumbing, and no technical jargon, for sure."

We asked Gambale how a CIO can best learn the language of the board. She urges CIOs to create close business relationships with their CFO, head of corporate strategy, and product development executives so they can understand the operating model of the company and clearly grasp what drives profitability. For example, at JetBlue, profitability is heavily dependent on the costs of fuel, labor, and airplanes.

12. Use Benchmarks

Having statistical analysis of the IT operations is still very important, certainly in supporter functions. CIOs need to show they use metrics to optimize the performance or their organizations.

Other members of the C-suite are accustomed to achieving best practices through industry benchmarking. It is difficult to determine whether the IT operation is performing to peak capacities without having some evidence of related performances of others in the industry and trades. Benchmarking data is typically available from CIO organizations as well as from industry organizations. The IT department should be required to participate in all aspects of benchmarking conversations with other business units as well.

Another excellent benchmark organization is ISO 9000. Many IT departments have utilized ISO 9000 concepts; ISO stands for the International Standards Organization, a worldwide organization that defines quality processes through very formal structures. It attempts to take knowledge-based information and transfer it into specific and documented steps that can be evaluated as they occur. Unfortunately, the ISO 9000 approach, even if realized, is challenging when such knowledge and procedures are undergoing constant and unpredictable change.

13. React to the Dynamics of the Market

We discussed Bradley and Nolan's concept of sense and respond. It is clear from our cases that successful CIOs understand that they cannot know the future and need to be very agile to changes in the market that affect their organization.

CIOs need to be good businesspeople. As such, they must understand how markets affect their world in IT. We spoke earlier of the notions of an S-curve and how it dictates indirectly how IT is viewed and measured. Furthermore, the S-curve is the basis of whether an IT initiative is at the driver or supporter phase. Responsive organizational dynamism needs to also be at the forefront of all CIO decisions, but the state of the market is most important. If there is anything we have learned it is that the market is very unpredictable. As such, CIOs must deal with a world of unpredictability. Thus, CIOs need to adapt to the concept of sensing an opportunity and responding dynamically. That is, the world of planning, getting requirements, implementing, and then considering future enhancements is no longer relevant for most IT projects.

We expect the acceleration of change to continue and the life cycle of S-curves to shrink, simply meaning that IT projects will be drivers for less time, then transform into supporters and reach obsolescence quicker. However, this accelerated life cycle also means that there will be more S-curves—meaning more IT projects that can change the relationships between the buyer and the seller. The advent of more and shorter IT projects should excite IT leaders because it means more opportunities to drive business value and participate in the supply-demand aspects of the market.

Conclusion

This chapter has summarized the results of what CIOs do to become successful. The question now is how to establish best practices to provide a blueprint for CIOs to follow and, more important, to measure their progress. Chapter 6 provides such models that not only define the mature CIO, but also his or her counterparts, the CEO and the middle managers of the business units. Here we will provide "maturity arcs" that are based on human development methods of assessing leadership growth.

Notes

1. R. Kegan, *In Over Our Heads: The Mental Demands of Modern Life* (Cambridge: Harvard University Press, 1994).
2. R. M. Grant, "Prospering in Dynamically-Competitive Environments—Organizational Capability as Knowledge Integration," *Organization Science* 7(4) (1996): 375–387; D. J. Collis, "Research Note—How Valuable Are Organizational Capabilities?" *Strategic Management Journal* 15 (1994): 143–152; Mark Dodgson, "Organizational Learning: A Review of Some Literatures," *Organizational Studies* 14(3) (1993): 375–394.
3. A. M. Langer, "Fixing Bad Habits: Integrating Technology Personnel in the Workplace Using Reflective Practice," *Reflective Practice* 2(1) (2001): 100–111.
4. D. Grant, T. Keenoy, and C. Oswick (Eds.), *Discourse and Organization* (London: Sage, 1998).
5. A. M. Langer, *Information Technology and Organizational Learning: Managing Behavioral Change through Technology and Education*, 2nd ed. (Boca Raton, FL: Taylor and Francis, 2011).
6. W. Pietersen, *Reinventing Strategy: Using Strategic Learning to Create and Sustain Breakthrough Performance* (Hoboken, NJ: John Wiley & Sons, 2002).
7. J. Deluca, *Political Savvy: Systematic Approaches to Leadership Behind-the-Scenes* (Berwyn, PA: EBG, 1999).
8. Ibid., p. xiv.
9. Ibid., p. xii.
10. Joe D. Batten, *Tough-Minded Management*, 3rd ed. (Eugene, OR: Resource Publications, 2002).
11. O. C. Ferrell, and G. Gardiner, *In Pursuit of Ethics: Tough Choices in the World of Work* (Springfield, IL: Smith Collins, 1991).
12. Langer, "Fixing Bad Habits."
13. R. W. Eichinger and M. M. Lombardo, "Education Competencies: Dealing With Ambiguity," *Microsoft in Education*, Training, www.microsoft.com/education/en-us/Training/Competencies/Pages/dealing_with_ambiguity.aspx.
14. J. Conger, in L. Keller Johnson, "Exerting Influence without Authority," *Harvard Business Update* (Boston: Harvard Business Press, 2003).
15. Langer, *Information Technology and Organizational Learning*.
16. Thomas L. Friedman and Michael Mandelbaum, *That Used to Be Us: How American Fell Behind in the World It Invented and How We Can Come Back* (New York: Picador, 2012).
17. C. K. Prahalad, and M. S. Krishnan, *The New Age of Innovation: Driving Cocreated Value through Global Networks* (New York: McGraw-Hill, 2008).
18. E. H. Schein, *Organizational Culture and Leadership*, 2nd ed. (San Francisco: Jossey-Bass, 1992).
19. E. Wenger, (1998) *Communities of Practice: Learning, Meaning and Identity* (Cambridge, UK: Cambridge University Press).

20. B. Elkjaer, "In Search of a Social Learning Theory." In M. Easterby-Smith, J. Burgoyne, and L. Araujo (Eds.), *Organizational Learning and the Learning Organization* (London: Sage Publications, 1999), 75.
21. H. C. Lucas, *Information Technology and the Productivity Paradox* (New York: Oxford University Press, 1999).
22. D. J. Teece, "Strategies for Managing Knowledge Assets: The Role of Firm Structure and Industrial Context." In I. Nonaka and D. Teece (Eds.), *Managing Industrial Knowledge: Creation, Transfer and Utilization* (London, UK: Sage, 2001), 125–144.
23. T. Bertels and C. M. Savage, "Tough Questions on Knowledge Management." In G. V. Krogh, J. Roos, and D. Kleine (Eds.), *Knowing in Firms: Understanding, Managing and Measuring Knowledge* (London: Sage, 1998).
24. I. Nonaka and H. Takeuchi, *The Knowledge-Creating Company: How Japanese Companies Create the Dynamics of Innovation* (New York: Oxford University Press, 1995), 3.

CHAPTER **6**

Lessons Learned
and Best Practices

The previous chapters provided many lessons learned about how chief information officers (CIOs) are successful. As a result, we lay the foundation for the formation of "best practices" to formalize the necessary attributes for rising to the CIO level and, more important, sustaining a leadership role. First, it is important to define what we mean by best practices and specify what components comprise that definition. Best practices are defined as generally accepted ways of doing specific functions and/or processes by a particular profession or industry. Best practices, in the context of the CIO, are a set of processes, behaviors, and organizational structures that tend to provide successful foundations to implement and sustain success. We stated earlier that CIOs needed to help create organizations that use responsive organizational dynamism (ROD) to successfully deal with the volatility of advancing technologies—technologies that challenge the organization to manage a constant state of dynamic and unpredictable change. We also discussed the need for CIOs to integrate with their C-suite colleagues by using strategic advocacy concepts and build the kind of executive collaborations that would allow them to successfully implement ROD. The case studies in Chapter 4 showed that these two issues were consistently the key reasons for the successful accomplishments of the selected CIOs.

Five Pillars to CIO Success—Lessons Learned

In 2011, 30 new graduate students at Columbia University started their development toward becoming tomorrow's CIOs. During the four-day inaugural course, we had a number of notable CIOs, board members, and chief executives from such companies as BP, JetBlue, Russell Reynolds, ICAP, Sealed Air, and Atlas, to name a few.

As we listened to each presentation, it became clear to me how consistent the messages were from these successful leaders with the results of our case studies in this book. The following are those five key issues discussed and why they are so important for CIO success and ultimately represent the lessons learned summarized best in Chapter 5:

1. **Communication is king:** No question, those CIOs that learn to effectively articulate information technology (IT) from a business perspective are winning the day. The discourse must be business lingo, not IT-converted speak. The more your language fits with those you support and help, the better you will integrate IT in the business. The question becomes how to speak the speak? CIOs recommend that CIOs spend time in the business. This is not just making trips, rather actually visiting the firm's clients and being part of production activities. In this way you can actually understand the true culture of the business and can develop insights to how IT can truly provide value. Typically, the more visibility you have as a CIO, the easier it is to sell your ideas and determine what you need to do to maximize support from the field.

2. **Help define your role:** This was an interesting point made by several CIOs. They stated that many chief executive officers (CEOs), chief operating officers (COO), and chief financial officers (CFOs) may not have the vision to understand what IT can really do to help the firm—and more important what your role needs to be to help accomplish your plan. CIOs need to help define their role—especially as a more strategic partner. We know that too many CIOs are viewed as the back-end support function, keeping the lights on; however, firms need the strategic direction of how IT can make a difference competitively. Their point was simple: If you wait to be asked, you may never receive the call. You need to sell your plan to senior management on how the CIO function can be used to help the business on the front end as well as the back end. Inevitably, the acceptance of such a plan can lead to redefining the CIO role and especially where it reports.

3. **Be patient:** Change in organizations takes time. Integration can take longer than you expect. Organizational culture evolves slowly, but if the change occurs organically, it will be more permanent. Remember that IT is a disruptive force—meaning that it affects employees, especially their roles and responsibilities. We know that organizations do not like change—so it should be no surprise that a new innovation proposed by the CIO may not be openly embraced—but in time

things can and will change. Those CIOs that are impatient and right-
eous do not last long.

4. **Persevere:** Don't think every idea will be accepted. More important,
   you likely don't get everything you ask for the first time. Every
   presenter spoke about their failures—and how much they learned
   from them. In many cases, it led the way to their success because they
   were able to rebound. Remember, anyone can sail a ship in calm
   waters, but you can never be a true captain until you sail through a
   storm! The most important aspect of perseverance is to always be
   impressive in how you handle yourself and explain your challenges to
   your C-level partners.

5. **Costs are important:** Many CIOs think that showing how IT can
   reduce costs is the name of the game. Perhaps, but our presenters were
   more focused on good fiscal control and sensitivity to expenditures
   than necessarily taking out costs for the sake of it. What your chief
   executive and board need to know is that you are a good businessperson, and establishing fiscal controls in your organization is the first
   test for any C-level person. The difference in fiscal control is that it
   does not necessarily rule out smart investment and acceptable risk taking. Remember the bottom line has two parts—revenues and expenses!

Thus, at Columbia University, the message was loud and clear. CIOs need
to communicate to better integrate with the business, be patient and persevere over their failures, and never forget to be a good fiscal partner! The question then is: What are the set of things that need to happen to create a template
for success?

Perhaps most important is that best practices can be obtained only by
creating a learning organization that can support the CIO; that is, it is not just
the perfect CIO that makes organizations successful, but rather the CIO's
ability to establish the necessary supporting cast of senior and middle managers. Therefore, Langer developed these best practices with the perspective
that they must operate across the three key levels of any organization: The
CIO, the CEO, and middle management personnel.[1] However, these multiple
tiers of best practices need to be integrated and to operate with one another
in order to be considered under the rubric. Indeed, best practices, contained
solely within a discipline or community, are limited in their ability to operate
on an organization-wide level. It is the objective of this chapter, therefore, to
formulate a set of distinctive yet integrated best practices that that can establish and support ROD by creating a balanced management structure. Each
component of the set of best practice needs to be accompanied with a maturity arc, which defines and describes the stages of development and the

dimensions that comprise best practices. Each stage will define a linear path of continued progress until a set of best practices is reached. In this way, organizations can assess where they are in terms of best practices and determine what they need to do to progress.

Ultimately, each maturity arc will represent a subset of the overall set of best practices for the organization. This concept is important in that it suggests that the CIO alone cannot create a sustainable, technology-ready organization. Does this mean that the successful CIOs we examined were only successful because they had the right support from their CEO and middle management teams? Not exactly, but our philosophy does advocate the need to have the right CEO in place or the ability, as emphasized earlier, to influence the CEO to understand what he or she needs to do to maximize the ability for the CIO to succeed. By middle management we mean what Langer defined as "line managers."[2] Line managers were defined as individuals who "usually manage an entire business unit and have return-on-investment responsibilities."[3] In other words, line managers run the day-to-day business. In some ways, the CEO and CIO can influence line management behavior and culture; however, in other ways they cannot without revolutionary patterns of change—typically meaning forced elimination of managers. Indeed, Langer's Ravell case study concluded "the success of organizational learning will depend on the degree of cross fertilization . . . and the ability of the community to combine new concepts and beliefs to form a hybrid culture."[4]

The CIO or Chief IT Executive

Langer used the title "chief IT executive" to represent the most senior IT individual in an organization.[5] While these titles are distinct among themselves, he found that they are not consistently followed in organizations. However, it is important to understand these titles and their distinctions, particularly because an organizational learning practitioner will encounter them in practice. These titles and roles are listed and discussed next:

- **Chief information officer (CIO):** This individual is usually the most senior IT executive in an organization, although not every organization has such a person. The CIO is not necessarily the most technical of people or even someone who has come through the "ranks" of IT. Instead, this individual is considered an executive who understands how technology needs to be integrated within the organization. CIOs typically have other top IT executives and managers who can report directly to them. As shown in the Siemens case study, there can be a number of alternate levels of CIOs, from corporate CIOs to local CIOs of a company division. For the purposes of this discussion, I take up the corporate CIO, who is considered part of the senior executive management team. My research on CEO perceptions of technology and business strategy shows that only a small percentage of CIOs report directly to the CEO of their organization, so it would be incorrect to generalize that they report to the most senior executive. In many cases, the CIO reports to the chief operating officer (COO). As stated earlier, the role of the CIO is to manage information with business needs and strategy. Technology, then, is considered a valuable part of knowledge management from the strategic perspective as opposed to just a technical one.

- **Chief technology officer (CTO):** This individual, unlike the CIO, is very much a senior technical person. The role of the CTO is to ensure that the organization is using the best and most cost-effective technology to achieve its goals. One could argue that the CTO is more of a research and development type of position. In many organizations, the CTO reports directly to the CIO and is seen as a component of the overall IT infrastructure. However, some companies, like Ravell and HTC, only have a CTO and view technology more from the technical perspective.

- **Chief knowledge officer (CKO):** This role derives from library management organizations because of the relevance of the word "knowledge." It also competes somewhat with CIO when organizations view technology more from a knowledge perspective. In larger organizations, the CKO may report directly to the CIO. In its purist role, the CKO is responsible for developing an overall infrastructure for managing knowledge, including intellectual capital, sharing of information, and worker communication. Based on this description, the CKO is not necessarily associated with technology, but is more often considered part of the technology infrastructure due to the relevance of knowledge to technology.

In order to define best practices for this function, it is necessary to understand the current information and statistics about what these people do and how they do it. Most of the statistical data about the roles and responsibilities of chief IT executives is reported under the auspices of the CIO.

From a best practices perspective, the following list from our case studies suggests what chief IT executives should be doing. The list emphasizes team building, coaching, motivating, and mentoring as techniques for implementing these best practices:

- **Strategic thinking:** Understanding the company's business strategy and competitive landscape to apply technology in the most valuable way to the organization.
- **Industry expertise:** Must have the ability to understand the product and services that the company produces.
- **Create and manage change:** Ability to create change, through technology, in the organization's operating and business processes in order to gain efficiency and competitive advantage.
- **Communications:** Ability to communicate ideas, to give direction, listen, negotiate, persuade, and resolve conflicts. Must be able translate technical information to those who are not technologically literate or are outside IT. Chief IT executives also need to be comfortable speaking in public forums and in front of other executives.
- **Relationships building:** Ability to interface with peers, superiors, and customers by establishing and maintaining strong rapport, bond, and trust between individuals.
- **Business knowledge:** Ability to develop strong business acumen and have peripheral vision across all functional areas of the business.
- **Technology proficiency:** Knowledge to identify appropriate technologies that are the most pragmatic for the business and can be delivered quickly at the lowest cost, produce an impact to the bottom line (ROI), and have longevity.
- **Leadership:** Must be a visionary person, inspirational, influential, creative, fair, and open-minded with individuals within and outside the organization.
- **Management skills:** Ability to direct and supervise people, projects, resources, budget, and vendors.
- **Hiring and retention:** Ability to recognize, cultivate, and retain IT talent.

While the previous list is not exhaustive, it provides a general perspective, and one that appears very generic; that is, many management positions in an organization might contain similar requirements. A survey of 500 CIOs (performed by *CIO* magazine) rated the top three most important concerns among this community in terms of importance:

1. Communications, 70%
2. Business understanding, 58%
3. Strategic thinking, 46%

What is very interesting about this statistic is that only 10% of CIOs identified technical proficiency as critical for their jobs. This finding supports the notion that CIOs need to familiarize themselves with business issues as opposed to just technical ones. Furthermore, the majority of a CIO's time today has been recorded as being spent communicating with other business executives (33%) and managing IT staffs (28%). Other common activities reported in the survey were:

- Operate the baseline infrastructure and applications.
- Act as technology visionary.
- Implement IT portions of new business initiatives.
- Design infrastructure and manage infrastructure projects.
- Allocate technology resources.
- Measure and communicate results.
- Serve as the company spokesperson on IT-related matters.
- Select and manage product and service providers.
- Recruit, retain, and develop IT staff.
- Participate in company and business unit strategy development.

The previous set of results serves to further confirm that chief IT executives define best practices based on understanding and supporting business strategy.

This survey also reported common barriers that chief IT executives have to being successful. The overarching barrier that most IT executives face is the constant struggle between the business expectation to drive change and improve processes and, at the same time, to reduce costs and complete projects faster. The detailed list of reported problems by rank follows:

Lack of key staff, skills sets, and retention, 40%

Inadequate budgets and prioritizing, 37%

Shortage of time for strategic thinking, 31%

Volatile market conditions, 22%

Ineffective communications with users, 18%

Poor vendor support and service levels and quality, 16%

Overwhelming pace of technological change, 14%

Disconnection with executive peers, 12%

Difficulty proving the value of IT, 10%

Counterproductive office politics, 6%

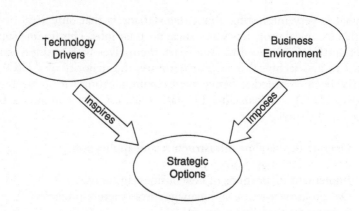

Figure 6.1   Chief IT executive role influences.

Chief IT executives also feel that their roles are ultimately influenced by two leading factors: (1) Changes in the nature and capabilities of technology; and (2) changes in the business environment including marketplace, competitive, and regulatory pressures. This can be graphically viewed in Figure 6.1.

Figure 6.1 has a striking similarity to ROD. It shows technology as an independent variable creating the need for ROD, which is composed of strategic integration and cultural assimilation, as shown in Figure 6.2.

The previous issues all suggest that the role of the CIO or chief IT executive is growing, and that their need to become better integrated with the rest of their organizations is crucial for their success. Much more relevant though is the need for ROD, and the role that the chief IT executive has as a member of the overall community. In order to create best practices that embrace organizational learning and foster ROD, a chief IT executive maturity arc needs to be developed that includes the industry best practices presented earlier integrated with organizational learning components.

The Langer Chief IT Executive Best Practices Arc

The Chief IT Executive Best Practices Arc is an instrument for assessing the business maturity of chief IT executives. The arc may be used to evaluate a chief IT executive's business leadership by using a grid that measures competencies ranging from essential knowledge in technology to more complex uses of technology in critical business thinking. Thus, the Chief IT Executive Best Practices Arc provides executives with a method of integrating technology knowledge and business by providing a structured approach of self-assessment and defined milestones.

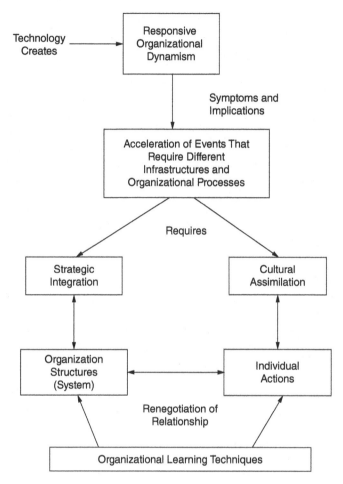

Figure 6.2 Responsive Organizational Dynamism.

The model measures five principal facets of a technology executive: Cognitive, organization culture, management values, business ethics, and executive presence. Each dimension or sector is measured in five stages of maturation that guide the chief IT executive's growth. The first facet calls for becoming reflectively aware about one's existing knowledge with technology and what it can do for the organization. The second calls for "other-centeredness" in which chief IT executives become aware of the multiplicity of technology perspectives available (e.g., other business views of how technology can benefit the organization). The third is "comprehension of the technology process" in which a chief IT executive can begin to merge technology issues with business concepts and functions. The fourth is "stable technology integration," meaning that the chief IT executive understands how technology can be used and is resilient to nonauthentic sources of business knowledge. Stage four represents an ongoing implementation of both technology and business concepts. The fifth is "technology leadership" in which chief IT executives have reached a stage where their judgment on using technology and business is independent and can be used to self-educate from within. Thus, as chief IT executives grow in knowledge of technology and business, they can become increasingly more other-centered, integrated, stable, and autonomous with the way they use their business minds and express their executive leadership and character.

Definitions of Maturity Stages and Dimension Variables in the Chief IT Executive Best Practices Arc

Maturity Stages

1. **Technology competence and recognition:** This first stage represents the chief IT executive's capacity to learn, conceptualize, and articulate key issues relating to cognitive technological skills, organization culture/etiquette, management value systems, business ethics, and executive presence needed to be a successful chief IT executive in business.
2. **Multiplicity of technology perspectives:** This stage indicates the chief IT executive's ability to integrate multiple points of view about technology from others in various levels of workplace hierarchies. Using these new perspectives, the chief IT executive augments his or her skills with the technology necessary for career success, expands his/her management value system, is increasingly motivated to act ethically, and enhances his or her executive presence.
3. **Comprehension of technology process:** Maturing chief IT executives accumulate increased understanding of workplace cooperation, competition, and advancement, as they gain new cognitive skills about technology and a facility with business culture/etiquette, expand their management value system, perform business/workplace actions to improve ethics about business and technology, and develop effective levels of executive presence.
4. **Stable technology integration:** Chief IT executives achieve integration with the business community when they have levels of cognitive and technological ability, organization etiquette/culture, management values, business ethics, and executive presence

appropriate for performing job duties not only adequately, but competitively with peers and even higher ranking executives in the workplace hierarchy.

5. **Technology leadership:** Leadership is attained by the chief IT executive when he or she can employ cognitive and technological skills, organization etiquette, management, a sense of business ethics, and a sense of executive presence in order to compete effectively for executive positions. This chief IT executive is capable of obtaining increasingly executive level positions through successful interviewing and workplace performance.

Performance Dimensions

1. **Technology cognition:** Concerns skills specifically related to learning and applying and creating resources in IT, which include the necessary knowledge of complex operations. This dimension essentially establishes the CIO as being technically proficient and forms a basis for movement to more complex and mature stages of development.

2. **Organizational culture:** The knowledge and practice of proper etiquette in corporate settings, with regard to dress, telephone and in-person interactions, punctuality, work completion, conflict resolution, deference, and other protocols in workplace hierarchies.

3. **Management values:** Measures the individual's ability to articulate and act upon mainstream corporate values credited with shaping the work ethic—independent initiative, dedication, honesty, and personal identification with career goals based on the organization's philosophy of management protocol.

4. **Business ethics:** Reflects the individual's commitment to the education and professional advancement of other persons in technology and other organizations.

5. **Executive presence:** Involves the chief IT executive's view of the role of an executive in business and the capacity to succeed in tandem with other executives. Aspects include a devotion to learning and self-improvement, self-evaluation, the ability to acknowledge and resolve business conflicts, and resilience when faced with personal and professional challenges.

Figure 6.3 shows the Chief IT Executive Best Practices Arc in chart form. Each cell in the arc provides the condition for assessment. The complete arc is provided in Figure 6.4.

Dimension Skill	Technology Competence and Recognition	Multiplicity of Technology Perspectives	Comprehension of Technology Process	Stable Technology Integration	Technology Leadership
Technology Cognition					
Organization Culture					
Management Values					
Business Ethics					
Executive Presence					

Figure 6.3 Chief IT Executive Best Practices Arc.

Dimension Variable	Technology Competence and Recognition	Multiplicity of Technology Perspectives	Comprehension of Technology Process	Stable Technology Integration	Technology Leadership
Technology Cognition	Understands how technology operates in business. Has mastered how systems are developed, hardware interfaces, and the software development life cycle. Has mastery of hardware, compilers, run-time systems. Has core competencies in distributed processing, database development, object-oriented component architecture, and project management. Is competent with main platform operating systems such as UNIX, WINDOWS, MAC Has the core ability to relate technology concepts to other business experiences. Can also make decisions about what technology is best suited for a particular project and organization. Can be taught how to expand the use of technology and can apply it to other business situations.	Understands that technology can have multiple perspectives. Able to analyze what are valid versus invalid opinions about business uses of technology. Can create objective ideas from multiple technology views without getting stuck on individual biases. An ability to identify and draw upon multiple perspectives available from business sources about technology. Developing a discriminating ability with respect to choices available. Realistic and objective judgment, as demonstrated by the applicability of the technology material drawn for a particular project or task and tied to functional/pragmatic results.	Has the ability to relate various technical concepts and organize them with nontechnical business issues. Can operate with both automated and manual business solutions. Can use technology to expand reasoning, logic, what-if scenarios. Ability to use the logic of computer programs to integrate the elements of nontechnological tasks and business problems. Ability to discern the templates that technology has to offer in order to approach everyday business problems. This involves the hypothetical (inductive/deductive) logical business skill.	Knowledge of technology is concrete, accurate, and precise, broad and resistant to interference from nonauthentic business sources. Ability to resist or recover from proposed technology that is not realistic—and can recover resiliently.	Methods and judgment in a multidimensional business world is independent, critical discernment. Knowledge of technology and skills in technology can be transferred and can be used to self-educate within and outside of technology. Can use technology for creative purposes to solve business challenges and integrate with executive management views.

Figure 6.4   Detailed Chief IT Executive Best Practices Arc. (Continued)

Dimension Variable	Technology Competence and Recognition	Multiplicity of Technology Perspectives	Comprehension of Technology Process	Stable Technology Integration	Technology Leadership
Organization Culture	Understands that technology can be viewed by other organizations in different ways. Uses technology as a medium of communication. Understands that certain technological solutions, Web pages, and training methods may not fit all business needs and preferences of the business. Has the ability to recommend/suggest technological solutions to suite other business needs and preferences	Seeks to use technology as a vehicle to learn more about organization cultures and mindsets. Strives to care about what others are communicating and embraces these opinions. Tries to understand and respect technologies that differ from own. Understands basic technological needs of others.	Can deal with multiple dimensions of criticism about technology. Can develop relationships (cooperative) that are dynamic and based on written communication and oral discourse. Ability to create business relations outside of technology departments. Has an appreciation of cyberspace as a communication space—a place wide open to dialogue (spontaneous), to give and take, or other than voyeuristic, one-sidedness. Ability to produce in teamwork situations, rather than solely in isolation.	Loyalty and fidelity to relations in multiple organizations. Commitment to criticism and acceptance of multiple levels of distance and local business relationships. Ability to sustain nontraditional types of inputs from multiple sources.	Can utilize and integrate multidimensions of business solutions in a self-reliant way. Developing alone if necessary using other technical resources. Can dynamically select types of interdependent and dependent organizational relationships. Ability to operate within multiple dimensions of business cultures, which may demand self-reliance, independence of initiative and interactive communications.

Management Values	Technology and cultural sensitivity. Global communication, education, and workplace use of technology can be problematic—subject to false generalizations and preconceived notions. Awareness of assumptions about how technology will be viewed by other organizations and about biases about types of technology (MAC vs. PC).	Can appreciate need to obtain multiple sources of information and opinion. The acceptance of multidimensional values in human character	Can operate within multiple dimensions of value systems and can prioritize multitasking events that are consistent with value priorities. Ability to assign value to new and diverse technology alternatives—integrating them within a system of preexisting business and technology values.	Testing value systems in new ways due to technology is integrated with long-term values and goals for business achievement. Some concepts are naturally persistent and endure despite new arenas in the technological era.	Use of technology and business are based on formed principles as opposed to dynamic influences or impulses. Formed principles establish the basis for navigating through, or negotiating the diversity of business influences and impulses.

Figure 6.4 (Continued)

Dimension Variable	Technology Competence and Recognition	Multiplicity of Technology Perspectives	Comprehension of Technology Process	Stable Technology Integration	Technology Leadership
Business Ethics	Using technology with honesty re: privacy of access and information. Development of ethical policies governing business uses of the Internet, research, intellectual property rights and plagiarism.	The use of information in a fair way—comparison of facts against equal sources of business information. Compassion for business information for which sources are limited because of inequality of technology access. Compassion for sharing information with other business units from a sense of inequality.	Consistent values displayed on multiple business communications, deliverables of content, and dedication to authenticity. Maintains consistency in integrating values within technology business issues.	Technology is a commitment in all aspects of value systems, including agility in managing multiple business commitments. Commitment to greater openness of mind to altering traditional and nontechnological methods.	Technological creativity with self-defined principles and beliefs. Risk-taking in technology-based ventures. Utilizing technology to expand one's arenas of business freedom. Exploring the business-liberating capacities of technology.

Executive Presence	Has accurate perception of one's own potential and capabilities in relation to technology in the business—the technologically realizable executive self.	Understands how other executives can view self from virtual and multiple perspectives. Understands or has awareness of the construction of self that occurs in business. Focuses on views of other executives in multiple settings. Understands that the self (through technology) is open for more fluid constructions, able to incorporate diverse views in multiple settings.	Operationalizes technology to unify multiple components of the self and understands its appropriate behaviors in varying executive situations.	Has regulated an identity of self from a multiplicity of executive venues. Methods of business interaction creates positive value systems that generate confidence about operating in multiple business communities.	Acceptance and belief in a multidimensional business world of the self. Can determine comfortably the authenticity of other executives and their view of the self. Can confirm disposition independently from others' valuations, both internally and from other organization cultures. Beliefs direct and control multidimensional executive growth.

Figure 6.4 Detailed Chief IT Executive Best Practices Arc.

Chief Executive Officer

When attempting to define chief executive officer (CEO) best practices, one is challenged with the myriad of material that attempts to determine the broad, yet important role of the CEO. As with many best practices, they are typically based on trends and percentages of what most CEOs do—assuming of course that the companies they work for are successful. That is, if their organization is successful, then their practices must be as well. This type of associative thinking leads to what researchers often call "false generalizations." Indeed, these types of inadequate methods lead to false judgments that foster business trends that are misinterpreted as best practices. Reputation is what would better define these trends, which usually after a period of time become ineffective and unpopular. We must also always remember the human element of success—certain individuals succeed based on natural instincts and talent, hard work and drive, and so on. These components of success should not be confused with theories that are scalable and replicable to practice; that is what best practices need to accomplish.

This section focuses on technology best practices of the CEO. These best practices will be based on my research, as well as other positions and facts that provide a defendable context of how and why they appear to be effective. However, as with the chief IT executive model, best practices cannot be attained without an arc that integrates mature organizational learning and developmental theories. Many of the CEO best practices are reconciled against previous interviews with CEOs. Other published definitions and support will be referenced in our presentation.

In February 2002, Hackett Benchmarking a part of Answerthink Corporation, issued its best practices for IT. Their documentation states: "In compiling its 2002 best practices trend data, Hackett evaluated the effectiveness (quality and value) and efficiency (cost and productivity) of the information technology function across five performance dimensions: Strategic alignment with the business; ability to partner with internal and external customers; use of technology; organization; and processes."[6] Their findings as they apply to the CEO function provide the following generalizations:

- There was an 85% increase in the number of CIOs that reported directly to the CEO. This increase would suggest that CEOs need to directly manage the CIO function because of its importance to business strategy.
- CEOs that supported outsourcing did not receive the cost-cutting effectiveness that they had hoped. In fact, most break even. This suggests that CEOs should not view outsourcing as a cost-cutting measure, but rather foster its use where there is identifiable business benefits.

- CEOs have found that IT organizations that have centralized operations save more money and have fewer helpline calls than decentralized organizations and without sacrificing service quality. This suggests the CEOs should consider less business-specific support structures, especially when they have multiple locations of business.
- CEOs are increasingly depending on the CIO for advice on improving the business with technology. Their view is that IT professionals then should have advanced business degrees.
- CEOs should know that consistent use of IT standards has enabled firms to trim IT development costs by 41%, which has reduced costs for end-user support and training operations by 17%.
- CEOs need to increase support for risk management. Only 77% of average companies maintain disaster recovery plans.

As we can see from these generalizations, they are essentially based on what CEOs are doing and what they have experienced. Unfortunately, this survey addresses little about what CEOs know and exactly what their role should be with respect to overall management, participations, and learning of technology. These best practices are particularly lacking in the area of organizational learning and the firm's abilities to respond to changing conditions as opposed to searching for general solutions.

Langer formulated a list of 11 key planks that represent the core of what constitutes a technology CEO's set of best practices:

1. The chief IT executive should report directly to the CEO.
2. CEOs should be actively committed to technology on an ongoing basis, as opposed to a project-by-project involvement.
3. CEOs should be willing to be management catalysts to support new technology-driven projects. They, in effect, need to sometimes play the role of technology champion.
4. CEOs should focus on business concepts and plans to drive technology.
5. In other words, technology should not drive the business.
6. CEOs should use consultants to provide objective input to emerging technology projects.
7. CEOs should establish organizational infrastructures that foster the creation of communities of practice. They need to create joint ownership of IT issues by fostering discourse between IT and business managers and staff.
8. CEOs may need to take control of certain aspects of technology investments such as setting milestones and holding management and staff to making critical project dates.

9. CEOs need to foster cultural assimilation, which may lead to reorganization since technology changes processes.
10. CEOs need to understand organizational learning and knowledge management theories and participate in organizational transformation.
11. CEOs need to understand how the technology life cycle behaves, with specific attention to the transition from driver activities to supporter functions. To that end, CEOs need to understand the short- and long-term investments that need to be made in technology.
12. CEOs should create organizations that can effectively operate within technological dynamism. This process will educate management and staff to handle the dynamic and unpredictable effects of emerging technologies. It will also foster the development of both middle-up-down and bottom-up management of technology.[7]

The issue is now to provide a linear development model for CEOs that enables them to measure where they are in relation to ROD and the best practices outlined earlier.

The CEO Best Practices Technology Arc

Similar to the Chief IT Executive Arc, the CEO Best Practices Arc is an instrument for assessing the technology best practices of CEOs. The arc evaluates a CEO's strategic uses of technology and leadership by using a grid that charts competencies ranging from conceptual knowledge about technology to more complex uses of technology and business and how they are integrated in strategic business planning.

As with all arc models, the CEO version measures five principal stages of a CEO's maturity with respect to business applications of technology: Conceptual, structural, executive values, executive ethics, and executive leadership. Each dimension or sector is measured in five stages of maturation that guides the CEO's executive growth managing technological dynamism. The first stage is in being reflectively aware about their conceptual knowledge with technology and what it can do for the organization. The second is "other-centeredness," where CEOs become aware of the multiplicity of business uses of technology and the different views that can exist inside and outside the organization. The third is "integration of business use of technology," where a CEO can begin to combine how business plans foster the need for technology. The fourth is "implementation of business/technology process," meaning that the CEO understands how business applications and technology are used together and is resilient to nonauthentic sources of emerging technology. Stage four represents an ongoing implementation of both technology and business applications. The fifth is "strategic uses of technology" in which CEOs have reached a stage where their judgment on using technology and business is independent and can be used to self-educate from within. Thus, as CEOs grow in knowledge of business uses of technology, they can become increasingly more understanding of the multiplicity of uses and more integrated in how they conceptualize technology; they can manage its implementation from an executive position and can apply new strategies to support new applications of technology in the organization.

Definitions of Maturity Stages and Dimension Variables in the CEO Technology Best Practices Arc

Maturity Stages

1. **Conceptual knowledge of technology:** This first stage represents the CEO's capacity to learn, conceptualize, and articulate key issues relating to business uses of technology, organizational structures available, executive value methods, executive ethical issues surrounding technology, and leadership alternatives needed to be a successful with technology applications.

2. **Multiplicity of business perspectives of technology:** This stage indicates the CEO's ability to integrate multiple points of view from management, staff, and consultants about technology applications in business. Using these new perspectives, the CEO augments his or her conceptual skills with technology, has an expanded view of what organizational structures might work best, expands his or her executive values about technology uses, is increasingly aware of the ethical dilemmas with technology, and enhances his or her leadership abilities.

3. **Integration of business uses of technology:** Maturing CEOs accumulate increased understanding of how technology can support the business and provide more competitive advantage and a more integrated understanding of how to use their conceptual skills about technology, the alternative organizational structures available, and how to combine their business executive value and ethical systems and develop effective levels of executive leadership.

4. **Implementation of business/technology process:** CEOs achieve integration when they can regularly apply their conceptual knowledge of technology, organization structures, executive values and ethics about technology, and executive leadership appropriate for performing their job duties not only adequately but at a level that provides a competitive advantage for the organization.

5. **Strategic uses of technology:** Leadership is attained by the CEO when he or she can employ conceptual skills, develop new organizational structures as necessary, establish new values and ethics that are appropriate for the organization, and create a sense of executive presence in order to lead the organization strategically. This CEO is capable of having new vision about how business and technology can be expanded into new endeavors.

Performance Dimensions

1. **Technology concepts:** Concerns conceptual skills specifically related to understanding how technology can be used in the business. This dimension essentially establishes the CEO as being technically proficient from a conceptual standpoint and forms a basis for movement to more complex and mature stages of business/technology development.
2. **Organizational structures:** The knowledge of the alternative organizational structures that can support the application of emerging technology in corporate settings, with regard to roles, responsibilities, career paths, and organizational reporting alternatives.
3. **Executive values:** Measures the CEO's ability to articulate and act on mainstream technological values credited with shaping the work ethic: Independent initiative, dedication, honesty, and personal identification with career goals based on the organization's philosophy of management protocol.
4. **Executive ethics:** Reflects the CEO's commitment to the education and professional advancement of organization's behavior as it relates to business uses of technology.
5. **Executive leadership:** Involves the CEO's view of the role of an executive in business and the capacity to succeed in tandem with his or her organizational resources. Aspects include a devotion to organizational learning and self-improvement, self-evaluation, the ability to acknowledge and resolve business/technology conflicts, and resilience when faced with personal and professional challenges.

Figure 6.5 shows the CEO Technology Best Practices Arc in chart form. Each cell in the arc provides the condition for assessment. The complete arc is provided in Figure 6.6.

Dimension Skill	Conceptual Knowledge of Technology	Multiplicity of Business Perspectives of Technology	Integration of Business Uses of Technology	Implementation of Business/ Technology Process	Strategic Users of Technology
Technology Concepts					
Organizational Structures					
Executive Values					
Executive Ethics					
Executive Leadership					

Figure 6.5   Developmental dimensions of maturing.

Dimension Variable	Conceptual Knowledge of Technology	Multiplicity of Business Perspectives of Technology	Integration of Business Uses of Technology	Implementation of Business/Technology Process	Strategic Uses of Technology
Technology Concept	Understands concepts and definitions about technology and how it relates to business. Has conceptual knowledge of the software development life cycle. Understands high-level concepts about distributed processing, database development, and project management. Understands the definition and role of operating systems such as UNIX, WINDOWS, MAC. Has the ability to relate technology concepts to other business experiences. Understands that different technology may be required for a particular project and organization. Can conceptualize how to expand the use of technology and apply it to business situations.	Seeks to manage by appreciating that technology can have multiple perspectives. Able to manage a process that requires validation about different opinions about business uses of technology. Can manage the different objective ideas from multiple technology views without getting stuck on personal biases. Has an ability to identify and draw upon multiple perspectives available from business sources about technology, particularly from independent sources. Developing a discriminating ability to create an infrastructure that can operate with multiple views. Committed to creating an organization that can learn through realistic and objective judgment, as demonstrated by the applicability of the technology material drawn for a particular project or task and tied to business outcomes.	Creates an organization that has the ability to relate various technical concepts and organize them with nontechnical business issues. Can manage by operating with both automated and manual business solutions. Can use technology to expand business reasoning, logic, and what-if scenarios. Establishes business templates that allow technology to offer everyday business solutions. This involves the hypothetical (inductive/deductive) logical business issues.	Organization's use of technology is concrete, accurate, and precise, broad and resistant to interference from nonauthentic technology business sources. Ability to resist or recover from faulty uses of technology that are not realistic without a supporting business plan.	Methods and judgment as a multidimensional CEO is independent, has critical discernment. Conceptual knowledge of technology can be transferred and can be used to self-educate within and outside of technology. Can use technology for creative purposes to create new business initiatives and integrate them with short- and long-term business goals.

Figure 6.6 CEO Technology Best Practices Arc.

Organi-zational Structures	Understands that technology can be viewed by other organizations in different ways and may need different organizational structures. Can use technology as a medium of communication. Understands that certain technologies may need to be managed differently and need specific types of structures and expertise. Has the ability to comprehend recommended/ suggested technological solutions to suite business needs and preferences	Seeks to manage technology as a vehicle to learn more about what alternative organization structures are available from others. Strives to create a learning organization that cares about what other staff perceive as solutions. Committed to cultural assimilation that can restructure the organization. Tries to understand and respect technologies that differ from what the organization is currently using. Understands that the organization has multiple and different technological needs.	Can deal with multiple dimensions of criticism about how technology can be used in the organization. Can develop relationships (cooperative) that are dynamic and based on written communication and oral discourse about how business can drive technological investments. Ability to create new business relations using technology with new and existing customers. Has an appreciation of cyberspace as a new market—a place wide open to dialogue (spontaneous), to provide new opportunities for business growth.	Commitment to open discussion of alternating opinions on technology and acceptance of varying types of structures to accommodate technology opportunities. Ability to sustain dynamic organizational structures.	Can design new structures to integrate multidimensions of business and technology solutions. Can dynamically manage different types of interdependent and dependent organizational relationships. Ability to manage within multiple dimensions of business cultures, which may demand self-reliance and confidence in independence of initiatives.

Figure 6.6 (Continued)

Dimension Variable	Conceptual Knowledge of Technology	Multiplicity of Business Perspectives of Technology	Integration of Business Uses of Technology	Implementation of Business/Technology Process	Strategic Uses of Technology
Executive Values	Understanding of technology and cultural differences. Conceptually understands that global communication, education, and workplace use of technology can be problematic—subject to false generalizations and preconceived notions. Management awareness of responsibilities to address assumptions about how technology will be viewed by other departments and customers.	Sets conditions that foster the need to obtain multiple sources of information and opinion about how technology values. The propagation organizationally of acceptance that there can be multidimensional values in human character.	Can manage multiple dimensions of value systems and can prioritize multitasking events that are consistent with value priorities. Ability to assign value to new and diverse technology business alternatives—linking them to legacy systems and processes.	Managing value systems in new ways because technology changes long-term values and goals for business goals and objectives. Recognition that some concepts remain unchanged despite emerging technologies.	Management of technology and business are based on formed principles as opposed to dynamic influences or impulses. Formed executive principles establish the basis for navigating through, or negotiating the diversity of business opportunities and impulses for investment in technologies.

Executive Ethics				
Understands that there is a need to use technology with honesty re: privacy of access and information. Supports the development of ethical policies governing business uses of the Internet, research, intellectual property rights and plagiarism.	Committed to creating an organization that uses information in a fair way—comparison of facts against equal sources of business information. Understands and is compassionate that business and technology information may have different levels of knowledge access. Recognizes the need for sharing information with other business units from a sense of inequality.	Consistent management values displayed on multiple business goals, mission, and dedication to authenticity. Maintains management consistency in combining values regarding technology issues.	Business and technology are a commitment in all aspects of management value systems, including agility in managing multiple business commitments. Commitment to greater openness of mind to altering traditional and nontechnological management methods.	Technology management creativity with self-defined principles and beliefs. Risk taking in technology-based ventures. Utilizing technology to expand one's arenas of business development. Manages the business liberating capacities of technology.

Figure 6.6 (Continued)

Dimension Variable	Conceptual Knowledge of Technology	Multiplicity of Business Perspectives of Technology	Integration of Business Uses of Technology	Implementation of Business/ Technology Process	Strategic Uses of Technology
Executive Leadership	Conceptualizes the need to have a leadership role with respect to technology in the business—the business and technologically realizable executive self.	Understands how other executives can view technology leadership differently. Understands or has awareness of the construction of self that occurs when taking on the integration of technology in business operations. Focuses on views of other CEOs in multiple settings. Understands that the self (through technology) is open for more fluid constructions, able to incorporate diverse views in multiple technology settings.	Manages technology to unify multiple parts of the organization and understands how the process behaves in different business situations.	Has developed an executive identity of self from a multiplicity of management venues. Method of management creates positive value systems that generate confidence about how multiple business communities need to operate.	Acceptance and belief in a multidimensional business world of the how to lead with technology. Can determine comfortably, authenticity of organization's executives and their view of the self. Can confirm disposition on technology independently from others' valuations, both internally and from other organizations. Beliefs direct and control multidimensional leadership growth.

Figure 6.6   CEO Technology Best Practices Arc.

Middle Management

Middle management can represent a number of management tiers and is perhaps the most challenging of the best practices to define. Langer stratified the different types of positions that make up middle managers into three tiers: Directors, line managers, and supervisors.[8] The objective then is to create the set of technology best practices for managers, so that they can effectively operate under ROD. It is also important for the CIO to attain these best practices to effectively establish the kind of organization that can integrate IT and non-IT personnel. That is, technology best practices must be designed to contain the eight insights and skills for effective management of technology:

1. Working with IT personnel
2. Providing valuable input to the executive management team including the CEO
3. Participating and developing a technology strategy within their business units
4. Effectively managing project resources, including technical staff
5. Leading innovative groups in their departments
6. Incorporating technology into new products and services
7. Proactive methods of dealing with changes in technology
8. Investigates how technology can improve competitive advantage[9]

As with CEO research, there is a myriad of best practices that have been offered as a method of dealing with the subject of "technology management."

Unfortunately, these practices usually are vague and intermingle management levels and departments; that is, it is difficult to know whether the best practice is for the chief IT executive, the CEO, or some other level of management. We know from the research from Bolman and Deal that middle managers feel torn by conflicting signals and pressures they get from both senior management and the operations that report to them[10]: "They need to understand the difference in taking risks and getting punished for mistakes."[11] According to a 2003 study performed by SRI Consulting Business Intelligence, best practices for middle managers need to cover the following eight areas:

1. Knowledge management
2. Alignment
3. Leadership and commitment
4. Organization
5. Human resources
6. Opportunity management

7. Leveraging
8. Performance assessment

The study covered more than 400 companies in the previous eight areas of concern. I extracted the following 10 middle management–related best practices from the study results and concluded that middle managers need to:

1. Understand how to take a strategy and implement it with technology; that is, they need to create tactics for completing the project.
2. Establish team-building measures for linking technology with staff's daily operations.
3. Foster the aggregation and collaboration of business unit assets to form peer groups that can determine joint efforts for implementing new technologies.
4. Stimulate their staffs by using innovative strategies of value propositions and reward systems.
5. Create multifunctional teams that can focus on particular aspects of how technology affects their specific area of expertise.
6. Follow common project management practices so that multitiered and department projects can be globally reviewed by senior management.
7. Form project teams that can respect and perform on an action basis, that is, teams that are action oriented.
8. Understand how to communicate with and use IT staff on projects.
9. Have a systematic process for gathering intelligence relating to pertinent technology developments.
10. Understands that customers are the drivers for technology tools provided by the organization.

Upon reviewing the different aspects of middle manager best practices with technology research, it appears that there are two focal points: (1) Those best practices that address the needs of senior management, the CIO, and the CEO, and (2) those that are geared toward the management of the staffs that need to implement emerging technology projects. This makes sense, given that the middle manager, notwithstanding whether they are a director, line manager, or supervisor, needs to deal with the productivity-related issues of the executives and the implementation-related ones of the staffs. They are, as Bolman and Deal stated, "torn" by these two competing organizational requirements. Table 6.1 represents the combined list of technology-based best practices organized by executive-level best practices and implementation best practices.

Table 6.1 Technology-based middle manager best practices.

Executive-based middle manager best practices	Implementation-based middle manager best practices
1. Provide valuable input to the executive management team including the CEO	1. Understand how to communicate with and use IT staff on projects
2. Incorporate technology into new products and services	2. Effectively manage project resources, including technical staff
3. Participate and develop a technology strategy within his or her business unit	3. Lead innovative groups in their departments
4. Act proactively when dealing with changes in technology	4. Understand how to take a strategy and implement it with technology
5. Focus on how technology can improve competitive advantage	5. Establish team-building measures for linking technology with staff's daily operations
6. Have a systematic process for gathering intelligence relating to pertinent technology developments.	6. Foster the aggregation and collaboration of business unit assets to form peer groups that can determine joint efforts for implementing new technologies
7. Understand that customers are the drivers for technology tools provided by the organization	7. Stimulate staffs using innovative strategies of value propositions and reward systems.
	8. Create multifunctional teams that can focus on particular aspects of how technology affects their specific area of expertise
	9. Follow common project management practices so that multitiered and department projects can be globally reviewed by senior management.
	10. Form project teams that can perform proactively

The matrix in Table 6.1 exemplifies the challenge that middle managers have in order to balance their priorities. In accordance with the research, the previous best practices are implemented using methods of knowledge management, alignment, leadership and commitment, human resources, opportunity management, leveraging, and performance assessment. As with the other best practices, the middle manager technology best practices are limited because they do not address the specific needs of ROD, particularly organizational learning theories (with the exception of knowledge management). This shortfall is integrated into another developmental arc model that combines these theories with the best practices defined earlier.

The Middle Management Best Practices Technology Arc

This arc can be used to evaluate a middle manager's strategic and operational uses of technology by using a grid that measures competencies ranging from conceptual knowledge about technology to more complex uses of technology and business operations.

The five principal stages defined by the arc determine the middle manager's maturity with business implementations of technology: Cognitive, organization interactions, management values, project ethics, and management presence. There are five stages of maturation that guide the middle manager's growth. The first is becoming reflectively aware about one's existing knowledge with business technology and how it can be implemented. The second is the recognition of the multiple ways that technology can be implemented on projects (e.g., other business views of how technology can benefit the organization). The third is the integration of business implementation of technology in which a middle manager can begin to combine technology issues with business concepts and functions on a project basis. The fourth is the stability of business/technology implementation in which the middle manager has integrated business and technology as a regular part of project implementations. The fifth is technology project leadership in which the middle manager can use his or her independent judgment on how best to use technology and business on a project-by-project basis. Thus, as middle managers grow in knowledge of technology and business projects, they can become increasingly more open to new methods of implementation and eventually autonomous with the way they implement projects and provide leadership.

Definitions of Maturity Stages and Dimension Variables in the Middle Management Best Practices Arc

Maturity Stages

1. **Technology implementation competence and recognition:** This first stage represents the middle manager's capacity to learn, conceptualize, and articulate key issues relating to cognitive business technological skills, organizational interactions, management value systems, project management ethics, and management presence.
2. **Multiplicity of business implementation of technology:** Indicates the middle manager's ability to integrate multiple points of view during technical project implementations. Using these new perspectives, the middle manager augments his or her skills with business implementation with technology career advancement, expands his or her management value system, is increasingly motivated to act ethically during projects, and enhances his or her management presence.

3. **Integration of business implementation of technology:** Maturing middle managers accumulate increased understanding of how business and technology operate together and affect one another. They gain new cognitive skills about technology and a facility with how the organization needs to interact, expand their management value system, perform business/technology actions to improve ethics about business and technology, and develop effective levels of management presence.

4. **Stability of business implementation:** Middle managers achieve stable integration when they have implemented all projects using their cognitive and technological ability; organization interactions with operations; management values with their superiors, peers, and subordinates; project ethics; and management presence appropriate for performing job duties not only adequately, but competitively with peers and higher-ranking executives in the organization hierarchy.

5. **Technology project leadership:** Leadership is attained by the middle manager when he or she can employ cognitive and technological skills, organization interactions, management, a sense of business ethics, and a sense of management presence in order to compete effectively for executive positions. This middle manager is capable of obtaining increasingly executive level positions through successful interviewing and organization performance.

Performance Dimensions

1. **Business technology cognition:** Concerns skills specifically related to learning, applying, and creating resources in business and technology, which include the necessary knowledge of complex operations. This dimension essentially establishes the middle manager as being "operationally" proficient with technology and forms a basis for movement to more complex and mature stages of development when managing technology projects.

2. **Organizational interactions:** The knowledge and practice of proper relationships and management interactions during technology projects. This pertains to in-person interactions, punctuality of staff, work completion, conflict resolution, deference, and other protocols in technology projects.

3. **Management values:** Measures the middle manager's ability to articulate and act upon mainstream corporate values credited with shaping technology project work ethic: Independent initiative, dedication, honesty, and personal identification with project goals based on the organization's philosophy of management protocol.

4. **Project ethics:** Reflects the middle manager's commitment to the education and professional advancement of other persons in technology and in other departments.

5. **Management presence:** Involves the middle manager's view of the role of a project-based manager during a technology project implementation and the capacity to succeed in tandem with other projects. Aspects include a devotion to learning and self-improvement, self-evaluation, the ability to acknowledge and resolve business conflicts, and resilience when faced with personal and professional challenges during technology implementations.

Figure 6.7 shows the Middle Management Technology Best Practices Arc in chart form.

Each cell in the arc provides the condition for assessment. The complete arc is provided in Figure 6.8.

The challenge of the Middle Management Best Practices Arc is whether to emphasize executive management concepts (more organizationally intended) or event-driven concepts (project-oriented). This arc focuses on project implementation factors and deals with best practices that can balance executive pressures with implementation realities. I suggest that senior middle managers, at the director level, who do not participate in implementation, set their own best practices on the model of the CEO maturity arc and best practices. In any event, yet another maturity arc appears to have too many overlapping cells.

Conclusion

The formation of best practices to implement and sustain ROD is a complex task for any CIO. It involves combining traditional best practice methods (that is, what seems to work for proven organizations) with developmental theory on individual maturation. The combination of these two components provides the missing organizational learning piece that supports the attainment of ROD. Another way of comprehending this concept is to view the Responsive Organizational Dynamism Arc as the overarching or top-level model.

The other maturity arcs and best practices represent the major communities of practice that are the subsets of that model. This is graphically depicted in Figure 6.9.

Thus, the challenge is to create and sustain each community and at the same time establish synergies that allow them to operate together. This is the

Dimension Skill	Technology Implementation Competence and Recognition	Multiplicity of Business Implementation of Technology	Integration of Business Implementation of Technology	Stability of Business/ Technology Implementation	Technology Project Leadership
Business Technology Cognition					
Organizational Interactions					
Management Values					
Project Ethics					
Management Presence					

Figure 6.7   Middle Management Technology Best Practices Arc.

Dimension Variable	Technology Implementation Competence and Recognition	Multiplicity of Business Implementation of Technology	Integration of Business Implementation of Technology	Stability of Business/Technology Implementation	Technology Project Leadership
Business Technology Cognition	Understands how technology operates during projects. Has conceptual knowledge about hardware interfaces, and the software development life cycle. Has the core ability to relate technology concepts to other business experiences. Can also participate in the decisions about what technology is best suited for a particular project. Can be taught how to expand the use of technology and can apply it to other business situations.	Understands that technology projects can have multiple perspectives on how to implement them. Able to analyze what is valid vs. invalid opinions about business uses of technology. Can create objective ideas from multiple technology views without getting stuck on individual biases. An ability to identify and draw upon multiple perspectives available from project sources about technology. Developing a discriminating ability with respect to choices available. Realistic and objective judgment, as demonstrated by the applicability of the technology material drawn for a particular project or task and tied to functional/pragmatic outcomes.	Has the ability to relate various technical project concepts and organize them with nontechnical business issues. Can operate with both business and technical solutions. Can use technology to expand reasoning, logic, and what-if scenarios. Ability to discern the templates that technology has to offer in order to approach everyday technology project problems. This involves the hypothetical (inductive/deductive) logical business and technology skills.	Knowledge of technology projects are concrete, accurate, and precise, broad and resistant to interference from nonauthentic business and technical project sources. Ability to resist or recover from proposed technology that is not realistic—and can recover resiliently.	Methods and judgment in multidimensional technology projects are independent and use critical discernment. Operational knowledge of technology and project management skills can be transferred and can be used to self-educate within and outside of technology. Can use technology for creative purposes to solve business and project challenges and integrate with executive management views.

Figure 6.8 Complete Middle Management Technology Best Practices Arc.

Organizational Interactions	Understands that technology projects require the opinions of other departments and staff in multiple ways. Understands that certain technological solutions and training methods may not fit all project needs and preferences of the business. Has the ability to recommend/suggest alternative technological solutions to suite other business and project needs and preferences.	Seeks to use technology projects as a vehicle to learn more about organization interactions and mindsets. Strives to care about what others are communicating and embraces these opinions on a project basis. Tries to understand and respect technologies that differ from own. Understands basic technological project needs of others.	Can deal with multiple dimensions of criticism about technology-based projects. Can develop relationships (cooperative) that are dynamic and based on discourse. Ability to create project relations with IT, other departments, and customers. Has an appreciation of project communication—to foster open dialogue (spontaneous), to give and take, or other than voyeuristic, one-sidedness about the project. Ability to produce in teamwork situations, rather than solely in isolation.	Loyalty and fidelity to relations in multiple organizations. Commitment to criticism and acceptance of multiple levels of IT and business relationships. Ability to sustain nontraditional types of inputs from multiple sources during projects.	Can utilize and integrate multidimensions of project solutions in a self-reliant way. Developing alone if necessary using other technical and nontechnical resources. Can dynamically select types of interdependent and dependent organizational relationships. Ability to operate within multiple dimensions of business cultures, which may demand self-reliance, independence of initiative and interactive communications during project implementations.

Figure 6.8 (Continued)

Dimension Variable	Technology Implementation Competence and Recognition	Multiplicity of Business Implementation of Technology	Integration of Business Implementation of Technology	Stability of Business/ Technology Implementation	Technology Project Leadership
Management Values	Technology and cultural sensitivity during project implementations. Global communication, education, and project use of technology can be problematic—subject to false generalizations and preconceived notions. Awareness of assumptions about how technology will be viewed by other departments and staff and about biases about types of technology used (MAC vs. PC).	Can appreciate need to obtain multiple sources of information and opinions during project implementations. The acceptance of multidimensional values in human character as value during project design and completion.	Can operate project within multiple dimensions of value systems and can prioritize multitasking events that are consistent with value priorities. Ability to assign value to new and diverse technology project alternatives—integrating them within a system of preexisting business and technology project implementation values.	Testing technology value systems in new ways during the project implementation is integrated with long-term values and goals for business achievement. Some project concepts are naturally persistent and endure despite new arenas in the technological era.	Use of technology and business during project implementation are based on formed principles as opposed to dynamic influences or impulses. Formed principles establish the basis for navigating through, or negotiating the diversity of business influences and impulses during the project.

| Project Ethics | Using technology on the project with honesty re: privacy of access and information. Development of ethical policies governing project uses of the Internet, research, intellectual property rights and plagiarism. | The use of information in a fair way—comparison of facts against equal sources of project information. Compassion for differences in project information for which sources are limited because of inequality of technology access. Compassion for sharing information with other business units from a sense of inequality. | Consistent values displayed on multiple project communications, deliverables of content, and dedication to authenticity. Maintains consistency in integrating values within technology business issues during project implementation. | Technology is a commitment in all aspects of value systems, including agility in managing multiple project commitments. Commitment to greater openness of mind to altering traditional and nontechnological methods on project implementations. | Technological project creativity with self-defined principles and beliefs. Risk-taking in technology-based projects. Utilizing technology to expand one's arenas of project freedom. Exploring the project management liberating capacities of technology. |

Figure 6.8 (Continued)

Dimension Variable	Technology Implementation Competence and Recognition	Multiplicity of Business Implementation of Technology	Integration of Business Implementation of Technology	Stability of Business/ Technology Implementation	Technology Project Leadership
Management Presence	Has accurate perception of one's own potential and capabilities in relation to technology projects—the technologically realizable manager.	Understands how other managers can view self from a virtual and multiple perspectives. Understands or has awareness of the construction of self that occurs in projects. Understands views of other executives and managers in multiple project settings. Understands that the self (through technology projects) are open for more fluid constructions, able to incorporate diverse views in multiple settings.	Operationalizes technology projects to unify multiple components of the self and understands its appropriate behaviors in varying management situations.	Has regulated an identity of self from a multiplicity of management venues. Method of project interaction creates positive value systems that generate confidence about operating in multiple organizational communities.	Can determine comfortably, authenticity of other managers and their view of the self. Can confirm project-related disposition independently from others' valuations, both internally and from other department cultures. **Has direct** beliefs and **controls** multidimensional management growth.[?]

Figure 6.8 Complete Middle Management Technology Best Practices Arc.

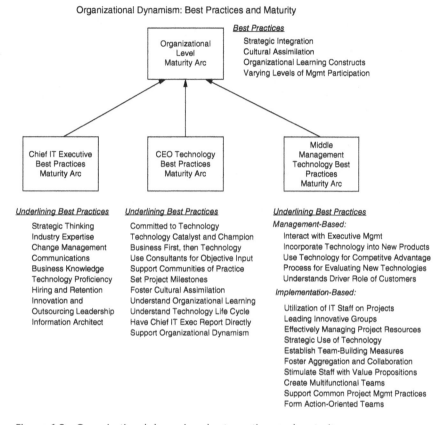

Organizational Dynamism: Best Practices and Maturity

Organizational Level Maturity Arc

Best Practices
Strategic Integration
Cultural Assimilation
Organizational Learning Constructs
Varying Levels of Mgmt Participation

Chief IT Executive Best Practices Maturity Arc

CEO Technology Best Practices Maturity Arc

Middle Management Technology Best Practices Maturity Arc

Underlining Best Practices
Strategic Thinking
Industry Expertise
Change Management
Communications
Business Knowledge
Technology Proficiency
Hiring and Retention
Innovation and
Outsourcing Leadership
Information Architect

Underlining Best Practices
Committed to Technology
Technology Catalyst and Champion
Business First, then Technology
Use Consultants for Objective Input
Support Communities of Practice
Set Project Milestones
Foster Cultural Assimilation
Understand Organizational Learning
Understand Technology Life Cycle
Have Chief IT Exec Report Directly
Support Organizational Dynamism

Underlining Best Practices
Management-Based:
Interact with Executive Mgmt
Incorporate Technology into New Products
Use Technology for Competitve Advantage
Process for Evaluating New Technologies
Understands Driver Role of Customers

Implementation-Based:
Utilization of IT Staff on Projects
Leading Innovative Groups
Effectively Managing Project Resources
Strategic Use of Technology
Establish Team-Building Measures
Foster Aggregation and Collaboration
Stimulate Staff with Value Propositions
Create Multifunctional Teams
Support Common Project Mgmt Practices
Form Action-Oriented Teams

Figure 6.9   Organizational dynamism: best practices and maturity.

organizational climate required, where the executive board, senior and middle managers, and operations personnel must form their own subcommunities, while at the same time have the ability for both downward and upward communication. In summary, this particular model relies on the CIO to drive the key management interfaces that are needed to support ROD.

Notes

1. A. M. Langer, *Information Technology and Organizational Learning: Managing Behavioral Change through Technology and Education*, 2nd ed. (Boca Raton, FL: Taylor and Francis, 2011).
2. Ibid.
3. Ibid., p. 111.
4. Ibid.

5. Ibid.
6. Hackett Benchmarking has tracked the performance of nearly 2000 complex, global organizations and identified key differentiators between world-class and average companies across a diverse set of industries. In addition to information technology, staff functions studied include finance, human resources, procurement, and strategic decision making, among others. Study participants comprise 80% of the Dow Jones Industrials, two thirds of the Fortune 100 and 60% of the Dow Jones Global Titans Index. Among the information technology study participants are Agilent Technologies, Alcoa, Capital One Financial Corporation, Honeywell International, Metropolitan Life Insurance, SAP America, and TRW (Source: *PR Newswire*, February 2002).
7. Langer, *Information Technology and Organizational Learning*.
8. Ibid.
9. Ibid.
10. L. G. Bolman and T. E. Deal, *Reframing Organizations: Artistry, Choice, and Leadership*, 2nd ed. (San Francisco: Jossey-Bass, 1997).
11. Ibid., p. 27.

CHAPTER 7

Implications for Personal Development

As noted repeatedly in the preceding chapters, the chief information officer's (CIO's) role is at a critical fork in the road. The consumerization of technology has gotten (not getting—but gotten) to a point where CIOs must transform themselves quickly to respond the needs of their organizations, particularly as it relates to the role of technology as a competitive advantage. We have seen in the case studies that CIOs must become better communicators to create important relationships with their C-suite colleagues. Furthermore, CIOs must integrate their IT organizations in such a way that they integrate seamlessly with the business and with their firm's clients. This important transformation has little to do with the technology itself; rather it is about creating the proper mindset in the IT organization— that is, a new IT culture is needed. Indeed, many CIOs agree that they need to integrate IT better in their organizations, yet so many fail to actually do it. The question, then, is why? We believe that to form a new IT culture starts with changing the current mindset of the management and staff. Methods to evolve behaviors and norms are related to a number of theories of strategic advocacy, a way to first evolve the personal development of the CIO, which we think can then change the culture of the IT organization as a whole. Specifically, we believe the reason why some CIOs have clearly accomplished success while others have not relates to the way they behave, not necessarily by what they know. The successful CIOs we interviewed figured out how to reinvent themselves by changing the way they manage, the way they communicate, and the way they perceive their overall role in their company. Therefore, there are two critical challenges that we see as critical for CIO success:

1. How can CIOs reinvent themselves using personal development methods to become a better business partner?
2. How can CIOs establish a natural evolution in their organizations that will lead to a fundamental shift in the way IT is managed and measured overall?

Addressing these questions is fundamental to the value proposition of the organization going forward; addressing them effectively requires strategic learning and political advocacy on the part of the CIO. In a world that is continuously "remade" through new mobile technologies, cloud computing, and social media, for example, it becomes increasingly critical for CIOs to become integrated into and have an influential voice in everyday conversations, not just at formal meetings. It is the everyday conversations that evolve an organization to be able to execute the fundamentals of Langer's responsive organizational dynamism (ROD) presented in Chapter 2. However, unlike other traditional executives at the C-suite who more often have backgrounds in finance and marketing, CIOs face a unique challenge to gain a different voice. This new voice must be one that is less scientific so they can overcome the stereotyped perspective of other members of the senior management team, who typically see technology as an administrative sideline support function. It is important to note that the transformative IT leader must continue to deal with the challenges from the support side, such as confidentiality and other security, as conveyed in earlier chapters. The support-side dilemmas are not unique, as we saw from our interview of the HR executive from Cushman & Wakefield in Chapter 4 that he, too, was challenged in the similar way as the CIO and with a growing emphasis on strategically managing talent in their organizations.

Thus, in order to provide a solution for the up-and-coming CIOs discussed in Chapter 5, we present three self-directed learning activities that can enhance a CIO's strategic insight while also fostering his or her personal development that will form a strategic mindset overall. This, then, is the vehicle to establish a personal development formula that we believe will lead to an easier transformation to the leadership skills needed for CIO success. The activities include:

1. Engaging in a process of developmental action inquiry.
2. Testing one's "business" acumen.
3. Thinking holistically in terms of situational analysis and synthesis of the organization's position.

First, we need to provide a rationale for undertaking these processes of personal development beyond using the tools and practices presented in prior chapters.

Rationale for a Self-Directed Learning Process of Personal Development

Chapter 3 presented a series of core tools and practices associated with developing a strategic mindset and engaging in strategic advocacy to address these challenges. The cases and lessons learned presented in subsequent chapters have further defined best practices and illustrated the necessary mindset in practice. This chapter addresses a corresponding—and in many ways the most challenging—aspect of strategic advocacy: Fostering the personal awareness necessary for developing a strategic mindset.

What makes it so challenging? For many CIOs this is a different way of thinking, a different perspective from how they have been trained, and, given that people typically gravitate toward professions that fit their aptitude, this training has been very compatible with their comfort zone. Through training and experience a habit of mind, in the case of technology an expert habit of mind and way of being, has been developed and reinforced. To repeat once more a crucial point made in Chapter 3, the challenge is not replacing this expert mindset. Rather, the challenge is making one's mindset more inclusive, with a capability for adopting a more strategic perspective under appropriate circumstances and, based on new insights and perspectives, adapting one's plans and approaches.

For most people, achieving this requires engaging in a conscious process of personal reflection and development, in effect bringing habit patterns that are applied unconsciously into objective, conscious awareness. Only then can these habit patterns be reflected on with attentiveness as to how they are shaping one's reactions and actions to new possibilities and one's comfort level with uncertainty and ambiguity. This is a process of personal cognitive development, one that goes beyond strategic advocacy per se and relates to one's ability for progressing through the developmental arc (see Chapter 6) and one's potential as a leader. Management is about creating control mechanisms, providing and analyzing information in the service of problem solving, and effectively distributing resources. Planning is a key management function. Leadership is about change, recognizing the need for enlisting support for key change initiatives, integrating diverse perspectives while making tough decisions, developing a following based on the value the leader is bringing to others, and bringing a sense of order under threatening circumstances. In short, strategic advocacy and leadership go hand in hand.

The effectiveness of tools and practices depends on the capability of the person applying them. The practices presented in Chapter 3 can simultaneously enhance one's strategic advocacy while contributing to fostering a more strategic mindset if one is intentionally engaging in a process of personal self-directed developmental learning. This chapter provides suggested guidelines for engaging in this intentional process of personal development along with some additional tools and practices that can further facilitate one's strategic thinking competencies. Ultimately, one's capability for strategic advocacy is a function of one's competency in using the tools and practices in interaction with one's mindset: Or

$$\text{Capability for strategic advocacy} = f\left(\text{Competency} \times \text{Mindset}\right)$$

Said simply, an expert mindset's coming into play early in the strategic thinking process constrains strategic insight. A strategic mindset enhances the use of the tools and practices, leading to richer insights and more nuanced actions taken.

Adopting a Developmental Action Inquiry Process for Both Strategic Insight and Mindset Awareness

The developmental action inquiry (DAI) process articulated by Bill Torbert and his colleagues is particularly applicable for the kind of personally developmental self-directed learning referred to earlier.[1] By developmental action inquiry Torbert means a process of engaging in action that is simultaneously inquiring and productive. It is a form of action learning[2] that incorporates principles of experiential learning,[3] action science,[4] and adult development.[5]

DAI requires intentionally engaging in three levels of inquiry as one works through cycles of action and reflection:

- First-person inquiry (awareness of one's own intentions, strategies, sensed performance, reactions, and assumptions).
- Second-person inquiry (building inquiry into one's interactions with others through mindful use of speech).
- Third-person inquiry (awareness of the larger system and the assumptions it shapes through the data provided from reactions to your actions).

All three levels of inquiry are highly relevant for enhancing one's capability for using the tools and practices of strategic advocacy.

First-Person Inquiry

The underlying rationale for engaging in first-person inquiry is that one's own intentions, strategies, sensed performance, reactions, and assumptions are an important factor in how receptive one is to highly adaptive or generative change. Over time, first-person inquiry can raise one's self-awareness of how they are reacting to the trends they are observing in the marketplace, new technologies, and the political context of the organization. When one is initially feeling resistance to an innovative idea, first-person inquiry can result in more openness, leading to a thorough assessment of the potential advantages of the proposed change. Relevant reflective questions to ask oneself include:

- Why am I resistant to really brainstorming the potential advantages?
- What feared losses are behind my felt need for countering with reasons why the idea won't work before really exploring the possible advantages?
- Are my reactions triggered by the idea, the threat of a possible loss or downsides I might experience, or the person who is presenting the proposal?
- In initially reacting to the suggestion, what analogies was I drawing on?

When mapping the political territory:

- What assumptions are you making in classifying someone as an ally or opponent?
- What "data" do you have in support of these assumptions?
- What alternative explanations might explain those "data"?

When discussing the map with close colleagues on your team:

- What personal reactions are you feeling?

In short, one's use of tools and practices such as the spectrum policy, reasoning by analogy, and the political mapping process is shaped by one's taken-for-granted, unexamined assumptions, intentions, and reactions. Through first-person inquiry these practices enable personal reflection that is both developmental and enhances the use of the practices themselves. Essentially, one is using immediate experiences as triggers for personal reflection.

Second-Person Inquiry

As noted throughout the preceding chapters, strategic thinking involves being able to engage a range of divergent viewpoints. Awareness of how one is reacting through first-person inquiry facilitates this. First-person inquiry is very challenging to do in isolation. Further, vetting the divergent viewpoints of others in shaping one's own strategic position and advocating for one's proposals involves engaging with others. Second-person inquiry involves consciously engaging with others through what Torbert refers to as the mindful use of speech:

- **Framing:** Explicitly stating one's intention in making a comment or presentation, including, for example, the dilemma being addressed, one's assumptions that may or may not be shared by others.
- **Advocating:** Stating the opinion, the action or strategy being proposed.
- **Illustrating:** Giving examples or providing a brief story that demonstrates the point.
- **Inquiring:** Questioning others about their reactions and thoughts with the explicit purpose to learn from them.

Observe how people often speak when they are seeking to influence others. Many begin by strongly advocating their position without really framing the discussion that makes clear to others their purpose or intention in any kind of thorough way that connects with others. Instead of inquiring, many people stay focused on what they have advocated. Become aware of how you often fall into this pattern, even when intentionally trying to explore divergent viewpoints.

A very basic but also important practice when engaging in second-person inquiry with one person or a small group of colleagues is paying attention to how one phrases questions when inquiring. Although the points made below seem very simplistic, the problem is that most people don't apply the points being made because of their ingrained habit patterns.

Everyone asks questions all the time. Unfortunately, questions are not always used effectively, especially in conversations where people are embedded in a complex, challenging environment and exploring diverse viewpoints. Next time you are in a meeting, pay attention to how people are phrasing their questions. Overwhelmingly, they will typically ask closed-ended questions— questions that start with "do," "did," "can," "have," "could," "are," and the like. The problem with this, beyond the fact that sometimes they don't elicit rich information, is that they are often loaded questions. When one's boss asks, "Did you like the meeting?" the preferred response is often assumed: "Yes, great." In contrast, phrasing open-ended questions like "what," "how," or "where" generally encourages a more open response. Also, particularly early in a dialogue, avoid questions that begin with "why." "Why" carries the connotation "justify yourself." "What is your rationale?," "What are your data for that?," or "Tell me more about that," stated with an even tone, are more likely to solicit their thinking without raising tensions. Closed-ended questions are useful when one is trying to "nail down" a specific answer or point from another person.

In purposeful and complicated conversations, questions are tools. As simple as the previous description of asking inquiring questions sounds, in practice using them effectively is a skill that can be challenging. We regularly observe strategy teams that, even after talking about the use of questions, immediately fall back into their old habit patterns during strategic conversions in their teams. As they get engaged in the content of the discussion, the old pattern emerges. A developmental practice, when engaged in conversations with a colleague where you want to remember the points made, is to ask if you can record the conversation. When you replay the conversation later, see whether you framed your comments before advocating: Did you illustrate and inquire? And how did you phrase your questions? Experiment with how your patterns were impacting the conversation.

Third-Person Inquiry

How the larger system is conceptualized depends on the scope and focus of one's strategic actions that are taken. The larger system can be the political territory captured on the map. As one acts, what is the impact in terms of reactions and dynamics among the stakeholders in the territory. The system can consist of the connections between different functions in the supply chain in response to changes introduced. Inquiry is a process of cycles of action and reflection. Under conditions of uncertainty and ambiguity, strategic learning is a process of "learning through," meaning inquiring and reflecting in real time on the unintended responses that emerge to navigate through the system and draw lessons from these responses.[6]

Testing One's "Business" Acumen

Returning to the comment of Chris Scalet quoted at the beginning of Chapter 3, "I would always start the conversation in terms of what is the meaning for the business . . . they are always business enabler projects," enacting this in practice requires a systematic and holistic understanding of the organization's strategic choices within the context of the larger environment. To be taken seriously in these conversations, the CIO needs to have business acumen: A holistic understanding of the marketing, financial, accounting, talent, and operational functions of the organization combined with an ability for making sound judgments and timely decisions. We have the word "business" in quotes to note that this acumen is relevant to any organization including educational, not-for-profit, community, and governmental, although the terminology and implications will vary from sector to sector. Accordingly, we will use the term "organizational acumen" in what follows.

A key developmental exercise for any manager is to test their acumen. Figure 7.1 provides a set of guiding questions for beginning this self-assessment. Answer each question as specifically as you can. Select, modify, or add questions to focus on your organization's institutional and market sector.

Market Knowledge and Impact

- What organizational capabilities are required for your organization to "win" in competition with your competitors/other contenders?
- In what specific ways do you and/or your function contribute to these capabilities?

Customer/Client/Literacy

- Who are your organization's three to five major customers/clients/users?
- If there are major potential customers/clients/users who do not choose your organization, why don't they?
- What is the value provided by your major competitors that attracts and retains their customers/clients/users?
- Why do your customers/clients/users choose your organization? (What do they like better about your organization?)
- How does/could your function contribute to customer/client/user experience?

Investor Relations

- Who are your organization's three to five major shareholders/funders, and what percentage does each provide?
- Why do they invest in your organization?
- For profit-sector companies:
  - What is your company's price/earnings ratio for the last decade, and how does it compare to your industry average and to the company with the highest P/E ratio?
  - Who are the major analysts who follow your company, and how do they view it compared to your competition?

Economic Context

- What are the major economic trends, and how will those influence your industry/institutional sector and organization?
- In terms of economic trends, how is the next five years likely to differ from the past five years?
- How does your organization compare to others in terms of productively, growth, and other performance variables?

Regulatory Context

- What pending legislation is likely to have a major impact on your organization?
- How does your organization influence this legislation?
- What is your organization and function doing to prepare for this legislation?

Value Proposition Assessment

- In what ways does the work done in your function link to the intangibles that:
  - Investors/funders value?
  - Customers/clients/users value?
- In what way is IT utilized to build long-term connections with target customers/clients/users?
- In what ways does your function create organizational capabilities that will turn strategy into action?
- In what ways does your IT strategy process link to business priorities/organizational strategic intent?

Figure 7.1 Testing your "business" acumen: Understanding your total organization with a holistic perspective.

Once you have completed the "test," two additional questions should be answered and acted on:

1. How can I verify my answers?
2. How can I learn the answers to those questions I couldn't answer?

Strategic thinking involves combining one's acumen to the trends and capabilities that are occurring in the environment and, through scenario learning, considering the implications. Over time, one's acumen can become an embedded mindset that is valuable if one is always thinking in terms of how current trends might change one's answers to the acumen questions. The trap is when the embedded mindset becomes a fixed frame of reference. As mentioned earlier, engaging in dialogue with others who hold diverse points of view is one way of maintaining this awareness.

Ram Charan offers a series of six simple questions to ask yourself and to explore strategic ideas with colleagues and peers:

1. What is happening in the world today?
2. What does it mean for others?
3. What does it mean for us?
4. What would have to happen first (for the results we want to occur)?
5. What do we have to do to play a role?
6. What do we do next?[7]

These questions should be a part of one's regular thinking. Avoiding the trap of a fixed frame of reference requires active engagement with first-person and second-person inquiry as one works through his or her organizational acumen and Charan's suggested questions.

Thinking Holistically in Terms of Situational Analysis and Synthesis of the Organization's Position

Pietersen makes the distinction between information and insight, writing that "insights involve looking a body of information and seeing the underlying truth . . . insight means seeing into."[8] Gaining insight requires serious inquiry. Charan's questions can be adapted to what Pietersen describes as "situation analysis." What are the key trends within:

- **Customer needs—trends in their expectations:** Consider the differences between now and in the past—what are the implications for the future. What do they and "will they" value most?

- **Competitors:** Taking into account people's answers to the organizational acumen test, in what distinctive ways do they serve their customers and how are they different from our organization? What are the key strategic drivers of their success? Considering Michael Porter's positioning model, what emergent technologies and/or substitute products and services raise a possible threat of new, nontraditional competitors and entrants into our market?[9]
- **Institutional, industry dynamics:** Which trends are impacting our industry (e.g., pharmaceuticals, transportation, high education, etc.) and changing the institutional logics and forms of operating?
- **The broader environment:** How are sociocultural–political trends evolving and at what pace? Where are the key uncertainties, and what is the possible impact on our organization? The most significant trends transcend the immediate institutional dynamics. In particular, how is technology impacting these trends, and what are the implications for the organization's "business" model and strategy?
- **Our own organizational reality:** What performance trends are evident over the past five years or so within business units, service lines, or programs? What are the implications in terms of strengths, weaknesses, opportunities, and threats (SWOT) or political, economic, social, and technological (PEST) analysis?
- **Technology trends and innovation:** To Pietersen's five sectors we add technology trends from Internet to cloud to new emergent technologies from engineering. Technology is driving many of the trends within the preceding sectors and an analysis of the next possible disruptive change is what the CIO is expected to add to the conversation (but within the context of the first five—remember the conversation is about the business, not technology).

Produce a story based on your analysis within each of the previous sectors of the organizational context that captures the key trends. Then, looking across the sectors, where are the disconnects in terms of divergence, and how do the trends connect in terms of convergence with a trend in one sector shaping or influencing a trend in another? Connect the "dots" across the sectors, creating a story or, under conditions of high uncertainty and ambiguity, stories that capture the synthesis that connects the insights that have emerged.[10] Strategic insight emerges through analysis of the trends within each sector, followed by synthesis across the sectors (see Figure 7.2).

This raises the question: What is one's objective in creating the synthesis? The objective of doing the synthesis is seeking insight into what is the

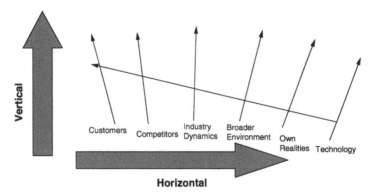

Horizontal

Finding the story vertically, then connecting the dots of the stories horizontally

Figure 7.2   The process of enacting synthesis for strategic advocacy from the CIO perspective.
Source: Based on W. Pietersen, Strategic Learning *(Hoboken, NJ: John Wiley & Sons, 2010).*

most important need that, if met by the organization, will solidify the relationship with the customer and result in having the customer work with our organization rather than others. One of the mistakes often made by organizations is only focusing on what Pietersen calls "table stakes," meaning providing the basic product or service. Table stakes gets one in the game; providing table stakes is important. However, they are expected. In terms of the IT function, "keeping the lights on" is table stakes. It has to be done reliably and is important. However, it doesn't build a strategic relationship with the user. Providing proprietary forums in a business unit that are drivers for its business and having dedicated staff serving them are satisfying a most important need. The focus in drawing on one's organizational acumen and synthesizing across the situation analysis is gaining insight into the customers' most important need and how the organization can meet it better than other, competing organizations regardless of whether it involves uses of technology. Credibility for one's strategic advocacy is built through being seen as a "business thinker." With credibility, the technology executive is positioned to effectively advocate when technology can be a driver meeting the most important customer need. Developing this perspective should guide one's developmental activities.

In practice, systematically working through Pietersen's situation analysis framework is a method for testing the viability of your organizational acumen. It is also a way of "updating" your acumen as well as suggesting provocative questions for conversations with executives throughout the senior executive suite. These conversations can be conducted as a form of second-person inquiry. Be aware of your use of speech:

- *Frame* the conversation within the story of the first five sectors.[11] What is the story line in terms of customer, competitor, industry, and broader environment along with the organization's realities?
- Next, make the connection with technological trends and how these trends might shape or alter that story, creating the frame for how technology can be more positioned as a driver within that story line, and how it would potentially alter it (*advocacy*); and provide some *illustrations*, perhaps in the form of a story.
- Then *inquire* into the other person's reactions. If they are skeptical, don't argue, but explore their reasoning.
- Then reframe and describe the possible impacts of not changing vs. moving forward on the broader system (*third-person inquiry*).

Remain mindful of your own reactions and how your intentions are producing them. In other words, use action inquiry to change the flow of the conversation. Strategic advocacy for change is a process of changing the conversations that are taking place in the organization.[12]

It is important to remember this is both a process of *personal development* and generating new strategic perspectives. Enhancing one's action inquiry competencies, testing and continuing to reflect on their organizational acumen, and engaging in situational analysis are ways of developing a more strategic mindset. These exercises are also tools for putting strategic advocacy into practice. The goal is to make them part of one's habit of mind—a way of thinking. Taken together, they comprise a framework for self-directed learning. Triangulating the content of each of these exercises provides for a holistic process of strategic learning (see Figure 7.3).

Obtaining the necessary information for organizational acumen and situation analysis, along with engaging in strategic advocacy conversations, begins with one-on-one conversations, sometimes spontaneously in the hallway; sometimes over breakfast, lunch, or dinner; or perhaps while on a trip. Other times these conversations involve office visits. The success of high-performing companies results as much from what happens behind the scenes as from leaders' more visible actions. This includes the kinds of conversations described earlier. One of the CIOs we interviewed had just come back from a trip abroad and shared with us how prior to our meeting he was having a conversation with the chief financial officer (CFO) regarding the business trends he had observed during his travels. This conversation began when the two crossed paths in the hallway and continued for a few minutes in the CFO's office, to

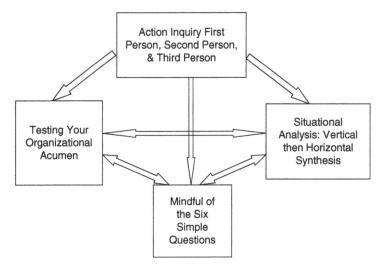

Figure 7.3   Triangulating the developmental practices.

be continued later. This was a classic example of how exchanges build and leverage social capital. (Of course, in this case, the social capital was already established.)Building a network of connections throughout the organization facilitates access to broader sources of information. Through the relationships that are built, a CIO or a technology manager can flesh out and keep current their organizational acumen and continue to revise their analysis and synthesis of the organization's situation.

Developing Strategic Mindsets Within the Technology Function

Beyond personal self-directed learning, engaging the management team of the technology group is a process of strategic learning that can be both developmental for the team and lead to new insights for positioning the function in the future. This can consist of a series of meetings with the focus on either the organization as a whole, or, in the case of the need for reassessing how the function is positioned in the organization, the technology function per se. The first meeting can frame the challenge of strategic thinking, as opposed to planning, and the need for a strategic mindset and strategic advocacy. In the second meeting, subteams can be created with each team assigned to document the trends in one of the sectors of the situation analysis: Customers or users, competitors or the challenge of new providers of the function's services, changes in the industries of their users, broader environmental changes, trends in technologies, and the function's own realities. Each team works over a period of a few weeks to a month or so, and then a third meeting is held with each team presenting their analysis. Over the next month, the teams work on synthesizing the findings. At the fourth meeting, these syntheses are presented, common themes identified, and implications for future action are discussed. The goal is to translate the story line that has emerged into a set of actions for engaging the broader organization through strategic advocacy. Depending on the outcome, action teams can be created or individual initiatives taken. Throughout the process the tools of strategic advocacy are presented and reflected on by the team.

The Balanced Scorecard

The challenge then is how to take the theories we have presented that outline strategic advocacy and put them into an applied framework as a way of measuring progress. While there a many instruments and processes that a CIO can use, we recommend the use of Langer's modified Balanced Scorecard, originally developed by Kaplan and Norton in the early 1990s.[13] While there has been much debate over the true effectiveness of the original Balanced Scorecard, we feel Langer's modified version is ideal to determine whether CIOs are communicating using the core concepts of strategic advocacy theory.

The original objective of the Balanced Scorecard was to provide a tool to solve measurement problems. The Balanced Scorecard is ideal for measuring outcomes that are not always financial and tangible. Furthermore, the Balanced Scorecard is a "living" document that can be modified as certain objectives or measurements require change. This is a critical advantage because as we have demonstrated, the role of the CIO often changes in scope and in objectives as a result of internal and external factions. Langer's modified Balanced Scorecard is designed to operate with technology and ROD as shown in Figure 7.4.

The objectives of this Balanced Scorecard are designed to create a strategy-focused organization. The CIO can use these objectives and measurements to derive whether he or she, via strategic advocacy, has provided the vision and strategy by using ROD. These measurements are based on the fundamental principles of any strategically focused organization and are consistent with strategic advocacy objectives. Thus, the ROD Balanced Scorecard

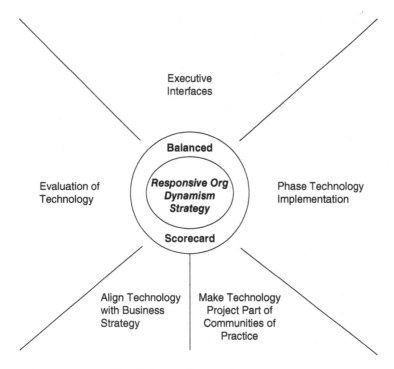

Figure 7.4   Langer's modified Balanced Scorecard.

can be used to determine a CIO's results across the five major components of the scorecard as follows:

1. **Evaluation of technology:** The first step is to have an infrastructure that can determine how technology fits into a specific strategy. Once this is targeted, the evaluation team needs to define it in operational terms. This principle requires the strategic integration of ROD.

2. **Align technology with business strategy:** Once technology is evaluated, it must be assimilated into business strategy. This involves ascertaining whether the addition of technology will change the current business strategy. This principle is also connected to strategic integration of ROD.

3. **Make technology project part of communities of practice:** Affected communities need to be strategically aware of the project. Organizational structures must determine how they relate rewards and objectives across departments. This principle requires cultural assimilation of ROD.

4. **Phase technology implementation:** Short- and long-term project objectives are based on driver and supporter life cycles. This will allow organizational transformation phases to be linked to implementation milestones. This principle maps to cultural assimilation of ROD.

5. **Executive interface:** CEO and senior managers act as executive sponsors and project champions. Communities of practice and their common "threads" need to be defined, including middle management and operations personnel, so that top-down, middle-up-down, and bottom-up information flows can occur.

The ROD Balanced Scorecard ultimately provides a framework to view strategy from four different measures:

1. **Financial:** Requires the inclusion of indirect benefits from technology, particularly Lucas specified nonmonetary methods of evaluating return on investment (ROI).[14] Risk must also be factored based on technology project specific issues.

2. **Customer:** Technology-based products are very integrated with customer needs and provide direct customer package interfaces. Further, Web systems that use the Internet are very dependent on consumer use. As such, technology can modify organizational strategy because of its direct effect on the customer interface.

3. **Internal business processes:** Technology requires business process reengineering (BPR), which is the process of reevaluating existing internal norms and behaviors before designing a new system. This new evaluation process will addresses customers, operational efficiencies, and cost.

4. **Learning and growth:** Organizational learning techniques, under the umbrella of ROD, need to be applied on an ongoing and evolutionary basis. Progress needs to be linked to the concepts of strategic advocacy and the "soft" skills necessary for the CIO to get the IT organization functioning across the components of the scorecard.

The major portion of the ROD Balanced Scorecard strategy is in its initial design, that is, evaluation of technology. During this phase, a strategy map and actual ROD Balanced Scorecard are created. This process should begin by designing a ROD Balanced Scorecard that articulates the business strategy. Remember that every organization needs to build a strategy that is unique and based on its evaluation of the external and internal situation. To establish and clarify this strategy definition, it is easier to consider drawing the scorecard initially in the form of a strategy map. A generic strategy map essentially

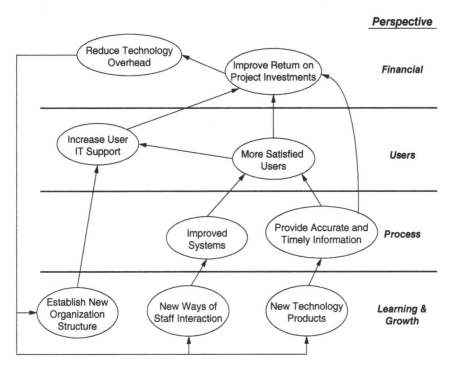

Figure 7.5   Strategy map.

defines the components of each perspective, showing specific strategies within each one, as shown in Figure 7.5.

There are two other important factors embedded in this ROD Balanced Scorecard technique. First, scorecards can be designed at varying different levels of detail. So a CIO can use this technique to complete a process for implementing innovations or communicating with various business units—each one could have a separate strategy map with an accompanying ROD Balanced Scorecard. Second, the scorecard can be modified to reflect unexpected changes during any milestone. These changes could be related to a shifting mission statement or external changes in the market that require a change in business strategy. Most important, though, are the expected outcomes and transformations that occur during the course of any project. Essentially, it is difficult to predict how organizations will actually react and transform. The Balanced Scorecard provides a checklist and tracking system that is structured and sustainable—but not perfect. Indeed, many of the important aspects for CIO success are more conceptual and dependent on many external variables, and this is why we feel it is a productive instrument as a road map for strategic advocacy. The salient issue here is that it allows a CIO to understand when such unexpected changes have occurred. When this does happen, CIOs need to have an infrastructure and a structured approach to examine what a change in their mission, strategy, or expectations means to all of the components of their organization. This can be described as a "rippling effect," where one change can "ripple" down, affecting many other parts of the whole. Thus, the ROD Balanced Scorecard, particularly using a strategy map, allows practitioners to reconcile how changes will affect the entire scheme and plan and what parts of advocacy are needed and with what specific sponsors.

Conclusion

Developing the capacity for strategic advocacy requires learning and development at the individual, team, and functional level. The processes described in this chapter provide a framework for engaging in this process. It requires commitment, self-direction, and a focus on critical reflection on trends, a willingness to become more comfortable with the ambiguity of addressing future possibilities. Developing this capacity is, however, critical to the future success of the organization, given the central role technology plays in driving the changes in today's world. The ROD Balanced Scorecard can be used to determine the process of where and when strategic advocacy can be effective.

Notes

1. D. Fisher, D. Rooke, and B. Torbert, *Personal and Organizational Transformations through Action Inquiry* (Boston: Edge/Work Press, 2003); D. Rooke, and W. R. Torbert, "The Seven Transformations of Leadership," *Harvard Business Review* 83(4) (2005): 66–77; and B. Torbert, *Action Inquiry: The Secrets of Timely and Transforming Leadership* (San Francisco: Berrett-Koehler, 2004).
2. J. O'Neil and V. J. Marsick, *Understanding Action Learning* (New York: AMACOM, 2007); L. Yorks, J. O'Neil, and V. J. Marsick (Eds.), "Action Learning: Successful Strategies for Individual, Team and Organization Development," *Advances in Human Resource Development* 1(2) (1999).
3. D. A. Kolb, *Experiential Learning: Experience as the Source of Learning and Development* (Upper Saddle River, NJ: Prentice Hall, 1984); A.Y. Kolb and D. A. Kolb, "Learning Styles and Learning Spaces: Enhancing Experiential Learning in Higher Education," *Academy of Management Learning and Education* 4(2) (2005): 193–212.
4. C. Argyris, *Knowledge for Action* (San Francisco: Jossey-Bass, 1993); and C. Argyris, R, Putnam, and D. Smith, *Action Science* (San Francisco: Jossey-Bass, 1985).
5. R. Kegan, *The Evolving Self: Problem and Process in Human Development* (Cambridge, MA: Harvard University Press, 1982); R. Kegan, *In Over Our Heads: The Mental Demands of Modern Life* (Cambridge, MA: Harvard University Press, 1994); B. Torbert, *Action Inquiry: The Secret of Timely and Transforming Leadership* (San Francisco: Berrett-Koehler, 2004).

6. A. Nicolaides and L. Yorks, "An Epistemology of Learning Through," *Emergence: Complexity and Organizations* 10(1) (2008): 50–61.

7. Ram Charan, *Sharpening Your Business Acumen Strategy & Business*, Booz & Co. (Boston: Harvard Business School Press, 2006).

8. W. Pietersen, *Strategic Learning* (Hoboken, NJ: John Wiley & Sons, 2010), 74.

9. M. Porter, "What Is Strategy?" *Harvard Business Review* 74(6) (1996): 61–78.

10. Pietersen, *Strategic Learning*, pp. 76–77.

11. Ibid., pp. 77–78.

12. P. Shaw, *Changing the Conversation in Organizations: A Complexity Approach to Change* (London: Routledge, 2002).

13. A. M. Langer, *Information Technology and Organizational Learning: Managing Behavioral Change through Technology and Education*, 2nd ed. (Boca Raton, FL: Taylor and Francis, 2011).

14. H. C. Lucas, *Information Technology and the Productivity Paradox* (New York: Oxford University Press, 1999).

CHAPTER 8

Digital Transformation and Business Strategy

Introduction

This chapter deals with digital transformation, which has had a huge impact on the way organizations compete in the 21st century. Digital transformation is defined as "the changes associated with the applications of digital technology in all aspects of human society" (Stolterman & Fors, 2004, 689). Technology leadership should not ignore digital transformation or perceive it as just another fade; IT organizations must now be part of the front office and involved in every aspect of business strategy. In fact, we believe that digital transformation will ultimately be the final force that truly integrates IT with business operations. There are apparent reasons that lead us to make this prediction. The success of digital transformation is predicated on the emergence of a number of newer computing platforms that integrate mobility, social media, cloud, and Big Data. The bottom line is that business leaders cannot accomplish this alone because of the technical complexity needed to develop sound competitive strategies, so an effective and seamless IT infrastructure is essential.

Unfortunately, if you ask a group of CIOs to define digital technology, one would likely get a myriad of definitions and interpretations from their points of view. The confusion among technical leaders as well as business executives certainly does not support a universal interpretation. The result is that most companies, while making some progress, are moving too slow. Dell Research (2017) recently interviewed 4,000 business leaders and found that 73% of them agree that technology must be a higher priority. Forty-five percent fear that their company will become obsolete in three to five years. Forty-eight percent are unaware of what their industries will be like; 78% feel threatened; and 62% see new entrants as competitors.

If we look at this solely from a business point of view, digital transformation *requires* organizations to implement technology in new ways just to survive—and we believe they are experiencing the phenomena. To survive, digital transformation mandates that the business go through another generation of reengineering, one that forces businesses to reexamine their entire supply chain of how they deliver their products and services. Some business leaders see digital transformation as the final step to eliminating paper while others see it as re-vamping a business to meet the demands of the digital economy, which is what we believe. Technology leaders then must figure out a strategy to integrate digital transformation with what Langer (2018) coined "digital re-engineering." Let's examine this further.

The first generation of re-engineering focused on upgrading legacy systems with newer applications and the seamless use of centralized database systems. The advent of digital transformation, on the other hand, requires that businesses understand the digital demands of their, or their customer's, consumers. Specifically, for many companies, the consumer is just another company (B2B); that is, the consumer is a provider to another company that inevitable supports a consumer. When Charlemagne built the Holy Roman Empire, his organization built roads throughout Europe that would always lead back to the central city of Rome, and this was famously coined as "all roads lead to Rome." Such is true for the consumer in the digital age. Whatever the business, the demand for products and services must inevitably lead back to the consumer, and there may be many ways to get that done! We will clarify the differences in dealing with direct and indirect consumers later in this chapter. What is important to recognize is that re-engineering is no longer limited to just the needs of the internal users, but rather the needs of the consumers of the business. Application systems then must continue to evolve to meet the needs of the consumer. The challenge is keeping ahead of what the consumer may or may not want. We must remember that the digital world can offer new things to consumers that they may never have envisioned for themselves. To make things more complex, needs also vary among different consumer groups by ethnicity, age, and gender, to name just a few.

As a result, technology leaders need to get closer to their consumer groups, even if the consumer is ultimately indirect. As a result, B2B companies need to extend their thinking to understand where the consumer exists in the demand chain. This requires technology leaders should view consumers as a new type of end user. The consumer is now the ultimate buyer of the organization's products and services. Langer (2018) established six approaches to getting closer to your consumer:

1. **Sales/Marketing:** These individuals sell to the company's buyers. Thus, they have a good sense of what customers are looking for, what things they like about the business, and what they dislike. The power of the sales and marketing team is their ability to drive realistic requirements that directly impact revenue opportunities. The limitation of this resource is that it still relies on an internal perspective of the consumer, that is, how the sales and marketing staff perceive the consumer's needs.

2. **Third-Party Market Analysis/Reporting:** These are outside resources that can research market trends among various industry sectors. These organizations have access to massive knowledge databases and use analysis tools that provide consumer behavior patterns. These third parties can generate reports that disclose how an organization compares with its competition and/or why consumers may be choosing alternative products. While using third party databases is invaluable, the data must be validated for accuracy to avoid making false generalizations about consumer behavior.

3. **Predictive Analytics:** An important concept in today's competitive landscape, predictive analytics is the process of using large data sets to predict future behavior patterns. Predictive analytics strategies are usually developed internally with the help from third-party products or vendors. The limitation is the risk that the prediction is not accurate.

4. **Consumer Support Departments:** Internal teams and outsourced service firms that directly support consumers are an excellent source. Specifically, these teams and firms deal with consumer questions regularly, respond to their problems, and have a real pulse of what is working and not working for the buyers of the business. These teams are an excellent source for what features and functions the system needs to provide to consumers.

5. **Surveys:** IT and the business staff can design surveys or questionnaires to receive select feedback from consumers. Surveys can provide significant value because they can be defined to target specific issues of interest to the business. Survey design and administration should be designed by professionals who understand how to format questions and are more objective.

6. **Focus Groups:** This approach is similar to the use of a survey. Focus groups are commonly used to understand consumer behavior patterns and preferences. They are often conducted by outside firms. The difference between the focus group and a survey is that surveys are very quantitative and use scoring mechanisms, such as a Likert scale, to evaluate results. Responders of the survey may not understand the question, which can result in unreliable information. Focus groups, on the other hand, are more qualitative and allow investigators to engage in conversations with the consumer.

Figure 8.1 reflects a graphical representation of the sources for determining consumer needs.

Figure 8.1   Sources for consumer behavior.

Table 8.1 further lists the methods and deliverables that technology leaders should consider when developing application system strategies.

Table 8.1 Langer's methods and deliverables for assessing consumer needs.

Analyst's Sources	Methods	Deliverables
Sales/Marketing	Interviews	Should be conducted in a similar way to typical end user interviews. IT should work closely with senior sales staff and set up interviews with key business stakeholders
	Win/Loss Sales Reviews	Review the results of sales efforts. Formal win/ loss review meetings should be conducted to determine important limitations of legacy systems.
Third-Party Databases	Document Reports Reviews	Obtain reports of consumer behavior patterns and determine shortfalls in current application systems.
	Data Analysis	Conduct targeted analytics on data sources to uncover information not available in existing reports.
	Predictive Analytics	Examine data by using analytic techniques that will expose trends in consumer behavior.
Support Department	Interviews	Interview support department personnel (internal and external) to identify possible application enhancements.
	Data/Reports	Review call logs and recorded calls between consumers and support personnel to determine common complaints.
Surveys	Internal and External Questionnaires	Work with business departments to design the survey. Target select populations of consumers.
		Use similar surveys targeted at consumers who are not existing customers and compare results. Differences between existing customer base and non-customers may expose new trends in consumer behavior.
Focus Groups	Hold Internal and External Sessions.	Internal focus groups can be completed by internal marketing staff. Select survey results that have unexpected results. Internal attendees should come from operations and sales. External focus groups should be facilitated by a third-party vendor and held at independent sites. Discussions with customers should be compared with internal focus group results.

Requirements Without User Input

Digital transformation has created an environment where it may be difficult to determine what consumers may want, especially in the future. The challenge then is to develop digital strategies without user input from the customer. IT may need to determine consumer needs without input.

To understand what might be the best approach to develop systems based on projections of consumer behavior, we need only to look at historical events. IBM's fall as the leading technology firm in the 1990s is an excellent example. Indeed, Microsoft overtook IBM because they were able to forecast a change in consumer behavior. Yet Google was able to take the analytics market share away from Microsoft. Let's also not forget the comeback Apple made when it created a new industry based on smart phone technology. Why do these changes in competitive advantage happen so quickly?

Technology continues to generate change, and that change is typically referred to today as a "digital disruption." The challenge in disruption is the inability to predict what consumers want and need; further, the consumer may not know! As a result, technology leaders will need to forecast the changes that are brought about by digital disruptions. Therefore, from our perspective, digital transformation is more about predicting consumer behavior than reacting to an existing market need. This is a significant shift for executives, given that the IT profession was built on the rule that good specifications accurately depicted what users want. Langer (1997) originally defined this as the "Concept of the Logical Equivalent." Perhaps this sounds like an oxymoron: How do we develop systems that the user cannot specify? To add to the complexity of the concept, requirements that depict consumer behavior may be different across global businesses as well as cultural norms. This reality essentially tells us that new software applications will need to be built with a certain amount of uncertainty.

To seek an example of how uncertainty translates in the tech industry, we need only to analyze the evolution of the electronic spreadsheet. The first electronic spreadsheet, called VisiCalc, was introduced by a company called Visicorp. It was designed for the Apple II and eventually the IBM personal computer. The Visicorp product was not created based on consumer input *per se*, rather by *creating* the need by foreseeing the value of a generic calculator and mathematical worksheet. Visicorp had to take a risk of offering a product to the market that consumers did not request. History shows us that it was a very good risk. The electronic spreadsheet, which is now dominated by Microsoft's Excel product, has gone through multiple product generations. The inventors of the electronic spreadsheet had a vision, and the market responded favorably. Future versions would be based on market input, but the

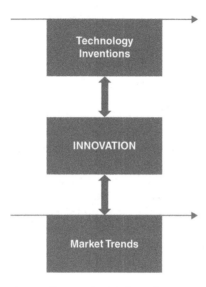

Figure 8.2   Technology, innovation, and market needs.

original concept was based on a forecasted need. Although Visicorp's initial vision of the market need was accurate, the first version was hardly 100% capable of providing consumers with all their inevitable requirements. For example, additional features, such as a database interface, three-dimensional spreadsheets to support budgeting, and forward referencing, are all examples of responses from consumers that resulted in new enhancements that responded to consumer feedback.

Allen & Morton (1994) established an excellent graphical representation of the relationship between technology inventions and market requirements (Figure 8.2).

Figure 8.2 shows the relationship between technology and market needs. The diagram reflects that innovations can occur as a result of new technology capabilities or inventions that establish new markets—like the electronic spreadsheet. On the other hand, the market can demand more features and functions and the technology organizations or developers need to respond to those needs—like the upgrades made over the years to spreadsheet applications. Responding to market needs are what most organizations have practiced over the past 60 years, usually working with their end-user populations (those internal users that supported the actual consumer). The digital revolution, however, is placing more emphasis on "generic" applications that resemble the object paradigm (one that requires applications to be able to fit into any business application). This trend will drive new and more advanced object-driven applications. These applications will reside in a more robust object functioning library that can dynamically link these modules together to form specific applications that can support consumer needs (what is now being called the "Internet of Things").

Porter's Five Forces Framework can also be a useful model. Porter's framework consists of five components:

1. **Competitors:** What is the number of competitors in the market, and what is the organization's position within the market?
2. **New Entrants:** What companies can come into the organization's space and provide competition?
3. **Substitutes:** What products or services can replace what you do?
4. **Buyers:** What alternatives do buyers have? How close and tight is the relationship between the buyer and seller?
5. **Suppliers:** What is the number of suppliers that are available which can affect the relationship with the buyer and also determine price levels?

Porter's framework is graphically depicted in Figure 8.3.

Cadle et al (2014) is a complimentary approach to Porter's model. This approach is especially applicable for the analysis and design process. Their solution can also be applied with Langer's Analysis Consumer Methods in Table 8.2.

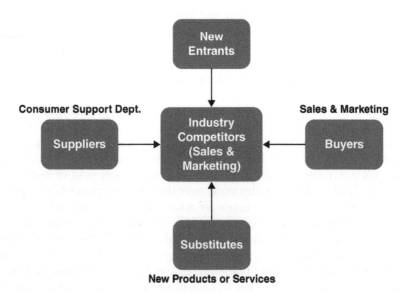

Figure 8.3   Porter's Five Forces Framework.

Table 8.2   Langer's Analysis Consumer Methods.

Porter's Five Force	Cadle et al.'s approach	Langer's Sources of Input
Industry competitors	How strong is your market share?	Third-party market studies
New entrants	New threats	Third-party market studies
		Surveys and focus groups
Suppliers	Price sensitivity and closeness of relationship	Consumer support and end-user departments
Buyers	Alternative choices and brand equity	Sales/marketing team
Substitutes	Consumer alternatives	Surveys and focus groups
		Sales and marketing team
		Third-party studies

The S-Curve and Digital Transformation

Digital transformation can be best understood and applied when used with the economic model called the "S-curve. The S-curve predicts the life cycle of a product or service and measures how consumer supply/demand behavior. A sample S-curve is shown below in Figure 8.4.

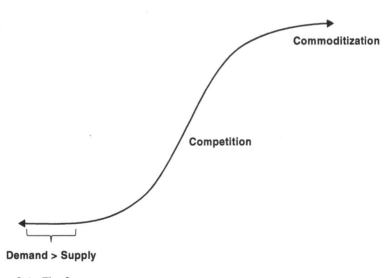

Figure 8.4   The S-curve.

Once a product or service has reached a level of market success, the beginning part of the S-curve predicts that demand exceeds supply. When demand exceeds supply, prices for the product/service are high. Businesses during this cycle should be aggressive and attempt to obtain as much market share as possible before competitors enter the market and drive prices down. To succeed at this objective, businesses need to take higher risks, spend more money, and worry less about short-term profits. The shape of the S-curve reflects how long the business can maintain the high price and competitive advantage. (The shape of the curve along the x-axis measures the expected time period.) Amazon is an excellent example of a firm that sacrificed short-term profits to gain more long-term market share.

No matter what strategy a firm takes, the S-curve predicts that competitors will inevitably enter the market and drive down prices. When this occurs, the market is less volatile and more predictable. When a product or service approaches the top of the S-curve, it has reached maturity and supply exceeds demand. The product or service is now seen as approaching a commodity, which means lower price is more important than the product brand. When the end of the S-curve nears, suppliers normally attempt to produce new features and functions to extend the life of the curve as shown Figure 8.5

Figure 8.5 establishes a new S-curve that hopes to extend the competitive life of the product or service. If the S-curve extension fails to establish a new market demand, then the product or service has likely reached the end of its useful competitive life. At this time the product or service should either be replaced with a new solution or considered for outsourcing to a third party who can deliver the product at a much lower price.

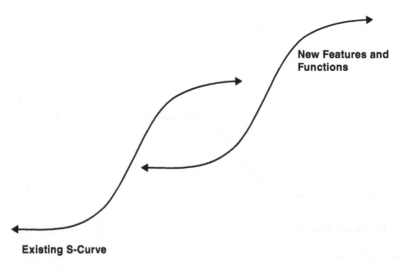

Figure 8.5   Extended S-curve.

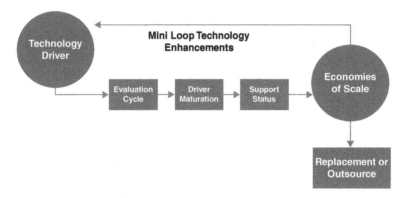

Figure 8.6   Langer's drive/supporter life cycle.

Langer's driver/supporter depicts the life cycle of any application or product as shown in Figure 8.6.

Organizational Change and the S-Curve

When designing a new product, the status of that product's S-curve should be carefully correlated to the source of the requirements. Table 8.3 shows the relationship of the S-curve position with the corresponding market input sources and their associated risk factors. Leaders need to determine the

Table 8.3   S-curve, application requirement sources, and risk.

S-curve position	Analysis input source	Risk factor
Early S-curve	Consumer	High: Market is volatile and uncertain.
High S-curve	Consumer	Lower: Market is less uncertain as product becomes more mature.
	End users	Medium: Business users have experience with consumers and can provide reasonable requirements.
Crest of the S-curve	End users	Low: Business users have more experience as product becomes mature.
	Consumer	High: Might consider new features and functions to keep product more competitive. Attempt to establish new S-curve.
End of S-curve	End user	None: Seek to replace product or consider third-party product to replace what is now a legacy application. Also think of outsourcing application.

organizational impacts of each position with a particular focus on the type of staff needed.

Communities of Practice

Communities of Practice (COP) have been traditionally used as a method of bringing together people in organizations with similar talents, responsibilities, and/or interests. These communities can be used to obtain valuable information about what might be required to improve business operations. Obtaining this knowledge can be associated with the challenges of obtaining dependable information from consumers. COP can be another way of bringing together similar types of consumers grouped by their interests and needs. During digital transformation COP can be another means of obtaining requirements by engaging in, and contributing to, the practices of specific consumer communities. This means that working with COP is another way of developing relations with consumers to better understand their needs. COP is also a valuable way of discovering challenges inside the organization that remain undocumented.

It seems logical that COP can provide yet another source of understanding how business users and consumers behave and interact. Indeed, the technology leader can use this knowledge to consider new organizational structures that can better support changing consumer needs. These changes in consumer behavior often require the realignment of business operations to meet market demands.

The relationship then between COP and digital transformation is significant because new products and services will be likely defined from informal input sources. While there are advanced computerized techniques available such as predictive analytic software and Big Data, using COP should also be part of the analysis process. So, COP along with these predictive analytics applications provides a more thorough umbrella of how to deal with the ongoing and unpredictable interactions established by emerging digital technologies.

The Technology Leader Role in the Digital Era

When we discuss the digital era and its multitude of effects on business strategy, one must ask how it impacts the role of the technology leader. Following are five critical factors to consider:

1. The IT leader must become more innovative. While the business has the problem of keeping up with changes in their markets, the IT needs to provide more solutions. Many of these solutions will not be

absolute and likely will have short shelf lives. Risk is fundamental. As a result, technologists must truly become "business technologists" by exploring new ideas from the outside and continually considering how to implement the needs of the company's consumers. As a result, the technology leaders will emerge as what Robertson & Robertson (2013) call an "idea broker." This entails the constant pursuit of external ideas and transforming these ideas into automated and competitive solutions for the business. Not all new ideas will succeed, which means that technology leaders will need to produce more initiatives than they will inevitably implement. Thus, technology investments must increase.

2. In order to keep in equilibrium with the S-curve the balance between quality and production will be a constant negotiation for software developers. Because of the shrinking S-curve, new applications will have shorter life cycles. This will place pressure to provide competitive solutions faster and leave less time to perform thorough quality assurance testing. As a result, fixes and enhancements to applications will be become more inherent after products go live in the market.

3. Dynamic interaction among users and business teams will require the creation of multiple layers of communities of practice. Organizations involved in this dynamic process must have autonomy and open purpose (Narayan, 2015).

4. Application analysis, design, and development must be treated and managed as a living process; that is, products are always evolving until they reach obsolescence (supporter end).

5. Organizations should never outsource a driver technology until the product reaches supporter status.

Technology Disruption on Firms and Industries

The world economy has quickly transformed from an analogue to digital society. This transformation requires businesses to move from a transactional relationship to one that that is "interactional" (Ernst & Young, 2013). However, this analogue to digital transformation, while essential for a business to survive in the 21st century, is difficult to accomplish. Langer's (2011) theory of responsive organizational dynamism (ROD), as discussed earlier in this book, is modified here to show that successful adaptation of new digital technologies called "digital dynamisms" requires cultural assimilation of the people that comprise the organization.

Dynamism and Digital Disruption

The effects of the digital dynamism can also be defined as a form of disruption or what is now being referred to as "digital disruption." The big question facing many enterprises is: *How can they anticipate the unexpected threats brought on by technological advances that can devastate their business?* There are mainly two disruption factors:

1. A new approach to providing products and services to the consumer
2. A strategy not previously feasible but now made possible using new technological capabilities

Indeed, disruption occurs when a new approach meets the right conditions. Because technology shortens the time to takes to reach consumers, the changes are occurring at an accelerated and exponential pace. Table 8.4 shows the significant acceleration of the time it takes to reach 50 million consumers:

Table 8.4   Acceleration of time to reach 50 million consumers.

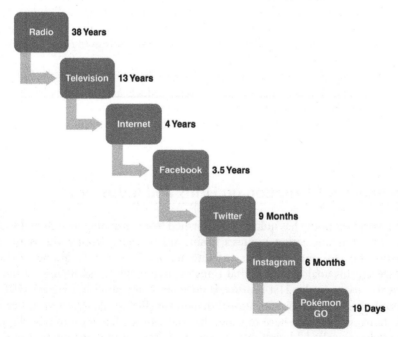

Figure 8.7   The shrinking S-curve.

The speed of which we can accelerate access has an inverse effect on the length of time the affect lasts. We use the S-curve to show how digital disruption shortens the competitive life of new products and services. Figure 8.7 represents how the S-curve is shrinking along the x-axis, which measures the life cycle of a product or service.

Figure 8.7 shows that as technology becomes more relevant in business, the life of a product or service shrinks. This means that businesses have less time to capture a market opportunity and far less time to enjoy the length of its competitive success. As a result, business leaders face a world that is changing at an accelerating rate, and they must figure out ways to cope with new waves of "disruptive" technologies that will affect their business. The bottom line is that digital disruption shifts the way competitive forces in the market deliver services and ultimately shortens the life of any given product or service, which forces firms to change the way they manage operations and measure success.

Critical Components of "Digital" Organization

A study conducted by Westerman et al (2014), which interviewed 157 executives in 50 large companies, found that there were four general capabilities that are key to successful digital transformation:

1. **A Unified Digital Platform:** Integration of the organization's data and processes across department silos is critical. One reason why web-based companies gain advantage over traditional competitors is their ability to use analytics and customer personalization from central and integrated sources. Thus, the first step towards a successful digital transformation is for companies to invest in establishing

central repositories of data and common applications that can access the information. This centralization of digital data is essential to competing in a global economy, since firms must be able to move data to multiple locations and be able to use that data in different contexts.

2. **Solution Delivery:** Many traditional IT departments are not geared to integrating new processes into their legacy operations. A number of firms have addressed this problem by establishing independent "innovation centers" designed to initiate new digital ideas that are more customer solution oriented. These centers typically focus on how new mobile and social media technologies can be launched without disturbing the core technology systems that support the enterprise. Some of these initiatives include partnerships with high-tech vendors; however, a number of executives were concerned that such alliances might result in dependencies because of the lack of knowledge inside the organization.

3. **Analytics Capabilities:** Companies need to ensure that their data can be used for predictive analytics purposes. Predictive analytics provides actors with a better understanding of their consumer's behaviors and allows them to formulate competitive strategies over their competitors. Companies that integrate data better from their transactional systems can make more "informed and better decisions" and formulate strategies to take advantage of customer preferences and thus turn them into business opportunities. An example is an insurance company initiative that concentrates on products that meet customer trends determined by examining their historical transactions across various divisions of the business. Analytics also helps organizations to develop risk models that can assist them to formulate accurate portfolios.

4. **Business and IT Integration:** While the integration of the IT department with the business has been discussed for decades, few companies have achieved a desired outcome (Langer, 2012). The need for digital transformation has now made this integration essential for success and to avoid becoming a victim of disruption. True IT and business integration means more than just combining processes and decision making, but rather the actual movement of personnel into business units so they can be culturally assimilated (Langer & Yorks, 2013).

How to Assimilate Digital Technology

When considering how to design an organizational structure that can implement digital technologies, firms must concentrate on how to culturally assimilate new social and physical reporting structures. These new structures must ensure the success of the strategic integration component of ROD.

This means that the process must allow for agility to effectively respond to changes in market demands. The intelligence of the consumer has resulted in what we now call the "consumerization of technology" that has created a continual need for new products and services. Thus, consumerization has increased what Eisenhardt and Bourgeouse (1987) defined as "high-velocity" market conditions.

Technology leaders must cope to avoid the negative effects of digital disruption. There are four overall components that appear to be critical factors of autonomy from disruption:

1. Companies must recognize that speed and ease of service can be more important than just the cost: We see that companies who offer varying levels of service options are more competitive. The more personal the service option, the higher the cost. Examples can be seen in the airline industry where passengers have options for better seats at a higher price, or a new option being offered by entertainment parks that now provides less wait time on shorter lines for higher paying customers. These two examples match the price with a desired service, and firms that do not offer creative pricing options are prime for disruption.

2. Empower your workforce to try new ideas without too much oversight. Companies are finding that many millennials have new service ideas but are blocked from trying them because of the traditional managers in power positions. Line managers need to allow their staffs to try new things and understand the risk factors in doing so.

3. Allow employees and customers to have choice of devices. Traditionally IT departments desire to create environments where employees adhere to standard hardware and software structures. While standard devices make it easier for IT to support internal users and provide better security across systems, it restricts agility. We see proprietary hardware and software in mobile devices for example that may require different versions of application software and security protocols. IT must figure out how to support multiple devices because both their customers and employees use multiple devices. Most important is to allow staff to use their personal devices when at work.

4. Similar to (3), organizations who force staff to adhere to strict processes and support structures are exposed to digital disruption. Organizational structures that rely on technological innovation must be able to integrate new digital opportunities seamlessly into their current production and support processes. Specifically, this means having the ability to be agile enough to provide services using different digital capabilities and from different geographical locations.

Conclusion

This chapter has provided a number of different and complex aspects of digital transformation and its effects on how organizations need to compete to survive in the future. The technology executive is by default the key person to lead these digital transformation initiatives because of the technical requirements that are at the center of successfully completing these projects. As such, these executives must also focus on their own transformation as leaders, allowing them to help form the strategic goals to meet the dynamic changes in consumer behavior. Ultimately many existing IT department structures must be diminished and reorganized to allow more agility.

References

Cadle, J., Paul, D., and Turner, P. (2014). *Business Analysis Techniques: 99 Essential Tools for Success* (2nd Ed). Swindom, UK: Chartered Institute for IT

Ernst & Young (2012). "The Digitization of Everything: How Organisations Must Adapt to Changing Consumer Behaviour" [White Paper]. Retrieved from http://www.ey.com/Publication/ vwLUAssets/The_digitisation_of_everything_-_How_organisations_must_adapt_to_changing_consumer_behaviour/$FILE/ EY_Digitisation_of_everything.pdf.

Langer, A. (2011). *Information Technology and Organizational Learning: Managing Behavioral Change through Technology and Education* (2nd Ed). Boca Raton, FL: CRC Press.

Langer, A. M. and Yorks, L. (2013). *Strategic IT: Best Practices for Managers and Executives*. Hoboken, New Jersey: John Wiley & Sons, Inc.

Narayan, S. (2015). *Agile IT Organization Design for Digital Transformation and Continuous Delivery*. New York: Addison-Wesley.

Robertson, S. and Robertson, J. (2012). *Mastering the Requirements Process: Getting Requirements Right* (3rd Ed). Upper Saddle River, NJ: Addison-Wesley.

Stolterman E. and Croon Fors, A. (2004). "*Information Technology and the Good Life.*" *Information Systems Research*. Springer US, 687–692.

Westerman, G., Bonnet, D., and McAfee, A. (2014). *Leading Digital: Turning Technology into Business Transformation*. Boston, MA: Harvard Business School Press.

CHAPTER 9

Integrating Gen Y Talent

Introduction

This chapter focuses on how technology executives must focus on succession planning and integration of millennials or Gen Y employees in the workforce. This chapter will also address the coming of the GIG economy, where full-time traditional employment may dramatically change in the 21st century. In addition, technology leaders must address how automation may affect employment in general, especially with the advances in artificial intelligence (AI) and machine learning (ML). Indeed, the evolution of robots along with sophisticated intelligent software is quickly becoming an important focus for organizations to consider as they weigh the challenges and costs of full-time workers. Perhaps the most immediate challenge facing technology executives is how to deal with the mix of multiple generations of people working in their organizations. Overall this chapter suggests that talent will come from many sources and needs to be integrated into organizations in nontraditional ways. Because of digital disruption, talent may come from self-employed people or third-party outsourcing agencies and be available on-demand and for temporary periods.

These "new employees" have been referred to as "Gen Y," "digital natives," and "millennials." These Gen Y employees are nontraditional workers that possess the attributes to assist companies to transform their workforce to meet the accelerated change in the competitive landscape, particularly because they have been born into a technology driven world, thus the name, digital native. There is some research about Gen Y behavior in the workplace; much of it at this time should be considered premature. Some reports suggest that Gen Y employees will not stay for long employment periods, require different types of work environments, and need free time off unlike their predecessors.

So, Gen Y employees appear to have the attributes that can provide a natural fit for the emerging digital-based workplace. Organizationally, the challenge for technology leaders is to figure out how to integrate them with baby boomer and Gen X employees, who occupy higher positions in most "legacy" firms. The primary strategy then for technology executives is to design new leadership models that maximize the potential contributions of these Gen Y employees so they can help transform the culture to help older companies compete. Given the recent acceleration of retirements, failure to assimilate Gen Y employees will create a shortfall of talent and an incongruent workplace that will have high turnover of their younger employees. Gen Ys also tend to seek more entrepreneurial workplaces. Firms need to realize that employees that have entrepreneurial aspirations need environments that embrace change; that is, become more "intrapreneurial."

We established in Chapter 8 that digital transformation is at the core of change and competitive survival in the 21st century. Chapter 8 did not address the necessary changes in personnel that are quickly becoming major challenges for legacy firms. Although we suggested changes in organizational structures, we did not address the need to integrate multiple generations or workers. This chapter is designed to discuss how these multiple generations need to "learn" to work together to form productive and effective organizations that can compete in the digital economy. Furthermore, this chapter will address how access to human capital will change in the future and the different types of relationships that individuals will have with employers. Digital technologies have created what is being coined the "GIG" economy. The GIG economy has established shorter fixed-term employment needs. Indeed, the GIG economy will require HR and IT leaders to form new and intricate employee relationships. We see the GIG economy expanding the presence of individual consultants and entrepreneurs who will service multiple clients.

As discussed in Chapter 8, companies need to transform their business from analogue to one based on digital technologies. This transformation requires moving from a transactional relationship with customers to one that is more "interactional" (Ernst & Young, 2012). Completing an analogue to digital transformation is difficult to accomplish to say the least. Responsive organizational dynamism (ROD) showed us that successful adaptation of new digital technologies requires strategic integration and cultural assimilation of the staff in the organization. These two components of ROD can be categorized as the essential roles and responsibilities of the organization that are necessary to utilize new technological inventions that can strategically be integrated in any business or department. ROD is the basis of why Gen Y employees need to be integrated with baby boomers and Gen X staff to effectively build change-ready organizations.

Employment in the Digital Economy

CapGemini and MIT (2013) research states that organizations need new operating models to meet the demands of a digital-driven era. Digital tools have provided leaders ways to connect at an unprecedented scale. Digital technology has allowed companies to invade other spaces previously protected by a businesses' "asset specificities" (Tushman & Anderson, 1997), defined as advantages enjoyed by companies because of their location, product access, and delivery capabilities. Digital technologies allow those specificities to be neutralized and thus change the previous competitive balances among market players. Furthermore, digital technology accelerates this process meaning that changes in market share occur very quickly. The research postulates five key indicators that are essential for successful digital transformation:

1. A company's strategic vision is only as effective as the people behind it. Thus, winning the minds of all levels of the organization is required.
2. To become digital is to be digital: Companies must have a "one-team culture" and raise their employees' digital IQs.
3. A company must address the scarcity of talented resources and look more to using Gen Y individuals because they have a more natural adaptation to take on the challenges of digital transformation.
4. Resistant managers are impediments to progress and can actually stop digital transformation.
5. Digital leadership starts at the top.

Eisenhardt and Bourgeois (1987) first defined dynamic changing markets as being in "high velocity." Their research showed that high-velocity conditions existed in the technology industry during the early 1980s in Silicon Valley in the United States. They found that competitive advantage was highly dependent on the quality of people that worked at those firms. Specifically, they concluded that workers who were capable of dealing with change and less subjected to a centralized totalitarian management structure outperformed those that had more traditional hierarchical organizational structures. While "high velocity" during the 1980s was unusual, digital disruption in the 21st century has made constant change the norm.

The dynamic digital drivers have accelerated new customer demands that have emphasized the need for organizations to adapt the strategic integration component of ROD. Specifically, the changing ways businesses need to deal with their customers and vendors requires an ongoing evaluation of the exiting processes in the firm. Most experts see digital technology as the mechanism that will require business realignment to facilitate new customer experiences. The driving force behind this realignment emanates from digital technologies, which serves as the principle accelerator of the change in transactions across all business units. Thus, there is a general need to optimize human resources efforts to help realign the way talent is identified, recruited, and maintained.

Attributes of Gen Y Employees

Gen Y are those individuals who are accustomed to the attributes of living in a digital world and are 18 to 25 years old, although there seems to be variances in the definitions of their age group. We know that Gen Y employees are more comfortable with change, particularly change brought on by new technologies. Such individuals, according to a number of commercial and academic researchers (Johnson Controls, 2010; CapGemini, 2013; Cisco, 2012; Saxena & Jain, 2012) have attributes and expectations in the workplace that support environments that are flexible, offer mobility, and provide collaborative and unconventional relationships. Gen Y workers therefore:

- Want access to dedicated team spaces where they can have emotional engagements in a socialized atmosphere.
- Require their own space; that is, they are not supportive of a "hoteling" existence, where they do not have a permanent office or workspace.
- Need a flexible life/work balance.
- Prefer a workplace that supports formal and informal collaborative engagement.

The research also states that 79% of Gen Y workers prefer mobile jobs, 40% want to drive to work, and females in this category want more flexibility at work than their male counterparts. This data suggests then that businesses will need to provide these requirements to Gen Y workers who now represent 25% of the workforce. In India, while Gen Y represents more than 50% of the working population, the required talent needed by businesses is extremely scarce, which could be a prediction of the level of competition to come over the next few decades. Of course, economic conditions always play a part in the supply and demand of talent.

Benefits of Gen Y Employees

We have established that Gen Y workers have many identities and capabilities that fit well in a digital-driven economy. Indeed, Gen Y people are consumers, colleagues, employees, managers, and innovators (Johnson Controls, 2010). They possess attributes that align with the requirements to be an entrepreneur, a person with technology savvy and creativity, and someone who works well in a mobile environment and is non-conformant enough to drive change in an organization. Thus, the presence of Gen Y personnel can help organizations to re-strategize their competitive position and to retain key talent (Saxena & Jain, 2012). Gen Y employees also bring a more impressive array of academic credentials than their predecessors.

Gen Y's natural instincts to deal with market change allows them to be better positioned to form new organization structures to accommodate evolving consumer needs. A major reason for Gen Y's willingness to change is their natural alignment with a company's customers. Swadsba (2010) posits that we are approaching the end of what he called the "work era" and into a new age based on consumption. Gen Y personnel are more apt to see the value of their jobs from their own consumption needs. Some say that Gen Y people see their employment as an act of consumption (Jonas & Kortenius, 2014). Gen Y employees therefore allow employers to acquire the necessary talent that can lead to better consumer reputation, reduced turnover of resources, and, ultimately, increased customer satisfaction (Bakanauskiene et al, 2011). Finally, Gen Y employees may have abilities to transform operations that are contained within silos into ones that are based more on function, an essential of being agile in the digital economy.

Integration of Gen Y with Baby Boomers and Gen X

The prediction is that 76 million Baby Boomers (born 1946–1964) and Gen X workers (born 1965–1984) will be retiring over the next 15 years. The question for many corporate talent executives is how to manage the transition in a major multigenerational workforce?

Baby boomers today still inhabit the most authoritative leadership positions in the world. Currently, the average age of CEOs is 56, and 65% of all corporate leaders are baby boomers. Essentially, corporations need to produce career paths that will be attractive to Gen Y employees. Thus, the older generation needs to:

- Acknowledge some of their preconceived perceptions of current work ethics that are simply not relevant in today's complex environments.

- Allow Gen Y to escalate in ranks to satisfy their ambitions and sense of entitlement.
- Implement more flexible work schedules, offer telecommuting, and develop a stronger focus on social responsibility.
- Support more advanced uses of technology, especially those used by Gen Yers in their personal lives.
- Employ more mentors to help Gen Y employees to better understand the reasons for existing constraints in the organizations where they work.
- Provide more complex employee orientations, more timely personnel reviews, and in general more frequent feedback needed by Gen Y individuals.
- Establish programs that improve the verbal communications skills of Gen Y workers that are typically more comfortable with nonverbal, text-based methods of communication.
- Implement more continual learning and rotational programs that support a vertical growth path for younger employees.

In summary, it is up to the baby boomer and Gen X leaders to evolve their styles of management to attract Gen Y employees. The challenge to accomplish this objective is not trivial given the wide variances on how these three generations think, plan, take risks, and, most important, learn.

Designing the Digital Enterprise

Zogby completed an interactive poll of 4,811 people on perceptions of different generations. Forty-two percent of the respondents stated that the Baby Boomers legacy would be remembered for their focus on consumerism and self-indulgence. Gen Y, on the other hand, are reported to be more self-interested, entitled narcissists who want to spend all their time posting "selfies" to Facebook. Other facts offer another perception of these two generations as shown in Table 9.1

Table 9.1 Baby boomers vs. Gen Y.

Baby boomers	Gen Y
Married later and less children	Not as aligned to political parties
Spend lavishly	More civically engaged
More active and selfless	Socially active
Fought against social injustice, supported civil rights, and defied the Vietnam War	Cheerfully optimistic
Had more higher education access	More concerned with quality of life than material gain

Research completed by Ernst and Young (2013) offers additional comparisons among the three generations as follows:

1. Gen Y individuals are moving into management positions faster due to retirements, lack of corporate succession planning, and their natural ability to use technology at work. Table 9.2 shows percentage comparisons between 2008 and 2013.

   The acceleration of growth to management positions among Gen Yers can be further illuminated in Table 9.3 by comparing the prior five-year period from 2003–2007.

2. While responders of the survey felt Gen X were better equipped to manage than Gen Y, the number of Gen Y managers is expected to double by 2020 due to continued retirements. Another interesting result of the research related to Gen Y expectations from their employers when they become managers. Specifically Gen Y managers expect: (1) An opportunity to have a mentor; (2) receive sponsorship, (3) have more career-related experiences, and (4) receive training to build their professional skills.

3. Seventy-five percent of respondents that identified themselves as managers agree that managing the multiple generations are a significant challenge. This was attributed to different work expectations and the lack of comfort with younger employees managing older employees.

Table 9.4 provides additional differences among the three generations.

Gen Y Talent from Underserved Populations

There has been much discussion of the outsourcing of jobs outside of local communities to countries with lower employment costs. This trend has led to significant social and economic problems, especially in the United States and in Western Europe. IT jobs in particular continue to migrate to foreign countries in the East who have lower labor costs and education systems that provide more focused skills training needed by corporations. Lager's (2012) research shows that most impacted by the loss of jobs have been the underserved or socially excluded Gen Y youth populations. Indeed, the European average alone for young adult unemployment (aged 15–25) in 2013 was nearly 25%, almost twice the rate for their adult counterparts (Dolado, 2015).

Table 9.2 Management roles 2008–2013.

Baby boomer (ages 49–67)	19%
Gen X (ages 33–48)	38%
Gen Y (18–32)	87%

Table 9.3   Management Roles 2003–2007.

Baby boomer (ages 49–67)	23%
Gen X (ages 33–48)	30%
Gen Y (ages 18–32)	12%

Another factor in the loss of local jobs can be attributed to expansion of the globalized economy, which has been accelerated by continued technological advancements (Wabike, 2014). As such, the effects of technology gains have negatively impacted efforts towards social inclusion and social equality. Langer in 2003 established an organization called Workforce Opportunity Services (WOS) as a means of utilizing a form of action research using adult development theory to solve employment problems caused by outsourcing. Langer's approach is based on the belief that socially-excluded youth can be trained and prepared for jobs in areas such as information technology that would typically be outsourced to lower labor markets. WOS has developed a talent-finding model that has successfully placed over 1,400 young individuals in such jobs. Results of over 15 years of operation and research have shown that talented youth in disadvantaged communities do exist and that such talent can economically and socially contribute to companies. The following section describes the Langer Workforce Maturity Arc (LWMA), presents data on its effectiveness, and discusses how the model can be used as an effective way of recruiting Gen Y talent from underserved and socially excluded populations.

Langer Workforce Maturity Arc

The Langer Workforce Maturity Arc (LWMA) was developed to help evaluate socially excluded youth preparation to succeed in the workplace. The LWMA, initially known as the Inner-City Workplace Literacy Arc:

> ". . . charts the progression of underserved or 'excluded' individuals along defined stages of development in workplace culture and skills in relation to multiple dimensions of workplace literacy such as cognitive growth and self-reflection. When one is mapped in relation to the other (workplace culture in relation to stages of literacy assimilation), an Arc is created. LWMA traces the assimilation of workplace norms, a form of individual development." (Langer, 2003: 18)

Table 9.4   Baby boomer, Gen X, and Gen Y compared.

Baby boomers	Gen X	Gen Y
Seek employment in large established companies that provide dependable employment.	Established companies no longer a guarantee for lifetime employment. Many jobs begin to go offshore.	Seek multiple experiences with heavy emphasis on social good and global experiences. Re-evaluation of offshoring strategies.
Process of promotion is well defined, hierarchical, and structured eventually leading to promotion and higher earnings—concept of waiting your turn.	Process of promotion still hierarchical, but based more on skills and individual accomplishments. Master's degree now preferred for many promotions.	Less patience with hierarchical promotion policies. More reliance on predictive analytics as the basis for decision making.
Undergraduate degree preferred but not mandatory.	Undergraduate degree required for most professional job opportunities.	More focus on specific skills. Multiple strategies developed on how to meet shortages of talent. Higher Education expensive and concerns increase about the value of graduate knowledge and abilities.
Plan career preferably with one company and retire. Acceptance of a gradual process of growth that was slow to change. Successful employees assimilated into existing organizational structures by following the rules.	Employees begin to change jobs more often, given growth in the technology industry and opportunities to increase compensation and accelerate promotion by switching jobs.	Emergence of a "GIG" economy and the rise of multiple employment relationships.
Entrepreneurism was seen as an external option for those individuals desiring wealth and independence and willing to take risks.	Corporate executives' compensation dramatically increases, no longer requiring starting businesses as the basis for wealth.	Entrepreneurism promoted in higher education as the basis for economic growth, given the loss of jobs in the United States.

Source: Langer (2018).

The LWMA addresses one of the major challenges confronting an organization's HR group: To find talent from diverse local populations that can successfully respond to evolving business norms, especially those related to electronic and digital technologies. The LWMA provides a method for measuring the assimilation of workplace cultural norms and thus can be used to meet the mounting demands of an increasingly global, dynamic, and multicultural workplace. Furthermore, if organizations are to attain acceptable quality of work from diverse employees, assimilation of socially or economically excluded populations must be evaluated based on (a) if and how individuals adopt workplace cultural norms and (b) how they become integrated into the business (Langer, 2003). Understanding the relationship between workplace assimilation and its development can provide important information on how to secure the work ethic, dignity, solidarity, culture, cognition, and self-esteem of individuals from disadvantaged communities and their salient contributions to the digital age.

Theoretical Constructs of the LWMA

The LWMA encompasses "sectors of workplace literacy" and "stages of literacy development," and the Arc charts business acculturation requirements as they pertain to disadvantaged young adult learners. The relationship between workplace assimilation and literacy is a challenging subject. A specific form of literacy can be defined as a social practice that requires specific skills and knowledge (Rassool, 1999). In this instance, workplace literacy addresses the effects of workplace practices and culture on the social experiences of people in their workday as well as their everyday lives. We need to better understand how individual literacy in the workplace, which subordinates individuality to the demands of an organization, is formulated for diverse groups (Newman, 1999). Most important is the ways in which one learns how to behave effectively in the workplace—the knowledge, skill, and attitude sets required by business generally as well as by a specific organization. This is particularly important in disadvantaged communities, which are marginalized from the experiences of more affluent communities in terms of access to high-quality education, information technologies, job opportunities, and workplace socialization. For example, Friedman et al (2014) postulates that the active involvement of parents in the lives of their children greatly impacts a student's chances of success. It is the absence of this activism that contributes to a system of social exclusion of youth. Prior to determining what directions to pursue in educational pedagogies and infrastructures, it is necessary to understand what workplace literacy requirements are present and how they can be developed for disadvantaged youth in the absence of the active support from families and friends.

The LWMA assesses individual development in six distinct "sectors" of workplace literacy:

1. **Cognition:** Knowledge and skills required to learn and complete job duties in the business world, including computational skills; ability to read, comprehend, and retain written information quickly; remembering and executing oral instructions; and critically examining data.
2. **Technology:** An aptitude for operating various electronic and digital technologies.
3. **Business culture:** Knowledge and practice of proper etiquette in the workplace, including dress codes, telephone and in-person interactions, punctuality, completing work and meeting deadlines, conflict resolution, and deference and other protocols associated with supervisors and hierarchies.
4. **Socio-economic values:** Ability to articulate and act upon mainstream business values which shape the work ethic. Such values include independent initiative, dedication, integrity, and personal identification with career goals. Values are associated with a person's appreciation for intellectual life, cultural sensitivity to others, and sensitivity for how others view their role in the workplace. Individuals understand that they should make decisions based on principles and evidence rather than personal interests.
5. **Community and ethnic solidarity:** Commitment to the education and professional advancement of persons in ethnic minority groups and underserved communities. Individuals can use their ethnicity to explore the liberating capacities offered in the workplace without sacrificing their identity (i.e., they can assimilate workplace norms without abandoning cultural, ethnic, or self-defining principles and beliefs).
6. **Self-esteem:** The view that personal and professional successes work in tandem, and the belief in one's capacity to succeed in both arenas. This includes a devotion to learning and self-improvement. Individuals with high self-esteem are reflective about themselves and their potential in business. They accept the realities of the business world in which they work and can comfortably confirm their business disposition independently of others' valuations.

Each stage in the course of an individual's workplace development reflects an underlying principle that guides the process of adopting workplace norms and behavior. The LWMA is a classificatory scheme that identifies progressive stages in the assimilated uses of workplace literacy. It reflects the perspective that an effective workplace participant is able to move through increasingly complex levels of thinking and to develop independence of thought and judgment (Knefelkamp, 1999). The profile of an individual who assimilates workplace norms can be characterized in five developmental stages:

1. **Concept recognition:** The first stage represents the capacity to learn, conceptualize, and articulate key issues related to the six sectors of workplace literacy. Concept recognition provides the basis for becoming adaptive to all workplace requirements.
2. **Multiple workplace perspectives:** Ability to integrate points of view from different colleagues at various levels of the workplace hierarchy. By using multiple perspectives, the individual is in a position to augment his or her workplace literacy.
3. **Comprehension of business processes:** Individuals increase their understanding of workplace cooperation, competition, and advancement as they build on their recognition of business concepts and workplace perspectives. They increasingly understand the organization as a system of interconnected parts.
4. **Workplace competence:** As assimilation and competence increase, the individual learns not only how to perform a particular job adequately but how to conduct oneself professionally within the workplace and larger business environment.
5. **Professional independence:** Ability to employ all sectors of workplace literacy to compete effectively in corporate labor markets; obtain more responsible jobs through successful interviewing and workplace performance; and to demonstrate leadership abilities leading to greater independence in career pursuits. Professionally independent individuals are motivated and can use their skills for creative purposes.

The LWMA is a rubric that charts an individual's development across the six sectors of workplace literacy. Each cell within the matrix represents a particular stage of development relative to that sector of workplace literacy, and each cell contains definitions that can be used to identify where a particular individual stands in his or her development of workplace literacy.

STAGES OF WORKPLACE LITERACY

Sectors of workplace literacy	Concept recognition	Multiple workplace perspectives	Comprehension of business processes	Workplace competence	Professional independence
Cognition					
Technology					
Business culture					
Socio-economic values					
Community and ethnic solidarity					
Self-esteem					

The LWMA and Action Research

While the LWMA serves as a framework for measuring growth, the model also uses reflection-with-action methods, a component of action research theory, as the primary vehicle for assisting young adults to develop the necessary labor market skills to compete for a job and inevitably achieve some level of professional independence (that is, the ability to work for many employers because of achieving required market skills). Reflection-with-action is used as a rubric for a variety of methods involving reflection in relation to learning activities. Reflection has received a number of definitions from different sources in the literature. Here, "reflection-with-action" carries the resonance of Schön's (1983) twin constructs: "reflection-on-action" and "reflection-in-action," which emphasize (respectively) reflection in retrospect and reflection to determine what actions to take in the present or immediate future (Langer, 2003). Dewey (1933) and Hullfish and Smith (1978) also suggested that the use of reflection supports an implied purpose. Their formulation suggests the possibility of reflection that is future-oriented, what we might call "reflection-to-action." These are methodological orientations covered by the rubric.

Reflection-with-action is critical to the educational and workplace assimilation process of Gen Y. While many people reflect, it is in being reflective that people bring about "an orientation to their everyday lives" (Moon, 2000). The LWMA incorporates reflection-with-action methods as fundamental strategies for facilitating development and assimilation. These methods are also implemented interactively, for example in mentoring, reflective learning journals, and group discussions. Indeed, as stated by De Jong (2014), "Social exclusion is multi-dimensional, ranging from unemployment, barriers to education and health care, and marginalized living circumstances" (p. 94). Ultimately, teaching socially excluded youth to reflect-with-action is the practice that will help them mature across the LWMA stages and inevitably achieve levels of inclusion in the labor market and in citizenship.

Implications for New Pathways for Digital Talent

The salient implications of the LWMA as a method of discovering and managing disadvantaged Gen Y youth in communities can be categorized across three frames: Demographic shifts in talent resources; economic sustainability; and integration and trust among vested local interest groups.

Demographic Shifts in Talent Resources

The LWMA can be used as a predictive analytic tool for capturing and culti-vating the abilities in the new generation of digital natives from disadvantaged local communities. This young talent has the advantage of more exposure to technologies that senior workers had to learn later in their careers. This puts them ahead of the curve with respect to basic digital skills. Having the capac-ity to employ talent locally and provide incentives for these individuals to advance can alleviate the significant strain placed on firms who suffer from high turnover in outsourced positions. By investing in viable Gen Y, under-served youth can help firms close the skills gap prevalent in the emerging labor force.

Economic Sustainability

As globalization ebbs and flows, cities need to establish themselves as global centers, careful not to slip into market obsolescence, especially when facing difficulties in labor force supply chains. In order to alleviate the difficulty in supplying industry-ready professionals to a city only recently maturing into the IT-centric business world, firms need to adapt to an "on-demand" GIG approach. The value drawn from this paradigm lies in its cyclical nature. By obtaining *localized* human capital at a lower cost, firms can generate a fundable supply chain of talent and diversity as markets change over time.

Integration and Trust

Porter and Kramer (2011) postulate that companies need to formulate a new method of integrating business profits and societal responsibilities. They state, "The solution lies in the principle of shared value, which involves creat-ing economic value in a way that also creates value for society by addressing its needs and challenges" (p. 64). Porter and Kramer suggest that companies need to alter corporate performance to include social progress. The LWMA provides the mechanism, theory, and measurement that is consistent with this direction and provides the vehicle that establishes a shared partnership of trust among business, education, and community needs. Each of the inter-ested parties experience progress towards its financial and social objectives. Specifically, companies are able to attract diverse and socially excluded local talent and have the constituents trained specifically for its needs and for an economic return that fits its corporate models. As a result, the community adds jobs, which reduces crime rates and increases tax revenue. The funding corporation then establishes an ecosystem that provides a shared value of performance that underserved and excluded youth bring to the business.

Global Implications for Sources of Talent

The increasing social exclusion of Gen Y youth is a growing problem in almost every country. Questions remain about how to establish systemic solutions that can create sustainable and scalable programs that provide equity in access to education for this population. This access to education is undoubtedly increasing employability, which indirectly contributes to better citizenship for underserved youth. Indeed, there is a widening gap between the "haves" and the "have-nots" throughout the world. Firms can use tools like the LWMA to provide a model that can improve educational attainment of underserved youth by establishing skill-based certificates with universities coupled with a different employment-to-hire model. The results have shown that students accelerate in these types of programs and ultimately find more success in labor market assimilation. The data suggests that traditional degree programs that require full-time study at the university as the primary preparation for labor market employment may not be the most appropriate approach to solving the growing social inequality issue among youth.

Conclusion

This chapter has made the argument that Gen Y employees are "digital natives" that have the attributes to assist companies to transform their workforce to meet the accelerated change in the competitive landscape. Organizations today need to adapt their staff to operate under the auspices of responsive organizational dynamism by creating processes that can determine the strategic value of new emerging technologies and to establish a culture that is more "change ready." Executives and board members recognize that digital technologies are the most powerful variable to maintaining and expanding company markets.

Gen Y employees provide a natural fit for dealing with emerging digital technologies; however, success with integrating Gen Y employees is contingent upon baby boomer and Gen X management to adapt new leadership philosophies and procedures suited to meet the expectations and needs of Gen Y employees. Ignoring the unique needs of Gen Y employees will likely result in an incongruent organization that suffers high turnover of young employees who will ultimately seek a more entrepreneurial environment. Firms should consider investing in nontraditional Gen Y youth from underserved and socially excluded populations as alternate sources of talent.

References

Bakanauskiené, I., Bendaravicliené, R., Krikstolaitis, R., and Lydeka, Z. (2011). "Discovering an Employer Branding: Identifying Dimensions of Employers' Attractiveness in University." *Management of Organizations: Systematic Research*, vol. 59, pp. 7–22.

Capgemini Consulting (2013). "Being Digital: Engaging the Organization to Accelerate Digital Transformation" [White Paper]. Retrieved from http://www.capgemini-consulting.com/resource-file-access/resource/pdf/being_digital_engaging_the_organization_to_accelerate_digital_transformation.pdf

Cisco (2012). "Creating an Office from an Easy Chair" [White Paper]. Retrieved from http://www.cisco.com/c/en/us/solutions/collateral/enterprise/cisco-on-cisco/Trends_in_IT_Gen_Y_Flexible_Collaborative_Workspace.pdf

De Jong, G. (2014). "Financial Inclusion of Youth in the Southern Provinces of Santander: Setting Up a Participatory Research in Columbia." In P.Wabike & J. van der Linden (eds.), *Education for Social Inclusion* (pp. 87–106). University of Groningen. Groningen, Netherlands.

Dewey, J. (1933). *How We Think*. Boston, MA: D C Heath and Co.

Dolado, J (ed.) 2015. *No Country for Young People? Youth Labour Market Problems in Europe*, VoxEU.org eBook. London: CEPR Press.

Eisenhardt, K. M., and Bourgeois, L. J. (1988). "Politics of Strategic Decision Making in High-velocity Environments: Toward a Midrange Theory."*Academy of Management Journal*, 31(4), 737–770.

Ernst & Young (2012). "The Digitization of Everything: How Organisations Must Adapt to Changing Consumer Behaviour" [White Paper]. Retrieved from http://www.ey.com/Publication/vwLUAssets/The_digitisation_of_everything_-_How_organisations_must_adapt_to_changing_consumer_behaviour/$FILE/EY_Digitisation_of_everything.pdf

Friedman, V. J., Razer, M., Tsafrir, H., and Zorda, O.2014. "An Action Science Approach to Creating Inclusive Teacher-Parent Relationships." In P.Wabike and J. van der Linden (eds.), *Education for Social Inclusion* (pp. 25–51). University of Groningen. Groningen, Netherlands.

Knefelkamp, L. L. (1999). In William G.Perry (Ed.), *Forms of Ethical and Intellectual Development in the College Years: A Scheme*. San Francisco: Jossey-Bass.

Johnson Controls (2010) "Generation Y and the Workplace: Annual Report 2010 [White Paper]. Retrieved from http://www.johnsoncontrols.com/content/dam/WWW/jci/be/global_workplace_innovation/oxygenz/Oxygenz_Report_-_2010.pdf

Jonas and Kortenius (2014). "Beyond a Paycheck: Employment as an Act of Consumption for Gen Y Talents (Master's Thesis). Retrieved from http://lup.lub.lu.se/luur/download?func=downloadFile&recordOId=4456566&fileOId=4456569

Langer, A. M. (2002). "Reflecting on Practice: Using Learning Journals in Higher and Continuing Education. *International Journal of Teaching in Higher Education* 7(3): 337–351.

Langer, A. M. (2003). "Forms of Workplace Literacy Using Reflection-with-Action Methods: A Scheme for Inner-City Adults." *Journal of Reflective Practice* 3(4): 317–333.

Langer, A. M. (2009). "Measuring Self-Esteem through Reflective Writing: Essential Factors in Workforce Development." *Journal of Reflective Practice* 9(10): 45–48.

Langer, A. M. (2011). *Information Technology and Organizational Learning: Managing Behavioral Change through Technology and Education*. Boca Raton, FL: CRC Press, Inc..

Langer, A. M. and Yorks, L. (2013). *Strategic IT: Best Practices for Managers and Executives*. Hoboken, NJ: John Wiley & Sons, Inc.

Langer, A. M. (2013). "Employing Young Talent from Underserved Populations: Designing a Flexible Organizational Process for Assimilation and Productivity." *Journal of Organization Design* 2(1): 11–26.

Newman, KS. (1999). *No Shame in My Game: The Working Poor in the Inner City*. New York: Vintage Books.

Porter, M. E., and Kramer, M. R. (2011). "Creating Shared Value." *Harvard Business Review* 890(1/2): 62–77.

Rassool, N. (1999). *Literacy for Sustainable Development in the Age of Information* (Vol. 14). Clevedon, UK: Multilingual Matters Limited.

Saxena, P., and Jain, R. (2012) "Managing Career Aspirations of Generation Y at Work Place." *International Journal of Advanced Research in Computer Science and Software Engineering* 2(7).

Schön, D.1983. *The Reflective Practitioner*. New York: Basic Books.

Swadzba, U. (2010). "Work or Consumption—Indicators of One´s Place in the Society." In *Beyond Globalisation: Exploring the Limits of Globalisation in the Regional Context* (conference preceedings). Ostrava: University of Astrava Czech Republic, pp. 123–129.

Tushman, M. L. and Anderson, P. (1997). *Managing Strategic Innovation and Change*. New York, NY: Oxford University Press.

Wabike P. (2014). University-Community Engagement: Universities at a Crossroad? In

Wabike, P. and van der Linden, J. (eds.), *Education for Social Inclusion* (pp. 131–149). University of Groningen. Groningen, *Netherlands*.

CHAPTER 10

Creating a Cyber Security Culture

Introduction

Most boards of directors now recognize the importance of dealing with cyber threats. Unfortunately, too many organizations are still focused on the technical ramifications of how to avoid being compromised. While the technical issues are certainly paramount in protecting an organization's data and processes, few have invested in how executive management can create an organization that is cyber ready. This chapter explores the important issues that executives must address on how to design an organization-wide strategy that deals with cyber attacks, especially ones that could devastate the reputation and revenues of any business. So the response to the cyber dilemma is not limited to inventing technical solutions, but rather establishing behavior patterns that use organizational learning approaches to transforming culture.

History

History shows us that there has been an interesting evolution of the types of attacks we have experienced as technology has advanced in capability. Prior to 1990, few organizations were concerned with information security except for the government, military, banks, and credit card companies, to name a few. In 1994, with the birth of the commercial Internet, a higher volume of attacks occurred and in 2001 the first nation-state–sponsored attacks emerged. These attacks resulted in 1997 with the development of commercial firewalls and malware. By 2013, however, the increase in attacks reached greater complexity with the Target credit card breach, Home Depot's compromise of its payment system, and JP Morgan's exposure that affected 76 million customers and 7 million businesses. These events resulted in an escalation of fear, particularly in the areas of sabotage, theft of intellectual property, and stealing of money. Figure 10.1 shows the changing pace of cyber security

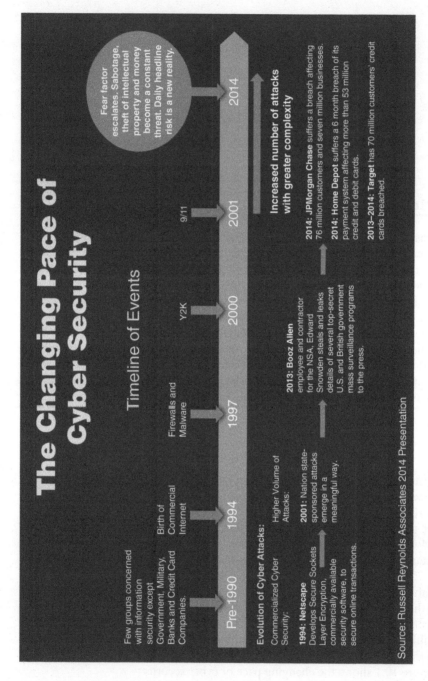

Figure 10.1   The changing pace of cyber security.

We agree with the conventional wisdom among cyber experts that no business can ever be compromise-proof from attacks. Technology leaders therefore need to realize that there must be: (1) Other ways beyond just developing new anti-software to ward off attacks, and (2) the need to develop internal and external strategies to deal with an attack when it occurs. These challenges in cyber security management can be put into three fundamental buckets:

- Learning how to educate and present to the board of directors
- Creating new and evolving security cultures
- Understanding what it means organizationally to be compromised

Each of these management tasks is summarized next.

Presenting to the Board

Board members need to understand the possible cyber attack exposures and what it means to the business. This requires some regular communications from those executives responsible for protecting the organization. Experienced security executives need to present the positive processes that are in place without overstating too much confidence since any firm can be compromised. On the other hand, technology executives should not scare the board either, as this will only create a lack of confidence in the organization's management. Most important is to always relate security to business objectives and above all avoid "tech" terms. Another important area of discussion is how third party vendors are being managed. Indeed, so many breaches have been caused by a lack of oversight of legacy applications that are controlled by third-party vendors. Finally, managers should always compare the state of security with that of the company's top competitors.

Designing a Cyber Security Culture

We know and much has been written that many cyber attacks often emanate from careless behaviors of staff. The first objective for managers is to present employees with best practices on how to avoid being compromised and the role they must play to maximize the data and systems they operate. While best practice documents are useful, they are not substitutes for having regular communication with staff. We recommend that these communications occur in the form of in-person meetings (or virtual meetings), so that staff can be updated on new threats and can engage in interactive conversations. However, mandating conformance is difficult and research has shown that transforming culture is best accomplished through ongoing relationship building, leadership that focuses on listening to staff, and the forming of task groups that can help form new cultures. Individual leadership remains the most important variable when transforming the behaviors and practices of any business.

Dealing with Compromise

Every firm should have a plan of what to do when breach occurs. The most important step in this process is to have short- and long-term goals for the organization. Ultimately, goals are the best plan to attaining a "risk" culture. The goals must deal with reality. For example, it is not realistic to achieve 100% protection; the reality is that the firm cannot maximize protection of all parts equally. So some entities may need more protection from cyber attacks than others. Without question, the business needs to maximize the protection of key company scientific and technical data first. The next level should address the control of network access with a priority on the level of exposure. Another area that needs to be addressed is oversight of all contractors and suppliers. It is especially important to keep tabs on these third parties (e.g., if they are merged/sold, disrupted in service, or even breached indirectly). Technology executives should especially pay close attention to Cloud computing organizations given these entities are typically storing vital company data and customer contact information.

Cyber Security and Responsive Organizational Dynamism

The new events and interactions brought about by cyber security threats can be related to the Langer's theory on technology dynamism. Recall that technology dynamism is also the basis of responsive organizational dynamism (ROD) discussed earlier in this book. Langer extends technology dynamism to address cyber security, which he labels "cyber dynamism."

Managing cyber dynamism is another way of managing the negative effects of cyber threats. As in ROD, *cyber* strategic integration and *cyber* cultural assimilation remain as distinct categories that present themselves in response to cyber dynamism. Figure 10.2 shows the components of *cyber* ROD:

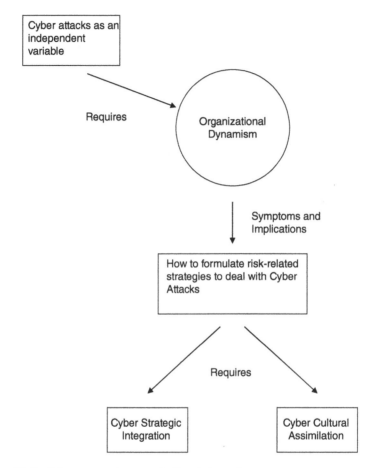

Figure 10.2   Cyber responsive organizational dynamism.
Source: Langer (2011).

Cyber Strategic Integration

Cyber strategic integration is a modified process that firms need to use to address the business impact of cyber attacks on its organizational processes. Complications posed by cyber dynamism via the process of strategic integration occurs when several new cyber attacks overlap and create a myriad of problems in various phases of an organization's ability to operate. Cyber attacks can also affect business confidence, which in turn limits the firm's ability to attract new customers. A compromise from a cyber attack can also result in reduction in productivity, which is difficult to identify. Therefore, it is important that organizations find ways to develop strategies to deal with cyber threats that answer the following questions:

1. How can we reduce occurrences by instituting aggressive organization structures that identify possible system weaknesses?
2. What new threats exist which may require ongoing research and/or collaborations with third party vendors?
3. What steps might be needed to combat new cyber threats?
4. What new systems architectures are needed that can maximize recovery from a breach?

In order to realize these objectives, technology executives must be able to:

- Create dynamic internal processes that can function on a daily basis to deal with new cyber attacks and understand their overall impact on all parts of the business.
- Monitor cyber risk investments and determine modifications to the current budget.
- Address the weaknesses in the organization in terms of how to deal with new threats should they occur and how to better protect key business functions.
- Provide a mechanism that enables the organization to deal with new cyber threats and integrates them into new procedures and behavioral patterns.
- Establish a system that integrates cyber risk accountability to other measurable parts of the organization.

The combination of evolving cyber threats with accelerated and changing consumer demands justifies the need for the strategic integration component of cyber ROD. Firms need to challenge their existing procedures by using strategic integration, or they risk losing market share due to a lack of consumer confidence. Experts agree that the danger of breaches from cyber attacks is very real and will continue, and firms must develop mechanisms that will force their business processes to be realigned to maximize protection of data and systems. The driving force behind this realignment emanates from cyber dynamisms, which serves as the principle threat across all operations.

Cyber Cultural Assimilation

Cyber cultural assimilation is a process that addresses the organizational aspects of how the security department is internally organized, its relationship with IT, and how it is integrated within the organization as a whole. As with technology dynamism, cyber dynamism is not limited only to cyber strategic issues, but *cultural* ones as well. A cyber culture is one that can respond to emerging cyber attacks in an optimally informed way, and one that understands the impact on business performance and reputation.

As one would expect, the acceleration of cyber attacks requires more dynamic management within and among departments, which cannot be accomplished through discrete communications between groups. Instead, the need for diverse groups to engage in more integrated discourse and to share varying levels of cyber security knowledge requires that new organizational structures be designed that address new social cultures.

In order to facilitate cyber cultural assimilation, organizations must have their staffs understand that cyber threats are part of daily life. The main objective is to design the best structure to support a broader assimilation of awareness about any given cyber threat; the next is about how that information can best be utilized by the organization to develop attack resilience. Technology leaders need to make sure that cyber staff is included in *all* decision-making processes. In other words, cyber assimilation must become fundamental to the day-to-day operation.

While many scholars and managers suggest the need for a separate entity responsible for cyber security governance, we feel such an approach creates fundamental problems. Specifically, central groups do not allow staff and managers to assimilate cyber security–driven change and understand how to design a culture that can operate under ROD. In other words, the issue of governance is misinterpreted as a problem of structural positioning or hierarchy when it is really one of cultural assimilation. As a result, many cyber security initiatives lean too much toward a prescriptive solution instead of the analytical approach to addressing the real problem. This does not suggest the need for a central department. A security team should be organized as a supporter—which aligns with Langer's driver/supporter theory.

Summary

This section has made the argument that organizations need to excel in providing both strategic and cultural initiatives to reduce exposure to cyber threats to avoid security breaches. Technology executives must extend their workforce to address the demands from accelerated threats brought on by cyber dynamisms. Organizations need to adapt their staff to operate under the auspices of cyber responsive organizational dynamism by creating processes that can determine the strategic exposure of new emerging cyber threats and to establish a culture that is more "defense ready." Most board members now recognize that cyber security has become one of the most powerful variables to maintaining and expanding company markets.

Organizational Learning and Cyber-Minded Application Development

Behavioral change leading to a more resilient cyber culture is just one of the challenges in maximizing protection in organizations. However, cyber culture does not cure cyber crime alone. Technology leaders need to redesign computer systems to be more resilient to protect against threats. We know that no system can be 100% protected. This challenge requires the need to use more analytics when designing applications and computer architectures. Indeed, security controls need to go beyond just limiting network access. How then do technology leaders participate in the process of designing secure applications through good design? We know that many cyber security architectures are designed from the office of the chief information security officer (CISO), a relatively new and emerging role in organizations. The CISO role, sometimes independent of the CIO (chief information officer) became significant as a result of the early threats from the Internet, the 9/11 attacks, and most recently the abundant number of system compromises experienced by companies such as JP Morgan Chase, SONY, Home Depot, and Target, to name just a few.

The challenge of cyber security must also address third-party vendor products that are part of most delivery systems. Third–party vendor design and compliance needs to be instituted and standards developed to ensure compliance. Further, firms need to do a complete review of the older and less resilient legacy applications that likely do not have adequate security software built into the architecture. In general, there is a need to design an enterprise-wide cyber security solution that connects all nodes of the system. Thus, cyber security architecture requires a re-evaluation of the firm's Software Development Life Cycle (SDLC) that includes strategic cyber security design, engineering, and operations integration.

Risk and Cyber Security

When designing against cyber security attacks, as stated earlier, there is no 100% protection assurance. Thus, risks must be factored into the decision-making process. A number of security experts often ask business executives the question, "How much security do you want, and what are you willing to spend to achieve that security?"

Certainly the recent compromises have increased investment in better security systems. This section provides guidance on how to determine appropriate security risks while these new investments are being made in the next generation of software and network systems.

Security risk is typically discussed in the form of threats. Threats can be categorized as presented by Schoenfield (2015):

1. **Threat agent:** Where is the threat coming from and who is making the attack?
2. **Threat goals:** What does the agent hope to gain
3. **Threat capability:** What threat methodology is the agent possibly going to use?
4. **Threat work factor:** How much effort is the agent willing to put in to get into the system?
5. **Threat risk tolerance:** What legal chances is the agent willing to take to achieve their goals?

Table 10.1 is shown as a guideline.

Table 10.1   Threat analysis.

Threat agent	Goals	Risk tolerance	Work factor	Methods
Cyber criminals	Financial	Low	Low to medium	Known and proven

Source: Schoenfield, 2015.

The nature of the cyber threat, its associated risks to disrupt operations, and the potential loss of data are primary factors that must provide important input to the security design especially at the application level. These application securities must address the following:

1. The user interface (sign in screen, access to specific parts of the application).
2. Command-line interface (interactivity) in on-line systems.
3. Inter-application communications, that is, how data and password information are passed and stored among applications across systems.

Risk Responsibility

Schoenfield (2015) suggests that someone in the organization is assigned the role of the "risk owner." There may be many risk owners, and as a result this role could have complex effects on the way systems are designed. For example, the top risk owner in most organizations today is associated with the CISO. However, many firms also employ a chief risk officer (CRO). This role's responsibilities tend to vary across industries.

Risk analysis at the application design level requires special governance. Application security risk is not trivial; it needs involvement from both the business and the consumer and must be integrated within the risk standards of the firm. For example, multiple layers of security often require users to re-enter secure information. Although this may maximize security, it can negatively impact the user experience and the robustness of the system interface in general. Performance can obviously also be sacrificed given the multiple layers of validation. There is no quick answer to this dilemma other than the reality that more security checkpoints will reduce user and consumer satisfaction unless cyber security algorithms become more invisible and sophisticated. However, even this approach would likely reduce protection. As with all analysts design challenges, the IT team, business users, and now the consumer must all be part of the decisions on how much security is required.

As my colleague at Columbia University, Steven Bellovin, states in his book, *Thinking Security*, security is about a mindset. This mindset to me relates to how we establish security cultures that can enable the analyst to define organizational security as it relates to new and existing systems. If we get the business leaders engaged in setting security goals in our applications, some key questions according to Bellovin (2015) must be answered:

1. What are the economics to protect systems?
2. What is the best protection you can get for the amount of money you want to spend?
3. Can you save more lives by spending that money?
4. What should you protect?
5. Can you estimate what it will take to protect your assets?
6. Should you protect the network or the host?
7. Is your Cloud secure enough?
8. Do you guess at the likelihood and cost of a penetration?
9. How do you evaluate your assets?
10. Are you thinking like the enemy?

The key to successful design in cyber security is recognizing that it will remain dynamic; the attackers are adaptive and somewhat unpredictable. This dynamism requires constant architectural change accompanied with increased complexity of how systems become compromised. Thus, analysts must be involved at the conceptual model, which includes business definitions, business processes, and enterprise standards. However, the analysts must also be engaged with the logical design, which comprises two sub-models:

1. **Logical architecture:** Depicts the relationships of different data domains and functionalities required to manage each type of information in the system.

2. **Component model:** Reflects each of the sub-models and applications that provide various functions in the system. The component model may also include third-party vendor products that interface with the system. The component model coincides in many ways with the process of decomposition.

In summary, the ROD interface with cyber security is more complex than many executives understand. Security is relative, not absolute, and technology leaders, in particular, must be closely aligned with how internal cultures must evolve with the changes in environments.

Cyber and Driver/Supporter Theory

Historically, security has been viewed as a supporter function in most organizations, particularly when it is managed by IT. However, the recent developments in cyber threats suggest, as with other aspects of technology, that security too has a driver role.

To excel in the role of security driver, leaders must:

- Have capabilities, budgets, and staffing levels using benchmarks.
- Align even closer with users and business partners.
- Have close relationships with third parties.
- Extend responsibilities to include the growing challenges in the mobile workforce.
- Manage virtualized environments and third-party ecosystems.
- Find and/or develop cyber security talent and human capital.
- Have a strategy to integrate millennials with baby boomer and Gen X managers.

References

Bellovin. S. M. (2015). *Thinking security: Stopping Next Year's Hackers*. Boston: Addison-Wesley.

Schoenfield, B.S.E. (2015). *Securing Systems: Applied Security Architecture and Threat Models*. Boca Raton, FL: CRC Press.

CHAPTER 11

The Non-IT CIO
of the Future

This chapter attempts to foresee the future of the chief information officer (CIO) position. We have presented in previous chapters the responsibilities challenging CIOs today, and using future trends we forecast some of the short- and long-term opportunities of the CIO. We see the position migrating toward more of a chief of automation's being functionally responsible for contracts, equipment management, general automation, and outsourcing while having a central role in conversations strategically leveraging emerging new technologies. We believe that the term "CIO" needs to be reinvented with less focus on the information technology (IT) side and much more emphasis on automation and innovations that will continue to drive new business opportunities while lowering costs.

The first aspect of attempting to forecast the CIOs of the future is to avoid trying to predict their new title, but rather to explore more the roles and responsibilities that these executives will need to manage. To be consistent with our research findings, we start with Langer's driver-support theory, which addresses much of the future needs of the position.

Driver-Side Responsibilities—New Automation

CIOs of the future will need to spend much of their time with the business, helping to develop strategic advantages through applications of automation and digital strategy. Note that we use the term "automation" as opposed to "IT" or even "technology." We think this is a critical shift in responsibilities. Indeed, not all automation implies information-based solutions. Automation needs are inclusive of equipment, media, engineering, and biotechnology, to name just a few. All of these automations need to be seamlessly integrated and managed through central sources to really provide effective cost savings as well as maximum strategic value. As we advocated in Chapter 1, ultimately the

CIO of the future will need to lead all kinds of business transformations in the organization. Indeed, no transformation can be accomplished without the uses of modern automation considerations.

Some of these transformations we foresee include:

- Sales and marketing
- Compliance
- Shared services
- Equipment and infrastructure
- Virtual offices and communications
- Talent management services
- Strategic information
- New innovations (disruptive technologies)
- Security and intelligence
- Business process integration
- Mobility

Each of these strategic automations will be expanded in this chapter.

Sales and Marketing

Technology continues to be a driving force on new ways of reaching customers and consumers. Salesforce, for example, has had major impacts on how salespeople penetrate new and old markets. Technology will continue to provide new techniques. The impacts of how to use automation applications such as Facebook have established new ways of how organizations build relationships with its buyers and sellers.

Because more and more customer information is now digital, having marketing information available is far more critical. Indeed, consumers are using the Internet and social media for commerce, and we see future activities to be continually being driven by automation capacities. The fascinating unknown is the extent of future need for traditional sales and marketing personnel. We believe technology will place tomorrow's automation executives at the forefront of driving sales revenues in many organizations. Simply put, markets have become too large for direct methods of penetration. The use of analytics and cloud technologies will dramatically change this. Recalling our interview with Passerini, IT was instrumental in creating an advanced approach to doing focus groups, and at lower cost.

So, will today's CIOs become tomorrow's chief marketing officers? Will technology inevitably drive sales? If so, we believe that both chief positions may indeed gravitate to a new "automation officer." Gartner previously predicted that by 2017 marketing officers would spend more on technology than the CIO. We have seen some evidence that this is true with the exponential growth of digital technologies that now is at the core of marketing through social media and mobile applications. However, with these two skills becoming more important for the customer advantage, we believe that it will likely be easier for the CIO to learn more about marketing needs than vice versa.

Results released by an IDG Research Services survey in 2010 showed that CIOs are already transitioning toward important support for sales and marketing—particularly with respect to "customer interaction." The survey showed that over two-thirds of CIOs stated a need to overhaul sales systems and processes and another 54% felt there was a need for better business intelligence. This trend continues to accelerate as we see more and more need for technology-savvy business executives. Again, the CIO is the logical person to seize the opportunity.

Compliance

We expect compliance, especially for regulatory bodies, to continue to increase as the power of technology touches more critical parts of consumer life. The costs to meet compliance requirements are significant and creating methods to reduce these costs while meeting the requirements is key for every business. This is particularly critical for public firms that must comply with Sarbanes-Oxley and Regulation Fair Disclosure (known as Reg FD). Furthermore, firms are pressed to preserve antidiscrimination compliance—all becoming increasingly more difficult with the way in which employees communicate across discoverable channels. In many ways, it appears that today's CIOs may need to handle the role of an "interrogator" in addition to their regular responsibilities. Yet we know that automation of communication has salient exposures—it drives corporate legal attorneys crazy with the apparent number of violations that occur in business every day.

In 2011, Michael Schrage wrote a blog in the *Harvard Business Review* titled, "Should CIOs Be Compliance Cops?" He states that there is a growing need to police employee compliance that may "offer an important opportunity for the CIO and IT to powerfully influence personnel and privacy policies at the firm." Schrage believes that CIOs should be wary of just becoming the "Big Brother," watching and policing activities; rather, they can take the opportunity to drive conversations of how to implement procedures and policies that can guide compliance instead.

Compliance requirements are not just limited to the United States. There are stringent European Union (EU) rules today that forbid firms from taking user data without first getting permission. Indeed, the EU plans to implement its new data laws effective May 2018, which will require CIOs to play a major role in compliance. To date, there are well over 100 federal and state regulations that are designed to protect the confidentiality, integrity, and availability of electronic data.[1] These regulations do not include yet another layer of rules that typically restrict industry-specific uses of information technology. Due to the significant data breaches, we only see further regulations globally. While the Chief Information Security Officer (CISO) role has emerged, we expect it to inevitably report to the CIO.

Intellectual property (IP) violations are yet another area of compliance that needs close focus from technology executives. The automation, in agreement with legal counsel, is becoming a major area of legal exposure. From a legal standpoint, CIOs need to prepare for the "growing need for standards and benchmarks by which automated search tools can be measured to show their reasonableness and defensibility when used in a legal context."[2] Therefore, technology leaders will need to take efforts along these lines and accelerate integration to protect IP and other legal exposures, both nationally and internationally. This can be accomplished only with advanced automation techniques that can uncover potential legal exposures.

Shared Services

Shared services are a growth area of responsibility for CIOs interested in expanding their responsibilities. Shared services are designed to allocate resources to one "shared department," rather than separate entities, each having their own dedicated resources. Given the opportunity to centralize and share resources, potential automations can also provide cost reductions simply because firms need less people. The challenge, of course, with shared services is to avoid the pitfalls of creating a bureaucracy and to provide quality services that meet local department needs.

Cloud computing is an example of an automation of shared services that resides within the domain of the CIO. It is likely that the continued advancements in cloud-type technologies will only expand the need for more shared service applications. Businesses are aware of this opportunity, and CIOs have an opportunity to be part of extending this service offering to the organization while expanding their domain of responsibilities. This is an important area of expansion because of the ultimate complexity of the Cloud and the predictable new innovations that will make it more robust. Some professionals have even labeled shared services as "hybrid IT."

It would be tunnel vision for future automation executives to think of shared services only as a new way of providing IT services at a reduced cost. Indeed, the overall mission to provide shared services is to cut costs. But strategic leaders see a lot more. The benefits of shared services should also provide opportunities for organizations to better share information across their own network of businesses, particularly in human resources (HR) and finance. This means that common practices and benefits learned from shared services will improve collaboration across departments and functions. Another way of stating this benefit is that shared services can provide a communication channel that improves collaboration. Improved collaboration can then increase productivity. Furthermore, shared services allow for more standardization of processes and services, especially for the internal users of the system. Standardization can also lay the foundation for better innovations, with continued improvements that can respond to ROD-based disruptions. Today, 90% of the top 1,000 companies have used some type of shared services model.

So evolving CIOs should be seeking opportunities to expand what is traditional IT shared services to a blend of corresponding functions—all of which will benefit from levels of automation. Technology executives of the future will treat shared services as an activity that continues to evolve and react to market needs as opposed to just an activity that supports a central service.

Equipment and Infrastructure

Obviously, CIOs are heavily involved in automation of technology infrastructure. Indeed, IT typically represents the largest part of a firm's capital expenditures. A number of CIOs have responsibilities for other equipment such as copy machines. Furthermore, some CIOs are now responsible for office space and other infrastructure facilities.

Overall, we see that technology executives will be responsible for integrating all machinery requirements and space allocations. This will likely be accomplished via sophisticated central portal systems that have the ability to dynamically improve the efficiency and return on investment (ROI) of products and services. These centralized systems will be able to access multiple points along a highway of networked locations around the world—it will be an "automation central." Using open and modular systems, technology executives will be able to:

- Centralize data management.
- Cross-reference systems.
- Do dynamic diagnostics on applications.
- Scale systems to meet peak demands.
- Simulate possibilities and predetermine how systems will perform.
- Provide better security and safety.

From a CIO perspective, the listed items fall under a larger category called infrastructure management (IM). IM typically includes systems management, network management, and storage management:

- **Systems management:** This is a look at the enterprise level of the organization and includes understanding the entire needs of the firm and providing for the purchasing of various equipment, software, and maintenance. Maintenance covers support, service updates, setup of equipment, and coordination of delivery.
- **Network management:** This represents the connectivity of multiple layers and types of computer equipment through various types of physical devices. Networks have traditionally been limited to applications support, but we see this area expanding into different types of requirements especially for security, data, video, and wireless devices. All of these new networks must have the necessary operating policies and procedures to be managed centrally but with a distributed architecture.
- **Storage management:** This is one of the significant challenges faced by organizations today. Storage management entails the overall ability to store and secure various forms of data and information. The storage of data is complex, especially as it relates to the kind of access needed and by whom. Storage also involves other than stored data files such as compressed music files or voice messages.

The necessity for technology executives to manage this growing area requires remote and sophisticated software that will ultimately reduce costs, protect information, and work to better integrate the wide variance of types of equipment in an enterprise.

Virtual Offices and Communications

The growth of virtual offices has been significant over the past 10 years and will likely continue to grow exponentially with the continual pressures to be global. Addressing virtual office challenges typically uncovers the need for improving communications among the offices themselves, especially across different countries and cultures.

IT has been the main driver of the growth of virtual teams simply because it makes it possible. It is IT that has vastly improved the development of competitive outsourcing abroad in such countries as India, China, Brazil, Ireland, and many others. These countries are not only physically remote, but they also present barriers of culture and language. These barriers often impede communications about project status and affect the likelihood of delivering a project timely and within forecasted budgets.

Despite these major challenges, outsourcing remains attractive due to the associated cost savings and talent supply. These two advantages are closely associated, and without a CIO's leadership it is difficult to maintain. Ultimately, because of technology, organizations need to continue to learn how to manage themselves using virtual technology, which is still an immature process in most firms.

Remote communications depends on the effective use of what we call "virtual teams." Virtual teams can be made up of workers anywhere, even those in the United States who are working from a distance rather than reporting to an office for work. A growing number of employees in the United States want more personal flexibility; in response, many companies are allowing employees to work from home more often—and have found the experience most productive. This type of virtual team management generally follows a hybrid model, with employees working at home most of the time but reporting to the office for critical meetings, an arrangement that dramatically helps with communication and allows management to have quality check points. However, working from home is impossible without the necessary technology to support important interactions as well as validation of work being performed.

However, the general consensus tells us that virtual teams render results. According to Bazarova and Walther, "virtual groups whose members communicate primarily or entirely via e-mail, computer conferencing, chat, or voice—has become a common feature of twenty-first century organizations."[3] Most important, we feel that the growing use of virtual teams will ultimately facilitate the complete integration of IT and non-IT workers—something that successful CIOs certainly advocate must happen for their long-term success.

Talent Management Services

Competing for the best talent is a critical objective for HR organizations. A number of firms have plans to overhaul their manual or existing systems in favor of more robust automated systems to access and track opportunities to find the best people. HR is now challenged to reinvent itself using predictive analytics to find the best people. Furthermore, many firms have established a talent acquisition role that focuses on new ways to solve the employment shortfalls. We also now see the need for nontraditional global workers that may be representing the next generation of workforce—now being coined the "GIG" worker. In our first edition we noted that Watson Wyatt, a consulting firm servicing the insurance and financial sectors, provided a survey in 2009 that found that 56% of the companies were planning to upgrade their systems to better technologies. These new systems will employ more advanced capabilities for integration of compensation, recruiting, performance management, learning management, career planning, and succession planning.[4] The Wyatt study also found that over 50% of companies still used manual solutions for a number of talent management activities, such as succession planning (53%), career development (48%), and workforce planning (55%). These surveys showed that many firms were unprepared for the impact of digital disruption.

So talent management automation is yet another strategic imperative for the support of future business growth, especially as it relates to performance efficiency. The question, of course, is why haven't HR executives implemented many of these performance improvements and why are many of them still doing it manually? The challenge stems from the historical inability for HR executives to gain support from the top. Next to the CIO, HR executives have similar challenges in that they are inevitably at the low end of the food chain for investments—HR is a supporter, and thus will always be evaluated on economies of scale and efficiency. In addition, HR has been unsuccessful in making a footprint as a strategic driver. We see HR functions becoming more of a compliance organization than a human development one. As a result, we believe that the technology executives of the future can provide more value given the need to automate and integrate talent management products throughout the enterprise. This is especially true given the widespread expansion of international personnel—pressuring firms to come up with products and services that inform employees and make them more aware and knowledgeable about the firms in which they work.

Another growing challenge for firms is the shortfalls in talent for skilled workers. As economies rebound there will be even more pressure to find and develop the right talent. This is further complicated by the growing number of skilled labor workers that will be retiring without a formidable inventory of younger workers to replace them. Indeed, the cost of replacing employees can be astronomical.

The talent dilemma is consistent with Prahalad's theory of $N = 1$ and $R = G$. Given global expansion of the workforce, the need for "on-demand" resources ($R = G$) requires more integrated automation for finding and maintaining an effective and agile workforce. This workforce is not necessarily limited to employees. $R = G$ does not specify employment resources, just resources. This means that firms will have integrated resources that include independent contractors, employees, and outside firms. It is difficult to imagine all of these requirements being solely handled by HR.

Finally, the advent of these expanded and dynamic HR talent responsibilities also feeds the need for robust reporting. These reports might include performance distribution, adherence to budgets, and exceptions. Such reporting will likely need to contain graphic displays, summary statistics, and detailed compensation data. The products must also allow for analytic capabilities to provide HR staff, managers, and executives with strategic reporting on demand.

Strategic Information

Strategic information is what we call the future of knowledge sharing in such a way that it provides strategic direction to firms. Today's popular term is "data analytics," or the ability to analyze data and provide strategic information for executives and managers. Among the CIO profession the term "Big Data" has emerged as the key to providing business with the strategic data they need to compete. To some extent strategic information falls under the theoretical study of knowledge management. In any case, the ability to provide strategic knowledge from both internal and external sources is invaluable for today's and tomorrow's firms. The impact of strategic knowledge can improve access to learning resources, improve decision making, and establish better communication channels in general. Our interviews with successful CIOs confirmed the current importance of analytics and Big Data. However, our future predictions are that data information is only one portion of the needs of tomorrow's businesses.

Our strategic information comprises the following components:

- Data analytics and Big Data
- Knowledge management
- Restructured work processes

Data Analytics and Big Data

As stated earlier, data analytics is perhaps the most relevant area of strategic information flow, particularly at the board of directors. Data analytics is a criterion for examining data with the focus of determining conclusions using scientific evaluation. Data analytics uses deductive methods to derive conclusions based on what is known in the data, as opposed to data mining, which is the process of determining what the data mean. Another aspect of analytics study is "predictive" analytics, which is really a part of the data mining camp. It focuses on predicting probabilities and trends based on analysis of the data. Big Data, on the other hand, looks at very large sets of data (data sets)—so large that the complexity of processing is a challenge and beyond the typical capacities of relational database technologies.

Knowledge Management

Because evaluating emerging technologies requires the ability to look into the future, it also requires tomorrow's technology executives to translate valuable tacit knowledge and to see creatively how these opportunities would be judged if implemented. Tacit knowledge is defined as the processes and procedures that are not documented in an organization, that is, the knowledge exists in individual minds. Examples of applicable tacit knowledge in this process are extracted from Kulkki and Kosonen:

- Cultural and social history
- Problem-solving modes
- Orientation to risks and uncertainties
- Worldview organizing principles
- Horizons of expectations[5]

So the challenge to organizations is to uncover how to transfer this "tacit" knowledge into "explicit" documented knowledge. Indeed, as Teece states: "Information transfer is not knowledge transfer and information management is not knowledge management, although the former can assist the latter. Individuals and organizations can suffer from information overload."[6] While this is a significant issue for many firms, the ability to have an organization that can select, interpret, and integrate information is a very valuable part of future knowledge management. This is why knowledge management is so important. Knowledge must be built on its own terms—which requires intensive and laborious interactions among members of the organization. CIOs are the logical choice to carry out this challenge.

Restructured Work Process

Restructuring the work process entails reduction of costs while increasing service levels. Typically, these improvements are results of reengineering efforts with the aid of automation. Indeed, restructuring projects, supported by advanced technologies, have proven to be an effective tool for sustaining business competencies and improved efficiency.

We know that restructuring takes time and resources. IT has the most experience of any organization in the design and development of new systems, which often require reengineering exercises with the business. Business analysts have been making a living by working with business units and developing alternative ways to gain efficiency and cost reduction through automation. Automation represents the most obvious way to achieve such improvements. Therefore, the process of reengineering and the need for restructuring simply match each other and suggest that IT be the driver of the effort. This represents a perfect opportunity for CIOs of the future.

New Innovations

Often, new innovations have been coined "disruptive" in that they establish new markets and networks. Thus, it disrupts existing markets and forces new evolutions of S-curves. Disruptive innovations are often "technology dynamisms" that require organizations to use "responsive organizational dynamism."[7] Technology dynamism has shown that it can change industries overnight and likely will continue to do so.

To us, the technology executives of the future will be the most influential people in the C-suite—if, of course, they adhere to the best practices that we offered earlier, in Chapter 6. Another important area relates to the work of Henry Chesbrough,[8] who pioneered the concept of "open innovation." Chesbrough presents a model that suggests that success with new innovations is heavily predicated on staying away from closed systems, like owning intellectual property, having the best people, and trying to invent everything inside your company.[9] He provides case after case showing that firms like Xerox failed to maintain their market leadership because they did not partner with outside firms and create an open framework to compete. Simply put, open innovation allows companies to be more agile and creative. It is also consistent with $N = 1$ and $R = G$—using resources from strategic alliances to ultimately place firms in an ongoing and evolutionary state. Gartner has continually recommended that CIOs establish formal operations to evaluate new technologies by setting up teams which are afforded the proper time to do the research they need to support the continual evolution of innovation opportunities. Much of these innovations, as stated in Chapter 1, will be driven by consumer demand. The following are Gartner's top 10 most disruptive technologies:

1. Multicore and hybrid processors
2. Virtualization and fabric computing
3. Social networks and social software
4. Cloud computing and cloud/Web platforms
5. Web mashups (Web applications with multiple data sources)
6. User interface
7. Ubiquitous computing (multiple devices and applications)
8. Contextual computing (location awareness)
9. Augmented reality (computer-enhanced real world)
10. Semantics (natural language and data mining)

This list provides examples of very advanced technologies that can have huge effects on competitive advantage—the challenge is how to bring such disruptions to the forefront of the business process. Who else but a well-prepared CIO could handle this complexity?

Security and Intelligence

The advent of the Internet, social media, and terrorism has dramatically changed the importance of security as it relates to the CIO function. Most of these security issues start with technological advances that allow individuals and groups to do things that can cause irreparable harm to organizations. These "harms" take on many complexities that start with the protection of data as well as the ways information is communicated to the consumer population. As with most security approaches, intelligence about risks is the first place to start—starting with intelligence helps determine security risks and allows organizations to put plans in place to avoid problems. Indeed, one of the regular agenda items with CIOs at board meetings is protection and security.

So, without question, security is a main concern for current CIOs. The typical issues relate to protecting the network and data files. Breaches against any of these can have great impacts on productivity as well as profitability and, most important, a firm's overall image. *CIO Insight's* magazine issued a report in 2012 "10 Security Concerns You'll Lose Sleep Over in 2011" that included the following:

1. **Viruses and spyware:** The ongoing challenge of preventing malicious hackers from attacking systems and data.
2. **E-mail-borne threats:** This relates to those unsolicited e-mails that work their way into firm systems and cause havoc.
3. **Spam:** Often, users think that spam is just a nuisance, but it too can have damaging threats. Most guidelines suggest that spam mail should be deleted by users immediately.
4. **Social threats:** Facebook and Twitter continue to lead the way and require internal policies of what information can be used on corporate machines.
5. **Smartphone connectivity:** These phones (iPhones and Androids) are designed for entertainment as well as corporate use (e-mail, calendar, etc.). CIOs need to be concerned about security threats making their way through the entertainment components and into their network systems.
6. **Gone phishing (the act of obtaining user information):** These scams have been around for a long time, and employees need to be reminded regularly to ignore and delete these phishings.
7. **Dangerous browsing:** The debate continues regarding whether corporations should limit Web site browsing. Notwithstanding this controversy, CIOs need to advise employees of the dangers when browsing unethical and dangerous web sites.
8. **Employee trustworthiness:** CIOs need to watch the honesty of employees; guarding against their stealing sensitive data for personal gains has escalated as a problem in recent years.

9. **Apps, apps, apps:** Downloading unprotected and unauthorized applications, especially on smartphones, continues to be of high risk.
10. **Tablets:** Like smartphones, tablets with entertainment applications expose the same security risks.[10]

What is interesting about these top 10 issues is that they essentially remain the same seven years later. We have articulated throughout this book the movement toward consumerization, even within companies. Security tends to limit this ability and as a result will continue to be a debate among executives. Indeed, we spoke to CEOs who are beginning to believe that the days of complete security are coming to an end. Simply put, data seem to be traveling everywhere.

Furthermore, the 10 hot issues represent only a small portion of the security challenges to come. CIOs will need to step up to integrate other forms of security that logically relate to automations issues, from ID theft protection to security access across locations and production systems. Virtually every form of manufacturing will contain software of some type, which will need centralized methods of determining ongoing exposure, formulating acceptable risks, and dealing with inevitable compromising of systems. Advance security will rely on the intelligence systems around us, similar to those activities taken against terrorists by the government. There are also sophisticated technologies that will be developed that need constant evaluation, including recent concerns about cloud protections. Here, we see new approaches taken by chipmakers, firmware, architecture, and server platforms.

Business Process Integration

Business process integration (BPI) represents the ability to synchronize multiple systems in real time. The linking of systems includes internal operations as well as third-party vendors and business partners. BPI has traditionally included components such as electronic data interchange (EDI), message-oriented middleware (MoM), and enterprise application integration (EAI).

The Gartner Group stated that, "Businesses that connect the design of information and business process with technology will exceed average sector performance by at least 15%." Today, for digital transformation to work efficiently it must break down the barriers among businesses. In a global context, this is critical, and thus we feel that the CIO will continue to be the main implementer of such efforts. Ultimately, the framework needed for successful transformation is the integration of data. This integration requires specific activities that can address the problems with silos of automation that can exist throughout the enterprise.

These self-contained automations need to either be redone (unlikely) or bridged via reengineering to ensure that data flows among its related components of the system and that security is maximized. Some of these data, unfortunately, in many organizations are still in manual or limited automation configuration, posing major challenges to accomplishing a fully integrated solution. Another important aspect of integration is performance. It is one thing to have the architecture that allows data to be shared; it's another to accomplish this productively in a way that employees can see the difference between effort and outcome.

Automating the business process is only one major component of the challenge. Integration also requires analysis and design. This design includes "flowing dependencies," which relate to processes that feed data to other systems. Furthermore, there are also dependencies where the output from one business unit is shared by other departments. Finally, there are dependencies where the same data are accessed by multiple departments but used for different purposes; that is, what the information means to one business unit might mean something different to another. This all translates into having personnel with the appropriate expertise to do business process reengineering (BPR). This requires a life cycle of understanding business needs, analyzing them for common architecture, and then propagating a design that caters to the organization as a whole. IT has been practicing BPR for decades and is best positioned to take on this challenge. Thus, the CIO of the future needs to expand his or her horizon and expand the IT reengineering methodology to include more expanded applications of automation and manual processes.

Ultimately, the need for reengineering through digital transformation requires the establishment of standards of operation and compliance—both of which are essential to create effective and efficient enterprise solutions that integrate together. Standards also feed the needs toward the goal of operational efficiency while maintaining quality and support. Standards also allows for the creation of process measures, which are required to properly analyze optimization versus quality.

Quality also heavily depends on a development methodology. BPI and the IT system development life cycle (SDLC) have remarkable similarities. BPI uses a five-stage process: Analyze, identify, simulate, validate, and deploy. The IT SDLC matches are analysis, design, prototype, test, and go live. We know that restructuring takes time and resources. IT has the most experience simply because it already has the core skills sets to expand BPI operations. Systems analysts make a living by working with operating units to determine how best to use automation to improve performance of their departments while reducing labor costs.

The process of reengineering and restructuring simply matches the future challenges of redistribution of labor across global markets. Looking at this process, it seems favorable for today's CIO to very well be ready for tomorrow's challenges of BPI.

Mobility

Perhaps mobility is still the largest challenge for firms today, not to mention the future. The dilemma is how to support the consumerization of technology through smartphones and tablets, yet at the same time protect firms from the problems they create. The most salient supporter of mobility has been the advent of cloud technology. Indeed, cloud automation has allowed for the access of applications, data, and videos from anywhere on a mobile device. The continual acceleration of change across mobile units will be staggering—hat is, the S-curve of mobility may have shorter and shorter life cycles. This all means that decisions and strategies regarding mobility will need to be rethought almost on a regular basis.

Indeed, the risks associated with mobile technologies opens up major potential threats to firms. A Veracode blog recently issued a number of vulnerabilities:

- **Sensitive data leakage:** Disclosing user location and personal information resident on the mobile device.
- **Unsafe sensitive data storage:** This includes passwords and other key information that needs to be encrypted.
- **Unsafe sensitive data transmission:** Mobile devices are accessible to eavesdroppers during user communications.
- **Hardcoded password/keys:** This information can be unencrypted by certain applications.

What is interesting about mobile threats is the dilemma of control versus freedom. We have articulated throughout this book the movement toward consumerization of technology. Security tends to limit this ability and, as a result, will continue to be a debate inside many firms. Indeed, we spoke recently to a CEO who now believes that the days of security may be coming to an end. Data seem to travel everywhere!

Organizations need to now accept that mobility has penetrated much faster than the Internet. Gartner had predicted that mobile phones would overtake PCs as the most common Web access device and that over three billion of the world's adult population would be able to conduct transactions via mobile devices or Internet technology. And context (location, presence, and social interactions) has become as important to consumer services as search engines are to the Web. Thus, using mobility provides significant access to the world. Its impact on advertising alone is significant for publishers, operators, network agencies, and advertisers. However, most firms have challenges, including:

- Lack of appropriate policies
- Proliferation of mobile devices without the ability to account for them properly
- Increased risks of unauthorized exposure of sensitive information

It appears again that the CIO is well positioned to deal with the proliferation of mobile devices and the forecast of growth of mobility in general. Most important is the need that future automation executives have to deal with the risks and rewards of mobility and the ongoing challenge of the rewards versus the risks.

Conclusion

This chapter has attempted to predict the roles and responsibilities of future technology leaders. Many have focused their predictions on the title of the new CIOs of the future. These new titles and responsibilities often suggest that the CIO role be cut up into pieces. Some of these roles now include:

- **Chief technology officer:** This role exists usually under the CIO, but many feel that the CTO should be a peer of the CIO and handle the technical issues of the IT department. In some companies, there is only a CTO—this exists in technology-driven firms.
- **Chief integration officer:** An interesting title and defined as someone who integrates technology with business applications.
- **Chief data scientist:** Leaders who focus on the meanings of the data, suggesting that data analytics and knowledge management are the most important aspects for business technology use.
- **Chief innovation officer:** This looks at the role as a driver only and focuses on new inventions and uses of technology.
- **Chief digital officer:** A role that concentrates on managing the digital technologies including social media and big data.
- **Chief information security officer:** A role that has emerged from the security breaches suffered by many top organizations. In many organizations, this individual reports directly to the CEO and the board of directors.
- **Chief administrative officer:** This looks at the role as a chief operating officer without the financial responsibilities.

Figure 11.1   Responsibilities of the non-IT CIO.
Source: "Adapting to the Data Explosion: Ensuring Justice for All." IEEE International Conference on Systems, Man, and Cybernetics, San Antonio, Texas, October 11–14, 2009.

The problem with these titles and responsibilities is that no one of them encompasses the total responsibilities we have articulated in this chapter. Figure 11.1 graphically represents the myriad of total responsibilities of the role as we see it developing.

We have advocated a title of chief of automation, but the question to be addressed is whether it really matters. The most important thing about the future leaders of automation and technology is in what they do and perform for their firms. We used "automation" because we feel strongly that the role needs to better align itself with the business and technology as opposed to the traditional IT department. We suggest that CIOs reinvent themselves as true C-level leaders and seek to bring value based on the needs of the entire business. Automation seems to embrace the entire realm of issues that we discussed, as well as those that have yet to be developed. However, it is our vision that the challenge of the CIO will remain as a role that continually looks at manual transactions and evaluates whether automating them will bring efficiency and drive new business. We also feel that it is important not to reduce the importance of the supporter side of the CIO. Just because the support role of the CIO does not directly drive strategy, it does not mean it is not significant, especially for reducing costs and improving efficiency. To be specific, driver strategies will never start out as being efficient or cost saving. Many of the responsibilities outlined in Figure 11.1 are indeed supporter responsibilities, which is why we stick to our feeling that the role is best described as an automation leader.

Another question often asked at CIO conferences is whether CIOs can become CEOs. We believe that the chief automation officer can become the CEO, simply because of the enormity and range of their responsibilities. The road to the CEO, in many firms, has traditionally been through sales and marketing simply because these individuals drive revenue. Figure 11.1 shows the amount of new business being driven by automation, so we believe that automation officers may be better suited for the CEO-level responsibilities to drive revenue using a myriad of diverse ways. In other companies, the CFO has been the road to the CEO position. Again looking at the operational responsibilities of an automation officer, we see equal levels of knowledge to handle the CEO function. This is why we titled this chapter "The Non-IT CIO of the Future."

Notes

1. J. Schectman, "New EU Privacy Rules Put CIOs in Compliance Roles," *Wall Street CIO Journal* (June 7, 2012).
2. "Adapting to the Data Explosion: Ensuring Justice for All," in *Proceedings of the 2009 IEEE International Conference on Systems, Man, and Cybernetics* (2009).
3. N. N. Bazarova and J. B. Walther, "Attribution of Blame in Virtual Groups," In P. Lutgen-Sandvik and B. Davenport-Sypher (Eds.), *The Destructive Side of Organizational Communication: Processes, Consequences, and Constructive Ways of Organizing* (Mahwah, NJ: Routledge/LEA, 2009), 252–266.
4. C. Burns, "Automated Talent Management," *Information Management* (2009), www.information-management.com/news/technology_development_talent_management-10016009-1.html.
5. S. Kulkki and M. Kosonen, "How Tacit Knowledge Explains Organizational Renewal and Growth: The Case at Nokia." In I. Nonaka and D. Teece (Eds.), *Managing Industrial Knowledge: Creation, Transfer and Utilization* (London: Sage, 2001), 244–269.
6. D. J. Teece, "Strategies for Managing Knowledge Assets: The Role of Firm Structure and Industrial Context." In Nonaka and Teece (Eds.), *Managing Industrial Knowledge*, 125–144.
7. A. M. Langer, "Responsive Organizational Dynamism: Managing Technology Life Cycles Using Reflective Practice," *Current Issues in Technology Management* 9(2) (2005): 1–8.
8. H. Chesbrough, *Open Services Innovation* (San Francisco, CA: Jossey Bass, 2011).
9. Ibid.
10. Don Reisinger, "10 Security Concerns You'll Lose Sleep Over in 2011," *CIO Insight*, January 5, 2011.

CHAPTER 12
Conclusion: New Directions for the CIO of the Future

This book has explored many conceptual aspects of the CIO position and how the role can help firms compete in a rapidly changing world.

Case studies were presented to show why certain CIOs have achieved success with their firms. It is most important, however, for us to represent the apparent skills that are common among successful CIOs that appear to work in almost any organization. Hence, there can be no boilerplate methodology for the process of how to be successful with technology; rather, it is a way of thinking and an ability to be strategic. Our research showed that there are 23 common attributes that CIOs must have for them to evolve the role in their firms. These attributes are more behavioral from an individual perspective, and philosophical from an organizational point of view.

In Langer's study of CEO perceptions of IT, he found that the role of IT was not generally understood in most of the organizations he surveyed, especially at the CEO level.[1] Little has changed according to the discussions and research we have had over the past year of writing this book. There appears to still be inconsistent reporting structures within the IT organization, and there is a fair amount of frustration of CIOs as effective "technology" strategists and as fiscally responsive members of their executive teams. Furthermore, there are still many non-IT executives who are not satisfied with IT performance, and while most agree that technology should play a larger role in marketing, few have been able to accomplish this. The general dilemma has still involved the inability of the CIO to integrate technology effectively into the workplace. Certainly, a principal target of this book is to answer the question of what CIOs need to do and in what directions their roles need to evolve regarding the firm as a whole. Other concerns center on general organizational issues surrounding who IT people are, where they report, and how they should be evaluated. CIOs must also provide better leadership with respect to guiding a company through the challenges of unproven technologies. While technology behaves dynamically, we still need processes that can validate its applicability to the organization by using sound business processes. Another way of viewing this dilemma is to accept the idea that certain technologies need to be rejected because of their inappropriateness to drive strategy.

The CIO function is somewhat unique in that it is often viewed from a project perspective; for instance, that which is required to deliver technology, along with the cultural impact it has on the organization, tend to be measured by project deliverables, due to the pressure to see measurable outcomes. From a project perspective CIOs can be seen as executive project managers, which requires them to communicate with multiple business units and management layers. They need to establish shorter project life cycles and respond to sudden changes to business requirements. No longer does a traditional project life cycle with static dates and deliverables work for today's fast-paced businesses. Rather these projects are living and breathing entities that must be in balance with what is occurring in the business at all times. Most important is that project measurable outcomes must be defined and in balance with expected organizational strategic goals.

Key to our philosophy is Langer's definition of the role of technology as a dynamic variable, which he termed "technological dynamism." "Responsive organizational dynamism" (ROD) represents Langer's attempt to think through a range of responses to the problems posed by technological dynamism, which is an environment of dynamic and unpredictable change resulting from the advent of innovative technologies.[2] This change can no longer be managed by a group of executives or managers; it is simply too complex, affecting every component of a business. A unilateral approach does not work; the problem requires a cultural transformation that we believe can be accomplished only by a technology executive. The question, then, for CIOs of the future is how they can create organizations that can respond to the variability of technologies in such a way that its responses become part of its everyday language and discourse of the firm. Not an easy task, yet this technological state of affairs is urgent for two major reasons. First, technology is not only an accelerator of change, it requires accelerated business responses. Organizations can no longer wait for a committee to be formed or long bureaucratic processes to make decisions on how technology will be adapted. Second, the market is unforgiving when it comes to missing business opportunities. Every missed opportunity for not responding in a timely fashion can cost an organization its livelihood and future. As stated by Johnson, Saveri, and Schmid:

> The global marketplace requires constant product innovation, quick delivery to market, and a large number of choices for the consumer, all of which are forcing us to rethink the way we structure our business organizations to compete. Indeed, many businesses are finding their traditional structure cumbersome—the way they work is more of an obstacle than help in taking advantage of global opportunities.[3]

While ROD is the overarching approach for a firm that can perform in a dynamic and unpredictable environment, there are two major components to that approach that we raise for further consideration. Langer discussed how technology as a variable is unique in that it affects two areas of any organization. The first is the technology itself and how it operates with business strategy. He called this the "strategic integration component" of ROD. The challenge here is to have organizations create processes that can formally and informally determine the benefit of new and emerging technologies on an ongoing basis. The second component is cultural assimilation, which is about managing the cultural and structural changes that are required when new strategies are adopted by the organization.

Creating an environment of ROD needs processes that can foster individual and organizational business integration of IT. The 24 techniques that were advocated by our case studies best fit the need, as they contain the core capabilities to assist organizations in reinventing themselves as necessary, and to build an organization that can evolve with technology, as opposed to one that needs to be reorganized. We have presented many strategic advocacy concepts and modified them to provide specific remedies to the challenges required to create ROD firms. We have also presented the complex issues of working with politics and understanding degrees of separation so that CIOs can use them in a way that can help them with their C-suite colleagues and other key leaders in business units. Indeed, understanding how to maneuver through complex organizational structures and people was clearly an advantage for the successful CIOs in our research. Our study of how strategic advocacy is fundamental for CIO success consists of eight key conclusions:

1. CIOs can contribute significant value to the business by engaging in strategic conversations and integrating technology drivers into the discussion. In the language of strategic thinking, technology, as a supporter or as "keeping the lights on," is table stakes. Other executives assume the CIO has people handling supporter functions. A CIO that can advance or enhance the strategic position of the organization by integrating strategic drivers in ways that further strengthen and/or expand customer commitment is meeting the most important need of the organization.

2. Business acumen is critical for CIO success. Leveraging technology as a strategic driver requires CIOs to be fluent in the business model of the firm. This requires knowledge of the larger competitive market and the trends among competitors, customers, and regulators. Furthermore, they need to understand their organization's own internal capabilities and performance measures, as well as the emerging technologies that are critical for framing strategic conversations. Most important is that the CIO must remember that these are business collaborations, not technology conversations.

3. Building alliances and social networks is a critical dimension of the CIO's role. CIOs must conceptualize these networks as social capital for having strategic conversations, access to credible path of conversations, and information about new insights of the business. It also allows access to important resources, both departmental and individual.

4. CIOs must have a strategic mindset, as opposed to relying solely on expert ways of thinking. Taking an outside-in perspective, noticing trends, emergent patterns, and exploring diverse perspectives is crucial for gaining both new business and political insights. Positioning strategic business insights is both a factual and a political act. Integrating these two requires formulating strategies that meet the needs of the overall business.

5. Positioning IT effectively involves simultaneously decentralizing driver activities and centralizing supporter functions. Both driver and supporter IT services will help build political capital.

6. CIOs are confronted with a need to be engaged in continuous learning—learning that is personally developmental in the sense that they are aware of their own habits and ways of thinking that emerge when they are outside their own comfort zones. This requires them to develop a comfort with "ambiguity" and "calculated risk taking." This means that CIOs must have outstanding communication skills by using effective patterns of speech and listening techniques.

7. The ability to constantly reflect on their actions is a precursor for CIOs to continue developing professionally and gaining new strategic insights.

8. The mindset of the technology leaders of the future is radically different from the way most CIOs perform today. Much of this dilemma is a result of their technical path to the CIO position as opposed to one that better prepares them for the realities of life at the C-suite. In addition, the IT function is itself in a process of continuous transition and transformation.

We believe that Langer's maturity arcs provide the necessary framework for the development of the future technology executive as described earlier. The use of these arcs can measure where individuals and organizations are in their trajectory toward the integration of emerging technologies in their business strategies. These maturity arcs also provide a basis for how to measure where the organization is, what types of corrections are necessary to consider, and what outcomes to expect. Indeed, providing measurable outcomes in the form of strategic performance is the very reason CIOs should consider embracing this model.

We also discussed a number of methods to manage technology business integration by modifying theories of knowledge management and change management, so that they specifically addressed the unique aspects of change brought about by new technologies. We looked at how the CEO needs to become more knowledgeable in technology, and, based on case studies and research, Langer provided sets of "best practices" to suggest that staff members cannot become part of a technology-based organization without the participation of the CEO and his or her executive committees. Langer formulated best practices for three major organizational structures along with corresponding maturity arcs to lay the foundation of what each community needs to do in order to properly participate in the transformations indicated for ROD. To this end, Langer proposes a road map that, if followed, could provide the mechanisms that lead to the kind of organizational transformation that is empowered to handle the challenges of new technologies. This process is summarized in Figure 12.1.

A theme of this book is the recognition of the importance of understanding the process of evolution. In the past, information traveled much slower, and there was more time to interpret its impact on the organization. Today, the wait is shrinking, and therefore evolution can and should occur at a quicker pace. Indeed, organizational evolution is intertwined with the dynamics of community legitimization.[4] Technological development for a particular population has widespread consequences for the rest of the organization. In these cases, technological innovations represent a form of collective learning that is different from direct learning from experience alone.[5] There are many of us who believe that effective management must be implemented through top-down approaches. Many such efforts to reorganize or reengineer organizations have had disappointing results. Many of these failures, we believe, are attributable to a dependence on management intervention as opposed to Langer's strategic integration and cultural assimilation components of ROD. Technology only serves to expose problems that have existed in organizations for decades: The inability to drive down responsibilities to the operational levels of the organization. Through automation advances, CIOs have a unique opportunity to truly address this dilemma.

Our case study interviews provide a pragmatic view toward the attainment of CIO excellence, assuming the correct support for the role in the firm exists. We advocated that CIOs must "redefine" their role and build toward a "natural evolution." However, we also admit that there needs to be some level of strategic support from the CEO for the position's potential to be realized in the business. Our case studies reflect that progress toward CIO support may be a gradual one. As such, we determined that organizational transformation must be addressed along the same basis—that is, transformation is a gradual process as opposed to a planned event with a specific outcome. We believe

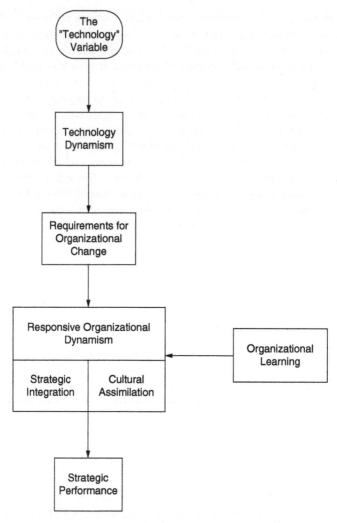

Figure 12.1   Responsive Organizational Dynamism road map.

that organizations should look at IT business integration in much shorter "chunks," as opposed to an immediate "big bang" approach, which rarely works and is difficult to measure. Our suggestion to better measure IT integration was through Langer's Balanced Scorecard, which provides a more evolutionary approach to success.

Another important concept in this book is the reconciliation between control and empowerment. As organizations find that their traditional structures are cumbersome when dealing with emerging technologies, they realize the need to empower IT and non-IT employees to do more dynamically. With this empowerment, employees may make more mistakes or seem less genuine at times. When this occurs, there may be a need for management controls to be instituted and power-centralized management styles to be incorporated. Unfortunately, too many controls end any hope of sustaining a creative organization that can foster the dynamic planning and needs of ROD. It also blocks the molding of true integration with the business, which requires common threads of discourse and language. Indeed, it is CIO discourse that lays the foundations for addressing the dilemma of control versus empowerment.

We are really beginning to experience the results of emerging technologies, particularly in global companies. We have seen a continual trend where offshore product development and maintenance continues to be at an all-time high and local employment down. The advent of this cycle lays a foundation for the new trends of the global worker operations, many of which are shifting from a labor-intensive process to needs for thinking, planning, and management. It is a perfect example of N = 1 and R = G so eloquently presented by Prahalad and Krishnan. However, we do see a recent movement to balance outsourcing with local resources. The challenge for CIOs is to find more ways to create pipelines of skilled workers, not only internationally, but also in local communities. Indeed, Randy Mott, the CIO of General Motors, continues to bring back 90 percent of its IT outsourcing abroad. We also see that the way individuals communicate or the rules of their engagement are quickly changing, particularly in the need to create more research and development (R&D) infrastructures that can respond quicker to innovation opportunities brought about by emerging technologies. We saw very clearly through our case studies that business strategy and technology are major investments and the acknowledgment by CIO leaders that IT was more about business than technology.

To address the lack of understanding of the technology life cycle, we presented Langer's concept of driver and supporter functions and mapped them to evolutionary business transformation. This life cycle is one that ties business strategy into technology and should be used to convey ROD to executives. Driver functions explain why strategic integration is so important and present a case that requires more marketing-based philosophies when investing in technologies. This means that early adaptation of technology requires, as Bradley and Nolan coined, "sense and respond" approaches, where IT organizations can experiment with business units on how a particular technology may benefit the business.[6] Siemens provided a good example of different ways of creating infrastructures that can support technology exploration, including Deasy's 90-day program there, where technology investments were reviewed periodically to see what adjustments are required to maximize the investment. It also provided a way to cancel those investments that were not paying off as originally forecasted. Understanding that changes along the way are needed or that there are technologies that do not provide the intended benefits must become a formal part of the process, and one that CEOs must recognize and fund. However, the supporter role is one that addresses the operational side of IT, such that executives and managers understand the difference. We treat the concept of supporter as an eventual reality—the reality that all technologies once adapted by operations must inevitably become a commodity. This realization paves the way to understanding when and how technologies can be considered for outsourcing based on economies of scale. The adaptation of this philosophy creates a structured way for CIOs to understand the cost side of the IT dilemma, and why it requires business units to integrate their own plans with those offered by emerging technologies. The supporter aspect of technology became the base of cultural assimilation because once a technology is adapted by operations, there must be a corresponding process that fosters its impact on organizational structures and cultural behaviors. It also provides the short- and long-term expected transformations, which ultimately link technology and strategic performance. The driver/supporter philosophy also shows the complexity of the many definitions of technology and that executives should not attempt to oversimplify it. Simply put, technology must be discussed in different ways, and CIOs need to rise to the occasion to take a leadership role in conveying this to executives, managers, and operations personnel. Organizations that can implement driver/supporter methods will inevitably be better positioned to understand why they need to invest in certain technologies and technology-based projects.

These general themes just discussed can be formulated as a marriage between business strategy and technological innovation and can be represented as follows:

- CIOs must change the business cycles of technology investment; technology investments must become part of the everyday or normative processes, as opposed to specific cycles based on economic opportunities or shortfalls. Emerging technologies tend to be implemented based on "stop and goes," or breakthroughs followed by discontinuities.[7]
- The previous experiences that organizations have had with technology are not a good indicator for its future use. Technology innovations must evolve through infrastructure, learning, and process evaluation.
- Technology is central to competitive strategy. CIOs need to ensure that technology opportunities are integrated with all discussions on business strategy.

- Managing technology innovations must be accomplished through linkages. Thus, CIOs must establish interfaces across the businesses by being very active with these units.
- Managing intellectual capital is of growing importance. Managing this knowledge requires CIOs of the future to create processes that transfer tacit knowledge to explicit knowledge.
- There are multiple and complex levels of management that needs to be involved in ROD. Successful CIOs must develop architectures, manage change, and deal with short- and long-term projects simultaneously. CIO leadership will understand that there are three primary levels (executive, middle management, and operations) in the business that constitute the infrastructure that best sustains the natural migration toward ROD.

This book looked at business strategy from yet another perspective, beyond its relationship with information technologies. Because business integration is required to foster ROD, strategy must also be linked to other types of technologies, which we called "automations." This expansion of the use of many types of technologies should then be seen as strategic automations, which if implemented helps organizations to continually adapt to the changing business environment, including changes brought about by all types of automation possibilities. However, due to the radical speed, complexity, and uncertainty, traditional ways of implementing strategy no longer ignore the nontraditional behaviors of technology. The old methods of determining business strategy were based on standard models that were linear and "plug-in." As stated earlier, they were also very much based on projects that attempted to design one-time efforts with a corresponding result. As Pietersen explains, "These processes usually produce operating plans and budgets rather than insights and strategic breakthroughs."[8] Technological dynamism has accelerated the need to replace these old traditions, and we have emphasized that organizations that practice ROD must:

- Evaluate and implement technology automations in an ongoing process and embed it as part of normal practices. This requires a change in business integration and culture.
- Comprehend that the process of ROD is not about planning; it is about adaptation and strategic innovation.
- Feed on the creation of new knowledge through business integration that leads to strategic organizational transformation.

Many scholars might correlate strategic success with leadership. While leadership, in itself, is an invaluable variable, it is just that. To attain ongoing evolution, we believe we need to move away from relying on individual leadership efforts and move toward an infrastructure that has fewer leaders and more normative behavior that can support and sustain ROD. Certainly, this fosters the important roles and responsibilities of CEOs, managers, and boards; but to have an ongoing process that changes the thinking and the operational fundamentals of the way the organization functions is more important and more valuable than individual leadership. That is why we raised the issues of discourse and language, as well as self-development as an important part of the future success of CIOs. Therefore, the CIO's ability to transform the business community is what will bring forth long-term strategic performance of any firm. However, the transformation must be expanded to include all types of automations for both drivers and supporter functions.

What this book really commits to is the importance of change management—the simple concept that people in organizations need to continually challenge their cultural norms if they are to develop what Mezirow calls "new meaning perspectives."[9] It is these new meaning perspectives that lay the foundation for ROD, so that managers and staff can continually challenge themselves to determine if they are making the best strategic decisions. Furthermore, it prepares individuals to deal with uncertainty as well as the ongoing transitions in the way they do their jobs. It is this very process that ultimately fosters success with dealing with the disruptions of new automation possibilities.

While on-the-job training is valuable, movement or rotations of IT personnel at work has merit for supporting real business integration. Specifically, the relocation of IT personnel to a business unit can serve to get IT staff more acclimated to business issues. This helps IT staff members to begin to reflect about their own functions and their relationship to the overall mission of the organization. CIOs like Passerini at Procter & Gamble took significant steps to accelerate real integration of IT by permanently integrating them in a non-IT business-specific department. This is why the CIO must be a "champion" who can demonstrate to IT staff that the process of business integration is not just lip service but a path to everyone's success in the department. If CIOs nurture the integration transformation properly, it will allow the business communities to become serious about technology best practices and the business's role in its development.

Although this book might suggest to readers that technology is the basis for the need for ROD, the needs for its existence can be attributed to *any* variable that requires dynamic change. As such, we suggest that readers begin to think about the next "technology" or variable that can cause the same needs to occur inside organizations. Such accelerations, if we are realistic, are not necessarily limited to technology automations. An example is the continual changes in consumer behavior or the loss of jobs due to corporate downsizing from acquisitions. These nontechnology variables present similar challenges in that organizations must be able to integrate new cultures and "other" business strategies and attempt to form new holistic directions—directions that need to be formed very quickly in order to survive. Indeed, trying to predict how consumers will react can be overwhelming. That is, consumers can also behave in a similar way as technology. The ability to adjust to consumer needs and shifting market segments is certainly not always related to technological change. Our point is that ROD is a concept that should be embraced notwithstanding whether technology seems to have slowed down or is not having an effect on a specific industry at a particular moment. Thus, we challenge CIOs or chiefs of automation, as we predict, to develop new strategies that embrace the need to become dynamic throughout all of their operations, and to create continual "reintegrations" of business units that plan for ongoing strategic integration and cultural assimilation.

This book has looked upon the advent of technology then to uncover a dilemma that has existed for some time. Perhaps a more general way of defining what ROD offers is to compare it to another historical concept called "self-generating organizations." Self-generating organizations are known for their promotion of autonomy with an "underlying organic sense of interdependence."[10] Based on this definition, a self-generating organization is similar to an organism, which evolves over time. This notion is consistent with the evolution of the CIO role because it inherently relates to the inner growth stemming from the organization as opposed to only its executives. The self-generating organization works well with business integration and ROD in the following ways:

- Traditional management control systems do not apply.
- Risks are higher given that staffs are granted a high degree of autonomy and empowerment, which will lead to processes that break with the controlling norms of the business and allow for IT integration.
- Adjustments and new processes from the CIO's efforts to integrate will be expected.
- These organizations tend to use political advocacy as a strong vehicle to support network building.
- Traditional hierarchical leadership models do not work because they are organized based on influence as opposed to control.

Self-generating organizations have been met with resistance in the past because managers view that they might be losing control. ROD, led by the CIO, provides a hybrid model that allows for self-generating infrastructures while providing certain levels of control within each business unit. In other words, it's more of a distributed leadership model; local control is maintained at the unit level. For example, ROD embraces the breaking of rules for good reasons; it allows individuals to fail, yet to reflect on the shortfall so that they do not repeat the same errors. Everything we have advocated in this book relating to IT drivers supports the idea of an IT batting average. It also allows employees to take risks that show promise and lead to more critical thinking that leads to strategic action. Local business units within an organization often balk at leadership edicts that are pushed down from the national or central organization. The self-generating organization allows for that local independence, so that these units can better respond to local consumer needs. Indeed, business units need to figure out what new innovations mean to their markets, observe the results, and make adjustments to meet the market requirements. Thus, seeing ROD as a form of self-generation is the basis for CIOs to sustain innovative infrastructures that can respond to dynamic variables like technology.

We believe that Vince's[11] organized reflection model modified by Langer[12] provides an analysis of how IT business integration could be used to sustain growth through evolution. Langer's modified model represents a matrix of how IT business integration can be measured across individuals, business units, and the firm as a whole. Langer's new framework is shown in Table 12.1.

Table 12.1 shows the three kinds of reflective practices that can operate in an organization: Individual, business unit, and firmwide. We emphasized that the extent of the CIO's success in business integration is directly related to the level of strategic advocacy, not only by the CIO but also across the IT staff. Much of strategic advocacy requires individuals to have ability to reflect about their actions and how others around them view what they say and what they do. The better they understand that, in accordance with the maturity arcs, the more effective the IT department will be as a whole in integrating with the business. The more learning that occurs through individual reflections, the sooner business integration will be absorbed in the firm. When this occurs at the IT management and staff level first, it will inevitably have a positive effect on the business unit and firmwide levels as well. Becoming more business integrated requires that the structured processes create and maintain links between strategic advocacy, individual reflection, and democratic thinking. These can be mapped onto the ROD arc, showing how, from an "organizing" perspective, strategic advocacy and reflective practices serve as a process to "outline what is involved in the process of reflection for learning and change."[13] Vince's model did not extend a structure for implementation for ROD. Langer's modification serves that very purpose, as shown in Figure 12.2.

Table 12.1   IT business integration matrix: Examples of reflective practices for IT integration using responsive organizational dynamism.

	Individual	Business unit	Firmwide
	Relationships among the person, the role, and the organization-in-the-mind.	Relationships across the IT boundaries of self/other and of subdepartments within IT.	Relationships between IT and other business units.
Peer Groups (nonmanagerial self-governing IT groups of at least three individuals).	Making connections for the self: review and reflection within IT community by friendship and mutuality of interests and needs.	Making connections in small groups with "others" across IT organization. Develop interpersonal communication and dialogue within IT communities.	Making connections with the entire organization: Reflection on ways that technology affects other groups in the organization.
Organizational Role Analysis (linking individuals with "others" inside the IT organization).	Organizational role analysis: Understanding the connections between the person, the person in IT, and his or her role in the organization.	Role analysis groups: The ways in which technology roles and the understanding of those roles interweave within an IT community or department.	Technology role provides the framework within which the person and the organization are integrated.
Business Unit Integration (groups of individuals united in actions that contribute to the production of IT ideas in practice).	Involvement: Providing personal experience as the vehicle to organize the use technology.	Engagement: Experience is used to apply technology across the IT organization. Understanding of importance of IT inter-department communication.	Establishment: Experience of power relationships as they react and respond to technology uses among communities of practice.
Firm Relations Conferences (reveal the complexities of feelings, interactions, and power relationships that are integral to the process of organizing technology implementations).	Experiencing and rethinking technology authority and the meanings and consequences of leadership and follower-ship.	Experience of defensive mechanisms and avoidance strategies across IT departments. Experience of organizing, belonging, and representing across IT organizations.	Experiencing the ways in which IT and the organization become integrated using collective emotional experience, politics, leadership, authority, and organizational transformation.

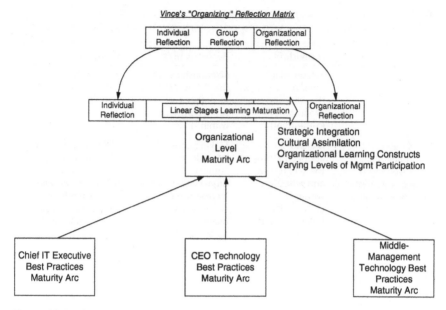

Figure 12.2   Organizational dynamism and organized reflection.

Figure 12.2 graphically shows how organized reflection maps to the linear stages of the ROD arc (the organizational level maturity arc), which in turn maps onto the three best practices arcs discussed in Chapter 6. Each of the management arcs represent a level of management maturity at the organizational level, with Vince's matrix providing the overarching concepts on how to actually organize the progression from individual-based thinking and reflection to a more comprehensive and systems-level thinking using strategic advocacy. The emphasis, overall, is that individual actions of IT staff alone may undermine collective governance of the CIO. Therefore, the movement from individual to organizational self-management remains a critical part of understanding how technology and other dynamic variables can foster new strategies for competitive advantage: A competitive advantage that must be led by the CIO but carefully intertwined with the actions of the IT staff. The actions then of the IT staff must be mapped onto business units and then toward the entire firm collectively.

Our overall message in this book is that the CIO of today can become the chief of automation of tomorrow. The opportunity is staggering; the rewards can be many, including the potential of becoming the main road to the CEO position. With this challenge come many pitfalls and a poor history of accomplishing business integration, but as Bynjolfsson and Saunders cleverly stated in their recent book *Race Against the Machine*: "The machine inevitably wins!"[14] If we believe that automation will win, the issue then is whether a new generation of CIOs can take advantage of the opportunity that has been afforded to them. We can be sure of one thing: If they don't, someone else at the C-suite will.

Notes

1. A. M. Langer, *Information Technology and Organizational Learning: Managing Behavioral Change through Technology and Education*, 2nd ed. (Boca Raton, FL: Taylor and Francis, 2011).
2. Ibid.
3. R. Johansen, A. Saveri, and G. Schmid, "Forces for Organizational Change: 21st Century Organizations: Reconciling Control and Empowerment," *Institute for the Future* 6(1) (1995): 1–9.
4. H. Aldrich, *Organizations Evolving* (London: Sage, 2001).
5. A. S. Miner and P. R. Haunschild, "Population and Learning." In B. Staw and L. L. Cummings (Eds.), Research in Organizational Behavior (Greenwich, CT: JAI Press, 1995), 115–166.
6. S. P. Bradley, and R. L. Nolan, *Sense and Respond: Capturing Value in the Network Era* (Boston: Harvard Business School Press, 1998).
7. M. L. Tushman and P. Anderson, *Managing Strategic Innovation and Change* (New York: Oxford University Press, 1997).
8. W. Pietersen, *Reinventing Strategy: Using Strategic Learning to Create and Sustain Breakthrough Performance* (Hoboken, NJ: John Wiley & Sons, 2002).
9. J. Mezirow, *Fostering Critical Reflection in Adulthood: A Guide to Transformative and Emancipatory Learning* (San Francisco: Jossey-Bass, 1990).
10. R. Johansen, A. Saveri, and G. Schmid, "Forces for Organizational Change: 21st Century Organizations: Reconciling Control and Empowerment," *Institute for the Future* 6(1) (1995): 1–9.
11. R. Vince, "Organizing Reflection," *Management Learning* 33(1): 63–78.
12. A. M. Langer, "Responsive Organizational Dynamism: Managing Technology Life Cycles Using Reflective Practice. In *Current Issues in Technology Management* 9(2) (2005): 1–8.
13. Vince, "Organizing Reflection."
14. E. Brynjolfsson and A. McAfee. *Race Against the Machine* (Lexington, KY: Digital Frontier Press, 2011).

BIBLIOGRAPHY

Adapting to the data explosion: Ensuring justice for all. In Proceedings of the 2009 IEEE International Conference on Systems, Man, and Cybernetics, 2009.

Aldrich, H. *Organizations Evolving*. London: Sage, 2001.

Allen, F., and J. Percival. "Financial Strategies and Venture Capital," in *Corporate Information Strategy and Management*, 2nd ed., edited by L. M. Applegate, R. D. Austin, and F. W. McFarlan. New York: McGraw-Hill, 2003.

Argyris, C. *Knowledge for Action*. San Francisco: Jossey-Bass, 1993.

Argyris, C., R. Putnam, and D. Smith. *Action Science*. San Francisco: Jossey-Bass, 1985.

Batten, Joe D. *Tough-Minded Management*, 3rd ed. Eugene, OR: Resource Publications, 2002.

Bazarova, N. N., and J. B. Walther. "Attribution of Blame in Virtual Groups," in *The Destructive Side of Organizational Communication: Processes, Consequences, and Constructive Ways of Organizing*, edited by P. Lutgen-Sandvik and B. Davenport-Sypher, 252–66. Mahwah, NJ: Routledge/LEA, 2009.

Beinhocker, E. D., and S. Kaplan. "Tired of Strategic Planning?" *McKinsey Quarterly*, 2: 48–57, 2002.

Bensaou, M., and M. J. Earl, "The Right Mind-Set for Managing Information Technology. In *World View: Global Strategies for the New Economy*, edited by J. E. Garten, 109–25. Cambridge, MA: Harvard University Press, 1998.

Benson, J. K. "The Interorganizational Network as a Political Economy." *Administrative Science Quarterly* 20 (1975): 229–49.

Bertels, T., and C. M. Savage. "Tough Questions on Knowledge Management," in *Knowing in Firms: Understanding, Managing and Measuring Knowledge*, edited by G. V. Krogh, J. Roos, and D. Kleine, 7–25. London: Sage, 1998.

Bolman, L. G., and T. E. Deal. *Reframing Organizations: Artistry, Choice, and Leadership*, 2nd ed. San Francisco: Jossey-Bass, 1997.

Bradley, S. P., and R. L. Nolan. *Sense and Respond: Capturing Value in the Network Era*. Boston: Harvard Business School Press, 1998.

Brynjolfsson, Erik, and Andrew McAfee. *Race Against the Machine*. Lexington: Digital Frontier Press, 2011.

Burke, W. W. *Organization Development: Principles and Practices*. Boston: Little Brown, 1982.

Burns, C. "Automated Talent Management." *Information Management*, http://www.information-management.com/news/technology_development_talent_management- 10016009-1.html 2009.

Carr, Nicholas. "IT Doesn't Matter." *Harvard Business Review* 81, no. 5: 41–49, 2003.

Charan, Ram. *Sharpening Your Business Acumen Strategy & Business.* New York: Booz & Co., 2006.

Chesbrough, H. San Francisco: Jossey-Bass, 2011.

Cillers, P. "Knowing Complex Systems," In *Managing Organizational Complexity: Philosophy, Theory, and Application*, edited by K. A. Richardson, 7–19. Greenwich, CT: Information Age, 2005.

Cohen, A. R., and D. L. Bradford. *Influence without Authority*, 2nd ed. Hoboken, NJ: John Wiley & Sons, 2005.

Cole, R. E. "The Macropolitics of Organizational Change." *Administrative Science Quarterly* 30 (1985): 560–85.

Collis, D. J. "Research Note—How Valuable Are Organizational Capabilities?" *Strategic Management Journal* 15 (1994): 143–52.

Conger, J. "Exerting Influence without Authority," in *Harvard Business Update*, edited by L. Keller Johnson. Boston: Harvard Business Press, 2003.

Deluca, J. *Political Savvy: Systematic Approaches to Leadership Behind-the-Scenes.* Berwyn, PA: EBG, 1999.

Dodgson, M. "Organizational Learning: A Review of Some Literatures." *Organizational Studies* 14, no. 3 (1993): 375–94.

Earl, M. J. "Business Process Engineering: A Phenomenon of Organizational Dimension. In *Information Management: The Organizational Dimension*, edited by M. J. Earl, 53–76. New York: Oxford University Press, 1996.

Earl, M. J. *Information Management: The Organizational Dimension.* New York: Oxford University Press, 1996.

Eichinger, R. W., and M. M. Lombardo. "Education Competencies: Dealing with Ambiguity." Microsoft in Education I Training. Microsoft. Web.

Eisenhardt, K. M., and L. J. Bourgeois. "Politics of Strategic Decision Making in High-Velocity Environments: Toward a Midrange Theory." *Academy of Management Journal* 31 (1988): 737–70.

Elkjaer, B. "In Search of a Social Learning Theory," in *Organizational Learning and the Learning Organization*, edited by M. Easterby-Smith, J. Burgoyne, and L. Araujo. London: Sage, 1999.

Fahey, L., and R. M. Randall, "What Is Scenario Learning?" In *Learning from the Future*, edited by L. Fahey and R. M. Randall, ch. 1. New York: John Wiley & Sons, 1998.

Fahey, L., and R. M. Randall, "Integrating Strategy and Scenarios," In *Learning from the Future*, edited by L. Fahey and R. M. Randall, ch. 2. New York: John Wiley & Sons, 1998.

Ferrell, O. C., and Gareth Gardiner. In *Pursuit of Ethics.* USA: Smith Collins, 1991.

Fisher D., D. Rooke, and B. Torbert. *Personal and Organizational Transformations Through Action Inquiry*. Boston: Edge/Work Press, 1993.

Friedman, T. L., and M. Mandelbaum. *That Used to Be Us*. London: Picador, 2012.

Gavitte, G., and J. W. Rivikin. "How Strategists Really Think: Tapping the Power of Analogy." *Harvard Business Review*, April 2005: 54–63.

Govindarajan, V., and C. Trimble. "Strategic Innovation and the Science of Learning." *MIT Sloan Management Review* 45, no. 2 (2004): 67–75.

Grant, D., Keenoy, T., and C. Oswick, eds. *Discourse and Organization*. London: Sage, 1998.

Grant, R. M. "Prospering in a Dynamically-Competitive Environment— Organizational Capability as Knowledge Integration." *Organization Science* 7, no. 4 (1996): 375–87.

Illbury, C., and C. Sunter. *The Mind of a Fox*, Cape Town, SA, 36–43. Human & Rousseau/Tafelberg, 2001.

Johnsen, R., A. Saveri, and G. Schmid. "Forces for Organizational Change: 21st Century Organizations: Reconciling Control and Empowerment." *Institute for the Future* 6, no. 1 (1995): 1–9.

Kegan, R. *In Over Our Heads: The Mental Demands of Modern Life*. Cambridge, MA: Harvard University Press, 1994.

Kolb, D. *Experiential Learning as the Science of Learning and Development*. Englewood Cliffs, NJ: Prentice Hall, 1984.

Kolb, A. Y., and D. A. Kolb. "Learning Styles and Learning Spaces: Enhancing Experiential Learning in Higher Education." *Academy of Management Learning and Education* 4, no. 2 (2005): 193–212.

Kulkki, S., and M. Kosonen. "How Tacit Knowledge Explains Organizational Renewal and Growth: The Case at Nokia," in *Managing Industrial Knowledge: Creation, Transfer and Utilization*, edited by I. Nonaka and D. Teece, 244–69. London: Sage, 2001.

Langer, A. M. "Fixing Bad Habits: Integrating Technology Personnel in the Workplace Using Reflective Practice. *Reflective Practice* 2, no. 1 (2001): 100–11.

Langer, A. M. "Reflecting on Practice: Using Learning Journals in Higher and Continuing Education. *Teaching in Higher Education* 7 (2002): 337–51.

Langer, A. M. *Information Technology and Organizational Learning: Managing Behavioral Change through Technology and Education*, 1st ed. Boca Raton, FL: Taylor & Francis, 2005.

Langer, A. M. *Information Technology and Organizational Learning: Managing Behavioral Change through Technology and Education*, 2nd ed. Boca Raton, FL: Taylor & Francis, 2011.

Langer, A. M. "Responsive Organizational Dynamism: Managing Technology Life Cycles Using Reflective Practice. In *Current Issues in Technology Management* 9(2) (2005): 1–8.

Leavy, B. "The Concept of Learning in the Strategy Field." *Management Learning* 29 (1998): 447–66.

Lovallo, D. P., and L. T. Mendonca. "Strategy's Strategist: An Interview with Richard Rumelt." *The McKinsey Quarterly*, 2007, www.mckinseyquarterly .com/Strategys_ strategist_An_interview_with_Richard_Rumelt_2039.

Lucas, H. C. *Information Technology and the Productivity Paradox*. New York: Oxford University Press, 1999.

MacMillan, I. C. *Strategy Formulation: Political Concepts*. New York: West, 1978.

Marsick, V. J., and K. E. Watkins. *Informal and Incidental Learning in the Workplace*. London: Routledge, 1990.

Mezirow, J. *Fostering Critical Reflection in Adulthood: A Guide to Transformative and Emancipatory Learning*. San Francisco: Jossey-Bass, 1990.

Miles, R. E., and C. C. Snow. *Organizational Strategy, Structure, and Process*. New York: McGraw-Hill, 1978.

Miner, A. S., and P. R. Haunschild. "Population and Learning, in *Research in Organizational Behavior*, edited by B. Staw and L. L. Cummings, 115–66. Greenwich, CT: JAI Press, 1995.

Mintzberg, H. "Crafting Strategy." *Harvard Business Review* 65, no. 4 (1987): 72.

Murphy, T. *Achieving Business Practice from Technology: A Practical Guide for Today's Executive*. New York: John Wiley & Sons, 2002.

Nahapiet, J., and S. Ghoshal. "Social Capital, Intellectual Capital, and the Organizational Advantage." *Academy of Management Review* 23 (1998): 242–66.

Nicolaides, A., and L. Yorks. "An Epistemology of Learning Through." 10, no. 1 (2008): 50–61.

Nonaka, I., and H. Takeuchi. *The Knowledge-Creating Company: How Japanese Companies Create the Dynamics of Innovation*, 3. New York: Oxford University Press, 1995.

Palmer, I., and C. Hardy. *Thinking About Management: Implications of Organizational Debates for Practice*. London: Sage, 2000.

Penton, H. *Material from conversation and presentation at a Saudi business school*, 2011.

Pettigrew, A. M. The *Politics of Organizational Decision-Making*. London: Tavistock, 1973.

Pettigrew, A. M. The *Awaking Giant: Continuity and Change in ICI*. Oxford, UK: Basil Blackwell, 1985.

Pfeffer, J. *Managing with Power: Politics and Influence in Organizations*. Boston: Harvard Business School Press, 1994.

Pietersen, W. *Reinventing Strategy: Using Strategic Learning to Create & Sustain Breakthrough Performance.* New York: John Wiley & Sons, 2002.

Pietersen, W. *Strategic Learning.* Hoboken, NJ: John Wiley & Sons, 2010.

Porter, M. "What Is Strategy?" *Harvard Business Review* 74, no. 6 (1996): 61–78.

Prahalad, C. K., and M. S. Krishnan. *The New Age of Innovation: Driving Cocreated Value through Global Networks.* New York: McGraw-Hill, 2008.

Prince, G. M. *The Practice of Creativity.* New York: Collier Books, 1970.

Richardson, K. A., and A. Tait. "The Death of the Expert?" In *Complexity and Knowledge Management: Understanding the Role of Knowledge in the Management of Social Networks,* edited by A. Tait & K. A. Richardson, 23–39. Charlotte, NC: Information Age, 2010.

Rooke, D., and W. R. Torbert. "The Seven Transformations of Leadership." *Harvard Business Review* 83, no. 4 (2005): 66–77.

Sampler, J. L. "Exploring the Relationship between Information Technology and Organizational Structure," in *Information Management: The Organizational Dimension,* edited by M. J. Earl, 5–22. New York: Oxford University Press, 1996.

Schectman, Joel. "New EU Privacy Rules Put CIOs in Compliance Roles." *Wall Street CIO Journal,* June 7, 2012.

Schein, E. H. *Organizational Culture and Leadership,* 2nd ed. San Francisco: Jossey-Bass, 1992.

Shaw, P. *Changing the Conversation in Organizations: A Complexity Approach to Change.* London: Routledge, 2002.

Stern, L. W., and T. Reve. "Distribution Channels as Political Economies: A Framework for Analysis." *Journal of Marketing* 44 (1980): 52–64.

Storey, J. "Management Control as a Bridging Concept." *Journal of Management Studies* 22 (1985): 269–91.

Szulanski, G., and K. Amin. "Disciplined Imagination: Strategy Making in Uncertain Environments," in *Wharton on Managing Emerging Technologies,* edited by G. S. Day and P. J. Schoemaker, 187–205. New York: John Wiley & Sons, 2000.

Teece, D. J. "Strategies for Managing Knowledge Assets: The Role of Firm Structure and Industrial Context," in *Managing Industrial Knowledge: Creation, Transfer and Utilization,* edited by I. Nonaka and D. Teece, 125–44. London: Sage, 2011.

Tichy, N. M., M. L. Tushman, and C. Fombrum. "Social Network Analysis for Organizations." *Academy of Management Review* 4 (1979): 507–19.

Torbert, B. Action Inquiry: *The Secrets of Timely and Transforming Leadership.* San Francisco: Berrett-Koehler, 2004.

Tushman, M. L., and P. Anderson. *Managing Strategic Innovation and Change.* New York: Oxford University Press, 1997.

Van Houten, D. R. "The Political Economy and Technical Control of Work Humanization in Sweden during the 1970s and 1980s." *Work and Occupations* 14 (1987): 483–513.

Vince, R. "Organizing Reflection." *Management Learning* 33, no. 1 (2002): 63–78.

Wamsley, G. L., and M. N. Zald. *The Political Economy of Public Organization.* Bloomington: Indiana University Press, 1976.

Wenger, E. *Communities of Practice: Learning, Meaning and Identity.* Cambridge, UK: Cambridge University Press, 1998.

Wideman Comparative Glossary of Common Project Management Terms, v2.1. Copyright R. Max Wideman, May 2001.

Yorks, L. "Toward a Political Economy Model for Comparative Analysis of the Role of Strategic Human Resource Development Leadership." *Human Resource Development Review* 3 (2004): 189–208.

Yorks, L., and A. Nicolaides. "A Conceptual Model for Developing Mindsets for Strategic Insight under Conditions of Complexity and High Uncertainty. *Human Resource Development Review* 11 (2012): 182–202.

Yorks, L., and D. A. Whitsett. *Scenarios of Change: Advocacy and the Diffusion of Job Redesign in Organizations.* New York: Praeger, 1989.

Zald, M. N. *Organizational Change: The Political Economy of the YMCA.* Chicago: University of Chicago Press, 1970.

Zald, M. N. "Political Economy: A Framework for Comparative Analysis," in *Power in Organizations,* edited by M. N. Zald, 221–61. Nashville: Vanderbilt University Press, 1970.

ABOUT THE AUTHORS

Dr. Arthur M. Langer is Professor of Professional Practice, Director of the Center for Technology Management, and the Academic Director of the Master of Science Programs in Technology Management at Columbia University. He is also an affiliated faculty member in the Department of Organization and Leadership at the Graduate School of Education (Teachers College). Dr. Langer's practice and research involves technology leadership, workforce development, adult mentoring programs, workplace learning, adult education, intellectual development, and transformative learning. Dr. Langer is also the Chairman and Founder of Workforce Opportunity Services (www.wforce.org), a nonprofit social venture that provides scholarships and careers to underserved populations around the world. Dr. Langer is the author of *Information Technology and Organizational Learning 3rd Edition* (2018), *Guide to Software Development: Designing and Managing the Life Cycle* (2012), *Analysis and Design of Information Systems* (2007), *Applied Ecommerce* (2002), and *The Art of Analysis* (1997) and has numerous published articles and papers relating to service learning for underserved populations, IT organizational integration, mentoring, and staff development. Dr. Langer consults with corporations and universities on information technology, staff development, management transformation, and curriculum development around the globe.

***

Dr. Lyle Yorks is Professor in the Department of Organization and Leadership, Teachers College, Columbia University, where he teaches courses in strategy development as a learning process, strategic human resource development, and research. He is also a lecturer in the Executive Master of Science Program in Technology Management at the School of Continuing Education, Columbia University, where he teaches a course in strategic advocacy. Dr. Yorks has over 30 years' experience working with organizations in diverse industries worldwide on projects involving training designs, strategic organizational change, and management development. Earlier in his career, Dr. Yorks was a senior vice president of Drake Beam Morin, a human resources consulting firm; a principal and consultant to the firm of Marshall-Qualtec, a consulting firm working in the area of organization restructuring and strategic change; and an internal consultant on the staff of the Corporate Systems and Methods Department, Travelers Insurance Companies. Dr. Yorks has also served as visiting faculty in various EMBA and executive education programs.

Articles authored and coauthored by Dr. Yorks have appeared in the *Academy of Management Review*, *Academy of Management Education and Learning*, *California Management Review*, *Journal of Applied Behavioral Science*, *Sloan Management Review*, and other scholarly and professional journals. His 2004 article "Toward a Political Economy Model for Comparative Analysis of the Role of Strategic Human Resource Development Leadership" in *Human Resource Development Review* received the Outstanding Article award. Dr. Yorks earned master degrees from Vanderbilt University and Columbia University and his doctorate from Columbia University.

INDEX

Page references followed by *f* indicate an illustrated figure; and page references followed by *t* indicate a table